T0144147

Storytelling for Interactive Digital Media and Video Games

Storytelling for Interactive Digital Media and Video Games

Nicholas Bernhardt Zeman

CRC Press is an imprint of the
Taylor & Francis Group, an **informa** business

CRC Press
Taylor & Francis Group
6000 Broken Sound Parkway NW, Suite 300
Boca Raton, FL 33487-2742

Printed on acid-free paper
Version Date: 20161111

International Standard Book Number-13: 978-1-4987-0384-0 (Paperback)

Library of Congress Cataloging-in-Publication Data

Names: Zeman, Nicholas B., author.
Title: Storytelling for interactive digital media and video games / Nicholas B. Zeman.
Description: Boca Raton, FL : Taylor & Francis, 2017.
Identifiers: LCCN 2016030793 | ISBN 9781498703840 (pbk. :alk. paper)
Subjects: LCSH: Video games--Authorship. | Narration (Rhetoric) | Video games--Design. | Storytelling in mass media.
Classification: LCC GV1469.34.A97 Z46 2017 | DDC 794.8--dc23
LC record available at https://lccn.loc.gov/2016030793

Visit the Taylor & Francis Web site at
http://www.taylorandfrancis.com

and the CRC Press Web site at
http://www.crcpress.com

Contents

Author

Nicholas Bernhardt Zeman is an assistant professor in media informatics at Northern Kentucky University, Highland Heights, Kentucky.

I

Story Fundamentals

CHAPTER 1

What Is a Story? Fundamental Components of the Story

YOU'VE JUST HAD A long day and finished dinner, and now you're slowly oozing into the warmth of your leather couch with the flashing light of the television in front you. What are you watching?

Or maybe you're on the exercise bike at the gym, trying to gouge out the minutes of grueling exertion and sweat by distracting yourself by hammering the remote control on your tiny, personal screen, caught between a rerun of *Friends* and *Buffy the Vampire Slayer.*

You could be at the bar having a few beers with a friend telling him or her about your day.

Or maybe you're snowboarding in Tahoe, earbuds in, listening to your favorite serial podcast episode.

No matter what you are doing, or who you are, as long as you are human, you spend a good portion of your free time listening to or otherwise engaging in stories and storytelling. It's a natural aspect of being human to engage in telling a story, just as it is to listen to other people's stories.

But why? Why don't we all just sit around and read math books and discuss calculus equations? It seems so much more constructive. Why do we prefer hearing about lightsaber duels, starship voyages, cowboys, and cartoon characters made from household utensils instead? What information is being transferred between us through the act of storytelling that couldn't be just as easily conveyed by reading a list? Why do we spend so much of our time engaged in this art, action, and activity that seems to frame us as a species?

That's a good question. And not one easily answered. Just because storytelling is an integral part of human communication doesn't mean that we *understand* the concept all that well. After all, you have a brain that processes all the creative information and stores it somewhere, but how well do you really understand your own brain? We're just starting to unlock the mysteries of cognitive reasoning and motivation from a scientific perspective. Who knows what science and medicine will discover in the future?

Stories and storytelling are not just *important* vessels of communication to the human species—I would argue that they are *essential* components of communication. I doubt that without some form of story and storytelling, our species would be able to communicate about anything at all in a meaningful sense. Our brains work in such a way as to make the method of communication vital in transferring information from one unit to another—unlike a computer interface, our brain is not (despite our inclination toward this belief) like a computer at all. Our brain, at its lowest "hardware" level, controls the basic functioning of our physical body, such as heartbeat, breathing, hunger, pain, and the circulatory system. But at its higher "consciousness" level, the brain is an incredible associative pattern-recognition machine, able to process multiple streams of data at once and do something that is really phenomenal, which is to creatively visualize things that have not happened or manifested in existence yet! This form of creative visualization is what really sets us apart from all other species and is part of what makes us able to communicate with one another using allegorical and representation elements of association such as a story. We literally communicate with associations based on emotion, common conceptual understanding, and complex verbal, visual and contextual clues that are far too subtle for even our conscious mind to be aware of.

Given the nature of how we think on an awareness conscious level, it really should be no surprise that we are wired to communicate meaningful information by association and pattern recognition, and not by memorization. The more we become aware of this general need for information that powers the creative and imaginative areas of our brain, the better we can become at crafting and telling stories for any purpose. When it comes to human–human communication, we can't think that our minds are like computers. Most of us don't really respond positively to lists, numbers, and figures in a meaningful way. Even financial analysts, accountants, and business managers, who deal with a constant stream of financial data, still go to the same movies as you do to relax! They don't watch a movie at home with a person in a three-piece suit standing in front of a white background reading the charts and the statistics of the latest *Avengers* movie! So it's a universal human trait. No matter how data driven you claim to be, you are still emotionally driven as well.

A 2012 *New York Times* article stated that "in a 2006 study published in the journal *NeuroImage*, researchers in Spain asked participants to read words with strong odor associations, along with neutral words, while their brains were being scanned by a functional magnetic resonance imaging (fMRI) machine. When subjects looked at the Spanish words for 'perfume' and 'coffee,' their primary olfactory cortex lit up; when they saw the words that mean 'chair' and 'key,' this region remained dark. The way the brain handles metaphors has also received extensive study; some scientists have contended that figures of speech like 'a rough day' are so familiar that they are treated simply as words and no more. A team of researchers from Emory University reported in *Brain & Language* that when subjects in their laboratory read a metaphor involving texture, the sensory cortex, responsible for perceiving texture through touch, became active. Metaphors like 'The singer had a velvet voice' and 'He had leathery hands' roused the sensory cortex, while phrases matched for meaning, like 'The singer had a pleasing voice' and 'He had strong hands,' did not" (Paul 2012).

These studies illustrate the power of metaphors and associations with the brain and the neurophysics behind them. Reading a list of things you did yesterday does not engage the brain in nearly as many meaningful ways as telling a story about what you did yesterday, replete with vivid descriptions that evoke associative memories from your audience.

1.1 BECOMING THE STORYTELLER

Before we delve into the deep, fundamental understanding of stories, how they operate, and what they consist of, we will need to free ourselves from the *chronic viewer syndrome*, or the habit of always seeing stories from the perspective of the passive audience. We watch movies, read books, watch television and Netflix chronically, and we often think of the nature of stories and storytelling from the *audience* perspective instead of the *storyteller* perspective. In this book, you are going to learn how to become an effective storyteller, using the arsenal of techniques and concepts laid out for you to be able to tell compelling stories of all kinds, in all formats, and for many different purposes. Becoming the storyteller requires one to step outside the story and to see it from all angles, like a Rubik's Cube. You can deconstruct the story and reassemble it any way you like in order to make it more interesting, appeal to a certain demographic, or just more entertaining. This book's intent is to allow you to unravel the thread and understand a story from all different angles in different circumstances for different purposes.

1.2 WHAT IS A STORY? FUNDAMENTAL COMPONENTS

Define a story for me in a single sentence (don't worry; this is an intellectual exercise; I won't be giving you an exam later). Having trouble? Can you really encapsulate the concept of a story into a single, one-sentence definition? *Merriam–Webster's Dictionary* defines *story* as follows:

> **story**
> *plural* **stories**
> **1**
> *archaic*
> **a:** history 1
> **b:** history 3
> **2**
> **a:** an account of incidents or events
> **b:** a statement regarding the facts pertinent to a situation in question
> **c:** anecdote; *especially* **:** an amusing one
> **3**
> **a:** a fictional narrative shorter than a novel; *specifically* **:** short story
> **b:** the intrigue or plot of a narrative or dramatic work
> **4**
> **:** a widely circulated rumor
> **5**
> **:** lie, falsehood
> **6**
> **:** legend, romance
> **7**
> **:** a news article or broadcast
> **8**
> **:** matter, situation

Wow. That's a lot of different definitions for a single word! That's because a *story*, as we understand it, is an incredibly mutable and nebulous thing. We know *what* it is, without being able to actually define it all that easily. The problem with a story, as we understand it, is that it has so many different components. We can't just define it in a single sentence. A story is a theoretical concept that is contained within certain objects (such as a book) or a performance (such a movie or a play). It is purely an object of communication, which in and of itself is completely subjective. So the word *story* may not have any objective definition whatsoever. That's the bad news.

The *good* news, however, is that the word *story can* be clearly defined! And it's up to me, the author of a book on creative storytelling, to define it. A story can be best defined by its essential components, and a few nonessential ones. Therefore, we can say that we are clearly defining a story by what it *can't* be without defining it by what it comes with. For that purpose, we are going to break the story down into three types of components: primary (or vital for the definition of *story* to apply), secondary (usually present but not necessary), and tertiary (sometimes present or often a common feature). It is only by understanding all these things that we can really begin to understand what a story is. And we can't understand anything else about a story unless we know what it is first.

1.3 PRIMARY COMPONENTS

1.3.1 Characters

A character is simply a participant in a story. A character is the vessel through which events and occurrences happen to and spring from. A character is an actor in the story who affects the narrative and is affected by it. What can be a character? Pretty much anything and anyone. If you want to write a story about some sponge that lives under the sea somewhere, go ahead (oh wait, somebody beat you to it...). But how do we convert a sponge into a *character*? Let's make sure that the sponge or the fly or the garbage can or *whatever* you want to make a character has some very specific attributes that will make it a viable character.

Assigning those attributes for a nonhuman character, or an inanimate object, will automatically humanize it and create a sympathetic response from your audience. This is known as *anthropomorphism*. Anthropomorphism is the act of assigning humanlike qualities to an object that isn't human, such as, say, a sponge. SpongeBob SquarePants is supposed to be an invertebrate animal, living on the bottom of the sea. Technically speaking, there isn't much human about him. In Figure 1.1, you can see what a *real* sea sponge looks like. In Figure 1.2, you can see what SpongeBob looks like. Can you spot the difference?

An anthropomorphic character must possess some specific characteristic in order to make it humanlike. Now, a character doesn't have to have

FIGURE 1.1 An actual photo of a sea sponge. It doesn't look very human, does it?

FIGURE 1.2 A wax museum sculpture of SpongeBob SquarePants. A sea sponge with legs, arms, and a face is now a character.

all these attributes in order to make it viable as a participant or an actor in a story, but it has to have at least the ability to draw an emotional reaction from the audience of the story. We as humans tend to create sympathetic and empathetic connections with things that we think of as having human characteristics, which is why the cartoon character SpongeBob has arms, hands, a face, a voice, *and* wears a pair of pants.

1.3.1.1 Has Emotions and Feelings

In order for a human being, who possesses strong emotions and feelings, to connect with a character in a story, that character has to also be perceived to possess feelings and emotions (Figure 1.3). If I tell you a story about a rocking chair, that chair had better be able to generate a sympathetic emotional response in the audience or the viewer of the story. Can a rocking chair be sad? Or angry? Of course, it can. Inanimate objects, along with animals and mystical beings such as gods and spirits, can be assigned emotional responses and feelings in all kinds of stories. What's really happening here is the projection of the audience's quite human responses to stimuli and certain situations onto fictional or inanimate objects. Without this emotional connection, it is very hard for the audience to connect with the character at all.

A great example of this is an IKEA ad, in which an aging IKEA lamp is replaced by a newer IKEA lamp, and the owners throw it out on the

FIGURE 1.3 IKEA lamps, showing no signs of emotions or anthropomorphic attributes. How could you make the audience feel sorry for a lamp?

street with the garbage as the lamp looks up, now soaked in the pouring rain, into the window where the new lamp is keeping the occupants in the light as they go about their usual business. The old lamp never actually moves, but the framing, the music, and the perspective all try and generate an emotional connection with a nonmoving, mechanical object. At the last minute, an IKEA employee comes out and asks why you feel so bad for a lamp, when it is just a lamp, making the point that you tend to feel emotional connection with an inanimate object simply because you are human. It's *because* of this human tendency that you, as the storyteller, will be able to manipulate the audience into certain feelings for certain characters.

1.3.1.2 Has a Method of Communication

Generally, our characters have some form of communication, either to other characters or to the audience. We can tell when the character feels things, thinks things, or is otherwise engaged in humanlike thought, feeling, or reasoning. This can be body language, audible sounds, or simple facial expressions (if your character has a face). The important thing here is that without a method of communication, the character has a hard time being seen as a viable character, and it is more like just a piece of furniture.

The bare minimum for an emotional state of being to be conveyed by a simple drawing or representation are eyes, eyebrows, and a mouth of some kind. Common emoticons are excellent examples of this, in the sense that they possess only mouths, eyes, and eyebrows but are able to convey a wide range of expressions and emotional information from an incredibly simple set of features.

1.3.1.3 Limbs/Method of Locomotion

Most characters of any sort have a way to move from place to place. This is not *necessary*, as you can tell a story about a mountain as your main character, who has no way of moving, and that can be an inanimate, nonmobile character in your story. But applying a method of movement and mobility to anything that doesn't already possess it (such as a rock or a sock puppet) can breathe life into a character (Figure 1.4). Locomotion is an essential human quality that makes us connect with the character.

1.3.1.4 Clothes, Accessories, Hair, Facial Features

Figure 1.5 is a picture of a regular potato, sitting on my desk. Does it evoke any emotions? Does it have feelings? Does it have a name? What

FIGURE 1.4 These pet rocks don't have any visible form of locomotion, but they have just barely enough human qualities to be considered characters.

FIGURE 1.5 Your basic Idaho potato. Nothing really interesting is going on here.

transformative experience could this potato undergo as part of an interesting story? Pretty much the only thing transformative that's going to happen to that potato is being sliced, getting fried in hydrogenated trans fats soybean oil, and becoming part of your very unhealthy lunch at your local fast food restaurant.

In Figure 1.6, you can see that I have taken a potato and dressed it up like a person with a marker and some plastic pieces from a Mr. Potato

FIGURE 1.6 Larry the Potato (my friend told me he looked a lot more like Trotsky the Potato, but let's call him Larry).

Head toy. How does this transform our starchy vegetable? Figure 1.5 is just the potato, naked and boring. Figure 1.6 is a character.

It may seem silly, but what happens when we put humanlike attributes on a basic, boring potato? Some simple human attributes scribbled onto the potato with a marker and a couple of plastic props have now imbued our potato with human characteristics, and we can create meaningful emotional connections with him. He can have friends. He can go to the prom. He can drive a car. He can even have a pet, and none of this would seem silly or strange to you, provided that he maintains those human characteristics. The idea that the potato in Figure 1.5 has a pet parakeet named Lilly would seem ludicrous to you; however, the potato in Figure 1.6 can have a dog, a cat, and a cow, and none of it would seem the least bit strange.

If you think about it in any kind of nontechnical language, it's actually pretty silly. You can clearly see that it's just a potato. But somehow giving it human attributes gives it some form of life! As if it was imbued with the spirit of life just for the sake of having human attributes. Would you throw the naked potato in the oven and eat it? Of course, you would. It's pretty much a lump of food. But would you throw the potato from Figure 1.6 in the oven and cook it (of course, the plastic would melt)? What if I call him Larry the Potato? Since I have given him a name, are you more or less likely to stick him in the oven (now that he has a name, he is not an *it* anymore)? The simple act of giving Larry some humanlike qualities completely transforms him from a piece of food to a sympathetic humanlike character with emotional attributes that we can connect to as human beings. He essentially becomes an avatar, or a representation of a human, no matter how vegetative his true nature is. And once we make that connection with any representation of humanity, it suddenly takes on human qualities and our reaction to it changes.

1.3.1.5 The Voodoo Principle

I once had a girlfriend give me a haircut and glue my hair to a pencil with a piece of cotton that she drew on with a little face. Many years later, I was moving and cleaning out a house, rummaging around through my drawers and found the little guy again. I wanted to throw it away—but I found that I simply couldn't manage to toss it into the garbage can. After all—it was somehow a representation of myself. And in that representation, I found myself connected to this silly, inanimate pencil with a tuft of my hair glued to it and a dumb look on its face. But is that so silly? Or is it simply a manifestation of how the human mind operates? We see things in terms of our own perception, and it makes complete sense that we would have empathy for a pencil with a face and a tuft of hair. Eventually, I buried it in the backyard (I did not, however, give it a funeral service).

The point of this is that attaching a human name and humanlike attributes to a potato or a pencil with a tuft of human hair is in fact breathing life into it—like Prometheus, you have created an entity and imbued it with a spirit, of sorts. This *spirit* can be entirely metaphysical or conceptual, but it is a spirit nonetheless, and suddenly that object becomes an entity, or what we call a person. The Voodoo Principle is the act of imbuing any inanimate object, animal, or even just a concept (such as a new car model or an app idea) with a spirit of its own by attributing it with a name and some human qualities. It is a powerful effect that can be seen across the full gamut of story-based content in traditional media as well as interactive media.

The inverse of the Voodoo Principle can clearly be seen as well, when we take a participant in a story and remove the spirit from them. When does this happen? Often when we are playing games that involve tremendous violence against other humanlike entities, we find it necessary to dehumanize the objects of that violence, by reversing the Voodoo Principle. We do this by removing individuality from the character or the participant and making them inhuman. Zombies? Aliens? Demons? Robots? Nazis? We suck the individuality (and hence the spirit) from otherwise perfectly viable bipedal entities by making them nondescript, subhuman, evil, mindless, and incapable of creating an emotional connection between the audience and themselves. Therefore, we can violently kill them in droves without fear of moral reprisal or feelings of personal guilt.

So here we can understand the first essential element of a story to be a character, or a participant, and we have seen that anything, imbued with a spirit through the Voodoo Principle (or removed of spirit through the reverse), can become a character, or an actor and a participant in your story. The story cannot exist without the participation and the experience of at least one character.

1.3.2 Narrative

What is a narrative as it pertains to storytelling? *Narrative*, as it is defined in terms of storytelling, is the transformative events that occur in the story. But what does this all mean? Is it essentially stuff that happens. Think of it this way—if I tell you a story where Larry the Potato is standing around on a street corner for an hour, and two cars pass by him during that hour, is it really a story? We have a character, we have a place and a time, and something does indeed happen. Even though our character, Larry the Potato, is standing still and not doing anything, we still have stuff that happens in a general sense. But the important distinction here is that we still don't have a narrative. We don't have an actual narrative because there has been no transformation. Nothing has occurred that has transformed any part of our story yet. What if there was somebody in one of the cars that knew Larry and waved at him? Well, now we have an actual transformation occur, because we have changed the nature of Larry's person in some manner. He has seen someone, or that someone has seen him, and now an acknowledgement of that moment has been made, and even though this is still an incredibly boring story, it's still a story because some transformation between the situation at the beginning of the story and the end of the story has taken place.

Narrative is the engine through which the story derives its locomotion. It is the manner in which the characters get from point A to point B, both figuratively and literally. If Larry decides to get a ride from the person driving the car who knows him, then he is literally moved from one place to another in our story. But he could just as easily recognize the person in the car as a hired assassin, pull out his potato gun and fire away, blowing up the car and causing a huge explosion as he jumps across the camera in slow motion. Although he hasn't transformed in time and space much, he certainly has completely transformed in terms of his actions, state of mind, and impact on the audience. Now here, at least, is a somewhat *interesting* story, especially if you know Larry and you thought he was just some ordinary, boring potato dressed in human clothes!

1.3.3 Perspective

What is perspective? By its nature, perspective is a kind of a mutable, subjective term. And by *subjective*, I mean that every perspective is subject to the individual *conveying* that perspective's opinion and personal experience. It is this very nature that makes perspective so vital and important in the definition and the construction of a story.

A story must contain at least one perspective to be considered a story, and it usually contains multiple perspectives. A perspective is the lens through which the events of the narrative are seen—either by a first-person narrator or a third-person outside view. The perspective is basically the teller of the story, and there is no reason that multiple people can't tell the same story. After all, if you and I witness an accident from different angles, our courtroom testimony might be drastically different from each other, because although we were in the same place at the same time, we had different *perspectives* of the event. I might have seen something you didn't see. You might have heard something I missed. And if we look at the footage from a security camera at the trial, we suddenly have another perspective in the mix. The camera perspective is considered unbiased because it is not human—it is not subject to personal interpretation. In stories, we can call this the God's-Eye view. The God's-Eye view allows us to see, hear, and know things in a film or a story that the characters themselves, even though they are the main participants in the story, don't actually know yet. Hitchcock would use this *God's-Eye perspective* quite frequently in his films to generate suspense, showing you an impending disaster about to happen while the recipients of that disaster would be totally unaware of it. He once used the idea that if we see two people talking on a park bench having a completely ordinary conversation, but the camera pans down to show a bomb underneath the park bench, the conversation they are having will suddenly generate an amazing amount of *suspense*, because *we* know there's a bomb there, but they have absolutely no idea. This is a great example of showing the audience of the story something the characters couldn't know and therefore creating a perspective that is for the audience's eyes alone.

1.3.3.1 First-Person and Third-Person Singular Perspectives

The first-person perspective is often used in literature and books. A first-person perspective is essentially the way we normally perceive the world when we're walking around—all we *know* is our own perspective, what we see or do or say or hear. We can't really ever know any other perspective than our own. If you want to get philosophical about it, we don't really have any way of knowing that anything else in the world exists outside of our own sensory perception. This is often termed *empiricism*—the idea that the entire world we live in is constructed strictly of our own interpretation of sensual data and that we can only know what we can prove based on that. In modern film terms, we all live in a *Matrix* or an illusory world constructed by mental interpretation of sound, air, light, and energy feedback from tactile sensations (known as *touch*). The evident fallacy of this way of thinking is clearly shown in Epicurus's argument about the estimation of the size of the sun, with which he had a clear disagreement with the Platonists, who used astronomical calculations to derive a size of the distant object based on something as abstract as math. Epicurus stated that if we must only work with our own observance, we must then conclude that the sun was an object about 2 feet in diameter.

This example of Greek philosophy and early science is a great elucidation of the division between the actual truth and the observable truth. It's also a great way to see how the perspective of your story can vastly change the nature of it—any first-person-only story has the advantage of making it personal through the primary character's eyes, but it also allows you, the storyteller, to only filter the world to the audience through that viewer, which makes it more personally connective in terms of literature, but fails to carry through in things such as film or television. There are few films, television series, or plays that see the world in a first-person perspective; rather, we like to watch multiple perspectives in a visual performance of a story. In speaking or writing, we can accept either a first-person or a third-person perspective, however.

A third-person perspective in terms of narrative, literary, or orally conveyed stories offers us the ability to tell a story through an individual's experiences, but *only* that individual's experiences. It is similar to the first-person perspective, but a little bit more removed since it keeps the personal thoughts and feelings buffered by a third party, the narrator, who at times might seem more or less impartial.

1.3.3.2 Multiple Perspectives

Multiple perspectives allow the storyteller to show the story through multiple lenses, carrying it into an ongoing narrative through multiple characters. Multiple third-person perspectives are the larger proportion of narrative television series, where we have many different characters progressing the narrative without other characters present. Think of the popular show *Game of Thrones*—we have an entire cast of characters, each caught in their own independent story, part of a web of other stories. Often, we follow one thread, with a cast of subcharacters, while being aware of multiple other threads happening simultaneously. There are certain, predefined structures for multiple perspectives in film, television, novels, and podcasts that allow the many different characters to interact with the audience at some point.

1.3.3.3 Revolving Multiple Perspective

Revolving multi-perspective is the most commonly used multi-perspective formatting. It takes a central narrative and lets the other characters revolve around it, swapping from one perspective to the other so that the audience can sew together the multiple planes and see the story from so many different angles (Figure 1.7). The perspective of the characters circles the narrative as they interact with it.

1.3.3.4 Convergent Multiple Perspective

A convergent multiple perspective structure follows the perspective of multiple individuals as they prepare to converge on the primary narrative—that is to say that entirely separate characters with no assumed association with one another are swapped until they converge at a specific point in time for the climax occurrence (Figure 1.8). The point of convergence is interesting because we now have experienced each of the converging characters' perspective and understood something about them.

1.3.3.5 Divergent Multiple Perspective

Divergent multiple perspectives are the inverse of convergent (Figure 1.9); the story begins with a central event, and the multiple perspectives are

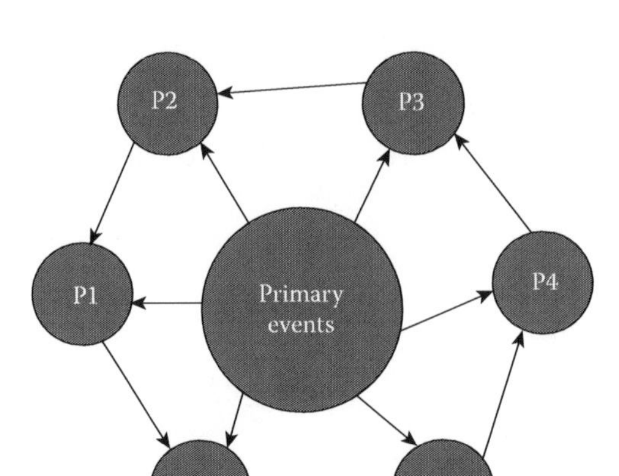

FIGURE 1.7 The revolving multiple perspective. Everyone gives their own account of the primary narrative, and the perspective will shift between them.

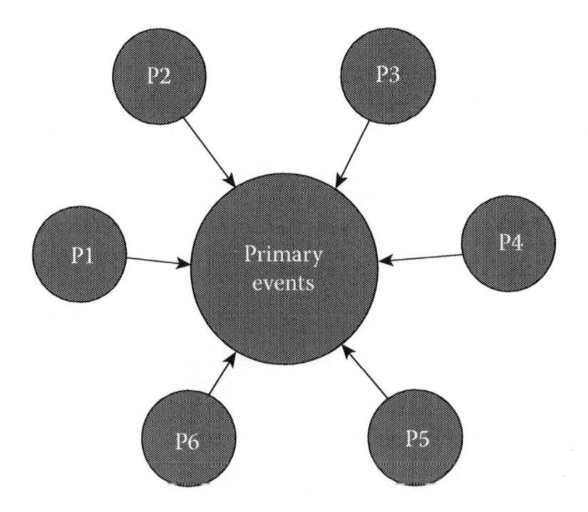

FIGURE 1.8 The convergent multiple perspective. The perspectives of multiple individuals are tracked as they all converge on a single place and time that creates the central narrative.

told through the following of participants in that event after the fact. The individuals may never meet again in the story, but the perspective will show how those events changed their life to some degree. The films *Crash* and *Fearless* are good examples of this perspective tracking, in which the lives of the victims of an accident are simultaneously tracked after the traumatic experience, but there is not necessarily a reconvening of the people in time and space.

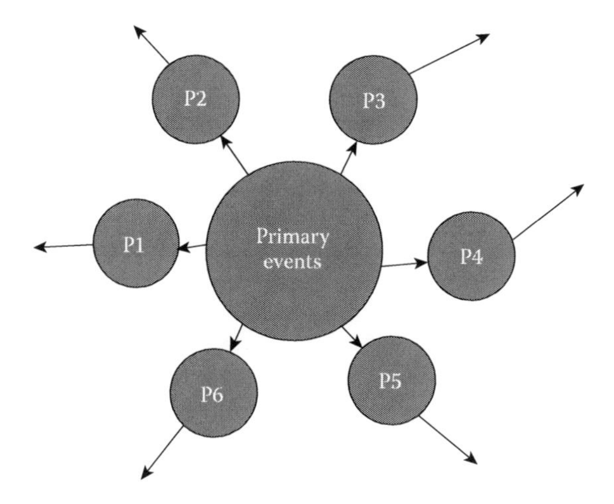

FIGURE 1.9 The divergent multiple perspective.

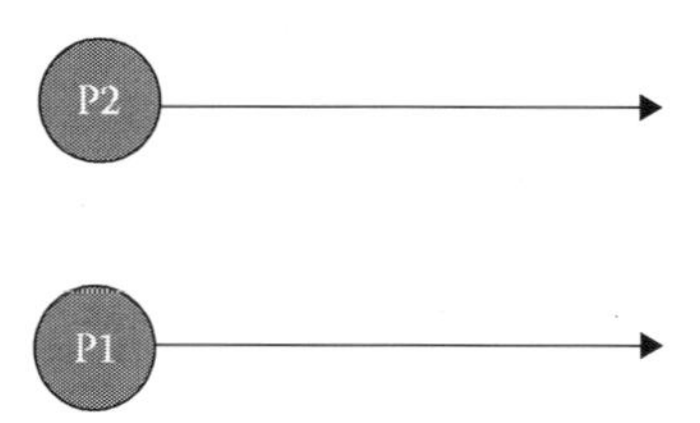

FIGURE 1.10 The parallel multiple perspective.

1.3.3.6 Parallel Multiple Perspective

A parallel multiple perspective is different from a convergent or divergent perspective because the characters will most often *not* cross paths in any way (Figure 1.10). The audience will get the perspective of each character, but there is no central narrative tying them together—two parallel narratives for two (or more) central perspectives. This is a structure often used to compare and contrast two different circumstances: rich and poor, African American or Caucasian, alien and human, etc. The structure allows the storyteller to show the audience the tremendous difference between the stimuli for each character and often make societal, racial, or prejudicial conclusions therein.

1.3.3.7 Relay Multiple Perspective

A relay race is characterized by the passing of a baton, or a tiny metal rod, from individual to individual as the race continues. No one racer carries the baton from beginning to end—it is a team effort! Similar to this, the

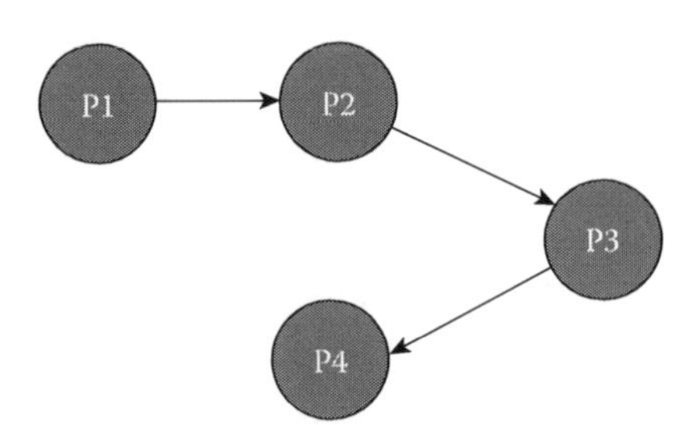

FIGURE 1.11 The relay multiple perspective. This is not often used, but it creates an interesting pan of a population, city, or other social community.

relay structure of multiple perspective allows the storyteller to create an entire ecosystem of people by moving the perspective from one person to another without ever repeating any one of them (Figure 1.11). This is used in the film *Slacker* by Richard Linklater, among others, and although it is not often used, it can be powerful in effect to shift the focus away from an individual to the larger community or environment as it pertains to certain cultural or socioeconomic circumstances. In the film *Slacker*, Linklater illustrates an overeducated, underambitious population and slice of life in Austin, Texas, in the early 1990s. Often this type of perspective shift is used to tell *slice-of-life* stories, where there's more of a setting in use than a specific character or narrative.

1.3.4 Sequence

Sequence is often the most misunderstood element of a story in terms of what it entails and how it is used. Sequence, in the case of storytelling, is not the sequence in which events take place temporally, but the sequence in which events are *told* to the audience. Remember that we must perform an exercise in removing ourselves from the common trap of *chronic passive audience syndrome*, a term I am coining here to describe the effect of being a constantly passive member of an audience when you watch television or stream your favorite show on Netflix. What happens is that you forget to think critically as a storyteller and you lose the ability to deconstruct stories and how they are engineered. Sometimes, of course, you want to lay around in your underwear and watch Hulu (the author may just do it on a regular basis), *but* when we need to think like a storyteller, we need to put our storytelling hat on (and maybe some pants, as well).

Sequence is a tool in your arsenal—you need to be able to put together a story in or out of sequence depending on the intended effect on the audience. Telling stories in a certain sequence can have a certain effect—it can fundamentally change the way the audience feels, generate suspense, defuse suspense, or increase the amount of humor. Telling stories out of sequence is a natural thing for humans to do.

Before we can delve into the auspices of sequence, let's return to our old friend Epicurus. Epicurus says that we can only firmly believe what we can personally experience. But here's the interesting thing—if that were true, we would live completely in the moment, only understanding what we know and feel *at that moment* and never anything else, which is what most cognitive scientists would call *goldfish experiences* (which explains why they can hang out in a plastic bag for days at the pet store without getting depressed). But Epicurus here is simply wrong—you can record and remember experiences and recall them at will. You can also construct or *imagine* events, people, situations, and worlds that never even existed at all. You are, in essence, the dreaming god Vishnu. Your imagination can create entire universes that don't exist anywhere but in your mind.

Events in the real world, in our perception, happen through the arrow of time. And the arrow of time only goes one way (forward). So I can tell you what happened to me yesterday but I can't tell you what will happen to me tomorrow. Our perception is able to access a forward direction in time but our memories and imagination have no such boundaries. Therefore, I can tell you what happened to me last week, a year ago, and 20 years ago in any sequence I desire. What's more, your brain has no problem whatsoever stitching these pieces together as they are conveyed—you don't usually need a map to understand how a flashback or even a flash-forward works. If I ask you what your day will be like tomorrow, I'm pretty sure that you can give me a great hour-to-hour play by play of a day in your life that you have yet to experience, and even if you throw in aliens and Greek gods, I will have little problem understanding what you're talking about.

This is because our brains are essentially pattern-recognition and association-making machines. They are not, contrary to popular depiction, like computers at all. If I were coding a piece of software to get stock market data for tomorrow today, it would most certainly break (or give me a compiler error). Why? Because a computer doesn't understand contextual imagination—I can't get data that hasn't been recorded yet. I can, of course, start giving in instructions to get the data when and if it's available, but we all know that it won't be available until it happens! This means it won't be in the future; it will be in the past.

If you tell me you are from the future (let's say that you're playing a practical joke on me) and know the stock market shifts tomorrow, and I ask you to tell them to me, you can absolutely do it. You may not be correct, and you might just be lying to me, but the point is that you can create a conceivably truthful situation in your own head, which can be conveyed to me in a series of images, a story, or just numbers. You can invent a future that may or may not happen.

So we as storytellers should have similar abilities—we construct a story as it happens in a temporal sequence, but we don't have to tell it back to you in that sequence. We can chop it up into pieces and tell you the pieces in any order we want. The fascinating thing about the brain is that it's able to put those pieces together and form a complete picture without much help. Look at Figure 2.18, a drawing by Matisse, and tell me what you see. Is it the image of a nude woman? How do you know that? It's not a photograph—indeed, if you look close enough, it's just a bunch of squiggly lines and some smudges. But your brain sees a nude woman. The reason for this is that a collection of lines in the shape of a silhouette will immediately register in your brain as a human form. Your brain interprets the patterns as being close to that of a human form, so it puts together the pieces in your brain as a definable image. This partly uses our imagination to construct the concept and partly our memory to recognize and remember what this form looks like. We can understand pieces and part of it out of sequence, because our brain has the ability to do this naturally and effortlessly on its own. *But* telling a story purely in a different sequence temporally as it happened can have a tremendous effect on the perception of the story by the audience! If you show a future scene in which a character is killed, but then later in the story have a scene with that character interacting with another, it can drastically change the impression or the feel of the scene. Why? Because you know that this character already dies fairly soon, and therefore, your empathy for him or her may be higher or lower (depending on how he or she died, I suppose).

So the important takeaway here is that sequence is a vital tool in the storyteller's arsenal; it allows you the flexibility to create a nonlinear world in which we can see events from the past, the present, and the future interchangeably. This can arguably get very confusing, especially if you don't interweave them properly. *Pulp Fiction*, a classic film by Quentin Tarantino, uses this out-of-sequence technique in order to show a central narrative through several characters' perceptions; with the connections stitched together in vignettes, which are individual stories that cross over one another at certain points. Several times the stories are told out of sequence, with certain chunks happening after others. This tells a story in an innovative way, which not only creates a more interesting flow for the audience, but also allows the story to flow like the brain's natural tendencies, which is to put together nonsequential temporal events quite easily from past to future.

1.4 SECONDARY COMPONENTS OF A STORY

1.4.1 Setting

Setting is the place and the time a story takes place. A setting can be familiar—like many films or television commercials are set in a modern, current time and a familiar city, town, state. A setting can also be unfamiliar—such as "long ago, in a galaxy far, far away…." The setting of a story creates an environment in which certain things are possible or an impossible and certain thing will connect with the audience because they are familiar or possibly connect with the audience because they are unfamiliar. Setting conveys a tremendous amount of information to the audience in a subtle fashion.

Setting is considered a secondary component to a story because it is not necessary to have a setting in order to tell a story—a story can occur with no defined place and time. Samuel Beckett's *Endgame* is a great example of a play with no defined place or time—it never creates any distinction in this regard and is indeed extremely existential in essence because it exists devoid of setting. Other stories without setting that we often are exposed to are commercials with the typical blank white background. We see stories occur in no definable area, part of the world, or even time period. All we see is a white background. This lack of setting actually focuses the audience's attention to the characters and the dialogue, instead of when and where it takes place.

Setting, of course, is often used and to great import when constructing a story. The setting of a story can impart certain feelings to the audience. It can be chaotic, such as in the middle of a war, or peaceful, if it takes place far away from civilization in some organic Eden devoid of strife. Setting can change over the course of a story, and most definitely, it can change often for specific purpose. It is common to have multiple settings in a story to compare and contrast elements of narrative or personalities of the characters involved.

Nostalgia is one very important product of a manipulated setting. Nostalgia is the feeling of fond memories attached to a certain period and time—most often in our youth. This is the reason there are so many nostalgic television shows and films, specifically set in a period and a place in which the people who were young during that time will emotionally connect with. The principles of nostalgia must be set to connect with happy feelings—one of a safe, warm, or good environment. This is most common in American and first-world countries where your parents or youreself can remember youth as a time of freedom from responsibilities and excitement during the transition from childhood to adulthood. This is why people can have strong positive emotional connections with toys and technology from their childhood. The nostalgic connection with events, technology, and social norms of our past must be a positive one, however! Very few people who grew up in abject poverty and constant violent warfare will be nostalgic for those events from their youth. It requires a positive emotional connection to be effective, which is why you see it most commonly used in American culture and other countries which were prosperous in the past.

Fantasy is another important concept of setting. Anything in the fantastical setting, including science fiction and future technology, can exist conceivably, and indeed, this type of setting is key to making it feasible in our imagination. Of course, there are plenty of stories about modern-world supernatural forces and science fiction elements, but they are somehow hidden or obfuscated from the "normal" people in the "normal" world. The *Harry Potter* series is a great example of this device—it's set in modern England, *but* the magical world exists as a separate and hidden aspect of the normal world in which most of us live. That setting is a very important distinction from otherworld fantasy, which need not conform to any modern-world aspects at all.

1.4.2 Tone

Tone is another secondary component of storytelling—it is elusive and subjective in some ways. Tone is the emotional color of the content of the story. Remember, we're only talking about the story as a concept at this point—it's easy to start thinking of *visual* tone in terms of color and saturation, but we are mostly looking at *content* tone. Is it a depressing story? Is it a happy story? Is it a romantic comedy? Is it a romantic tragedy? What's the difference between the two? You can see that tone is something that we inherently get but something that's moderately difficult to pin down.

Tone comes from character interaction, narrative, and perspective. If the events in the story happening to the characters are events that the characters don't want, it can be funny, sad, or depressing, depending on *how* we tell the story. If I start laughing and tell you I have this great joke to tell you, but it ends up being about a man whose wife dies of cancer and then he kills himself, you might ask what the hell was so funny about that? But maybe I keep laughing, and the fact that I think a depressing story is funny *is* the part that's funny.

Tone sets the emotional mood in the audience. You want to create a story that communicates emotional information through the events and the character's reaction to those events. You can paint your emotional palette by using the events and the responses to impart emotional sensation into the audience.

Tone is not necessary for a story—often, stories try to leech the tone from them in order to tell it in a factual or a journalistic manner. This is a manipulation or a desaturation of the emotional tone in order to allow the audience freedom to imprint their own emotions into the events and the characters. In contrast, the tone can be highly exaggerated, with the characters doing or saying things that project the tone deliberately. In a performed play, there often can be different performances by different casts and different directors with highly different tones being used. Often, this can lead to completely different *interpretations* of what is essentially the same story—a performance can take on an extremely different meaning depending on the nature of the tone of the actors.

1.5 TERTIARY COMPONENTS

1.5.1 Intended Audience

The intended audience is something very unique and specific—I define it as a tertiary component of a story because it can be very specific, very broad, or completely absent. Intended audience matters more when you are trying to tell a certain story to a certain group that will resonate with them through association and emotional connection. For instance, if you were making an antidrinking and driving campaign commercial for women specifically, you might want to make the driver in the story a woman. Or you might want to show the primary character drinking with her female friends. Do you want to get more specific? Then target it toward upscale, single, career women. What will they be drinking? Beer from a bottle? Or wine from a glass? Red wine or white wine? Are they in Manhattan? Maybe instead you will show them with a martini. Do you see how complex this can get? In the world of competitive advertising, this is big business! You'd better bet that advertisers are targeting very small demographics for very specific purposes, and the digital revolution and the access to piles of data are only helping this process along. With access to social media information, the people in the advertiser's world are hard at work, figuring out just what kind of story to tell just what audience.

How do we identify our audience? We can break it down into several categories:

- *Gender*—Although we strive to end gender double standards in terms of civil rights, you can bet that women and men see the world differently and are interested in different products. So, of course, targeting a story to a demographic is going to have gender as a primary concern.
- *Race*—Race is a big player in the intended audience. Certainly, racial profiling is bad for police or Homeland Security, but it plays heavily into advertising.
- *Socioeconomic status*—Socioeconomic status is even a bigger player than race. Your socioeconomic status is often driven by your upbringing, and not necessarily your current income. Are you likely to respond positively to blue-collar images of physical labor and beers or white-collar images of business development and cocktails?
- *College education*—College education matters in terms of your audience because there are some ideas, concepts, and information that some will have and others will not. Basic curricula in colleges often have a wide swath of humanities, languages, and conceptual mathematics that everyone must learn, but those who did not go would not be familiar with.
- *Political ideology*—Politics and party affiliation will determine a lot about how people identify with a story. In fact, telling a story with the wrong political narrative will result in an almost instant rejection of anything else in that story. Literally, you can take the same commercial, advertisement, or otherwise and stick a Mitt Romney or an Obama sticker on the preroll, and half of the audience will simply ignore everything else coming after! It's a knee-jerk reaction from political affiliation, which can be a huge factor in constructing a story if targeting your audience is important.

- *Religion*—Religion, of course, can determine a lot about storytelling and personal connection. Many religions have vastly different attitudes and rules about premarital sex, abortion, contraception, capital punishment, and multitudes of other societal constraints. Knowing just what the targeted demographic find appropriate or inappropriate is key in connecting them to your story.
- *Age*—Age, of course, is a key determinant in your story. If the targeted demographic is younger, older, or of a particular generation, they might be more or less likely to respond to certain storylines, stimuli, or character archetypes more strongly. For instance, a 70-year old man is not going to respond to a modern-style cartoon character. Try using a style that would appeal to him based on the principles of nostalgia or familiarity.
- *Marital status*—Married and unmarried people often have vastly different priorities in certain categories, especially in considering products that are designed to attract a member of the opposite sex! If you're marketing products to single men, your story will have to be adjusted accordingly.
- *Having children*—Having children, by nature, strips the parent of certain priorities while enhancing other concerns, especially if the children need products or services they can't purchase themselves (such as diapers or baby formula) and the parents must choose these products for them.
- *Income*—Would you try to sell a homeless man a Mercedes? Why not? You get the point. Income is a key factor in a lot of products—and *not* a factor in others. Things such as cigarettes don't have to advertise to high-income people. It's a universally affordable product to all income levels (or used to be).
- *Ethnic culture*—Ethnic background is similar to religion, but less by sets of rules and more by sets of associations. If a person comes from an ethnic background, they may or may not agree with the common religious practices or ideas, but they will connect with things such as food, clothing, music, speech patterns, and perspectives.

So what *is* a story, after all? As you can see, the *what* is pretty complex. A story isn't just an object we can hold in our hand; it's a concept that requires a certain amount of information connected in certain ways. A story is the model our mind constructs through these essential components when they are conveyed to us in a certain way. We use these components to build a metaphysical universe in our head containing those elements. Don't forget (and you will hear me repeat it many times in this book) that our brain is an associative machine. It works by making association between various things and building patterns. A story is a way to construct an object in our mind by giving it multiple patterns and connections to put together like a jigsaw puzzle.

REFERENCE

Paul, A. M. (2012, March 17). Your brain on fiction. *New York Times*.

CHAPTER 2

Who's Telling the Story? Teller/Audience Relationship and the Told

ONE THING WE HAVE to carefully consider in exploring the art of storytelling is the person *telling* the story. Who *is* telling the story? How do we identify them? What is their defining characteristic? What is their relationship to the person *listening* to the story? All these things are vital in how the story affects the audience, and even how the *audience affects the storyteller*, which in turn affects the story.

Sometimes, the storyteller is easily identified; it's the person talking to you. In this case of a person-to-person story, you can clearly identify the storyteller (the person at the bar) and the audience (which is you). But what if you are telling a story with your buddy to some person at that same bar? Now you *and* your buddy are the storytellers, and the person is the one listening.

If you are sitting around a campfire with a bunch of people and one person is standing up telling the story, you can pretty much clearly identify the storyteller. But sometimes the storyteller is harder to identify. If you go see a play at a theater, there isn't necessarily a clear narrator. Often times, our plays are told through the actors and the dialogue.

Sometimes we have a narrator; sometimes we don't. The original Greek tragedies were performed with a chorus, who often substituted for the God's-Eye View. The chorus would tell the audience what was happening everywhere, as the players on stage performed their roles. In this manner, the storytelling can come from multiple perspectives: the actors and the chorus.

When we watch films or television, the storyteller becomes even more nebulous or fractured at times. When watching traditional sitcoms or narrative dramas, there is often a diffusion of narrative. You don't have one particular person telling you the story. The teller in this situation is the camera, often showing you different perspectives of different situations but generally centered around one or two central characters (see Chapter 1 for multiple perspective narratives). In reality television (see Chapter 3), you often have multiple storytellers *including* the camera, which serves as an impartial perspective.

The reason identifying the storyteller is so important is because we need to gauge the relationship between them and the audience! This relationship can alter or affect the story being told in so many ways.

When we start talking about storytelling, we have to become acutely aware of the relationship between the teller and the audience. The teller is the medium through which the story is conveyed—whether it is a person at a bar, a cast on a stage at a play, a radio, a podcasting mobile device, a television, or a movie theater. The teller is the medium through which you receive the story.

2.1 DIRECTION OF INPUT

The audience is the receiver of the story. It's whoever is paying attention to it. The audience can be passive (such as when watching television) or active (such as when applauding for a play). Some formats of storytelling allow for input from the audience directly to the teller, and some are completely passive for the audience. A story *always* moves in the direction of the audience, but you would be surprised at how much storytelling involves input coming *back* from the audience! This is called *bidirectional* storytelling. Figure 2.1 shows a simple illustration of a teller and the audience and the information that passes between them. Sometimes the direction of input is entirely unidirectional, as it is in the case of television or films. In this case, we can consider the audience fairly passive, with no feedback to the teller (Figure 2.2).

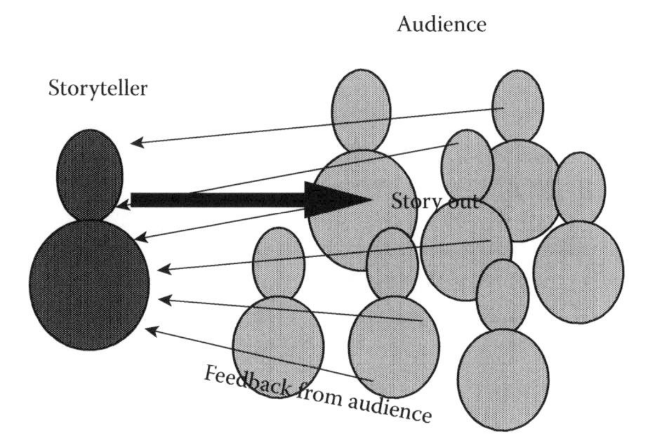

FIGURE 2.1 Diagram showing an oral tradition or an egalitarian form of storytelling. The storyteller and the audience are on the same level and in the same physical space.

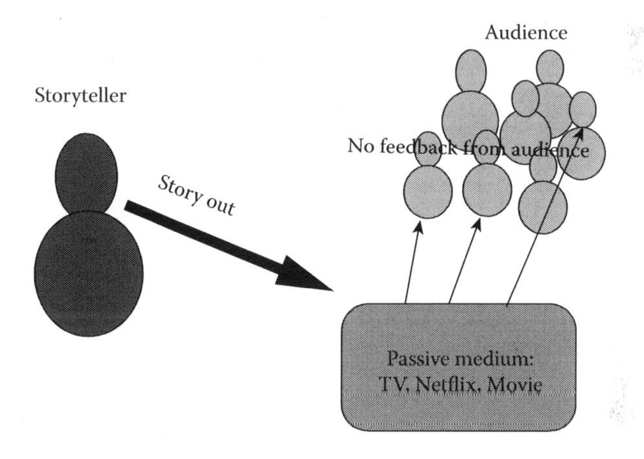

FIGURE 2.2 A medium that separates the audience and the storyteller by time and space, without some level of interaction is considered a passive medium, and the effect of audience feedback and input is lost. This is how the majority of twentieth century storytelling has been produced.

2.2 HEIGHT OF TELLER

Often, we will participate in a storytelling in an egalitarian manner—a person at a bar tells us some story about what happened yesterday. He or she and you are on the same conceptual level. He or she is at the bar, with you, in front of you, doing the same thing you are in the same manner. Now, *if* he or she were a celebrity, or a famous person, you might think of him or her as larger than life or above you in some way. Conversely, if this person was homeless or acting like a complete idiot, you would see him or her as beneath you, or inferior.

In this example you have stumbled across the concept of the storyteller height versus the audience height. The teller of a story can be equal, inferior, or superior to the audience. All these have vastly different effects on the story and the delivery of that story.

We use inferior storytelling often for comedic purposes. If you go see a comedy with Jack Black or Seth Rogen, you can be fairly sure that they are going to act stupid or buffoon-like at some point, at which point you will laugh. Why is this the case? It's because you need to feel superior to the people telling the story, or the characters in the story. There really was a purpose behind the jester at a king's court. Because the Jester told stories in an inferior position, they could be entertaining and funny without being offensive. Often in comedies, you will see people acting stupid or ridiculous in order to tell a story in a comedic manner. We like to feel superior to the storyteller or characters in a story.

Equality in terms of height between teller and audience is an attempt to relate to the audience on their own terms. You will often see this in commercials and advertisements. The narrator comes off as a regular person, or just another normal person ... just like you. Of course, we know that this person is an actor paid to pretend to be just like you, but as long as he looks, talks, and acts similar to you, you can feel like you're both on the same level. In this way, advertisements entice you to buy a product because you feel comfortable with the person telling you to do it. It's an old trick to get you to identify with the spokesperson.

A storyteller in the superior position, or talking down to you in some manner, is often used for the purposes of education or a documentary. The storyteller, or narrator, is telling you information from a top–down perspective; they are imparting information to you from a position of knowledge and power. I call this the *Morgan Freeman Effect*. It's when the storyteller uses a superior perch to tell you a story for very specific purposes. Usually, those purposes are to make you receptive to listening to something that is going to teach you or impart you with information. You become receptive to the information that they are speaking to you about because you view the storyteller as an authority figure who is more knowledgeable than you are.

2.3 DISTANCE OF TELLER

The distance between the storyteller and the audience is a figurative concept—although real-life distance can have an influence! You can see in Figure 2.1 that the physical closeness of the audience can influence the amount of feedback they give the storyteller. The more input an audience has (and the more real time the input is), the *closer* they feel to the teller. And the closer in literal distance the audience is to the source of the story, the closer they *feel* to the story. A completely passive audience experience, say in a movie theater, makes you feel far away from the source of the story. Conversely, a ghost story by the campfire will make you feel very close to the source of the story indeed—they're right next to you! The distance matters in terms of interaction with the teller and the story. The digital world has made us able to interact with the storyteller in multiple ways, often even in real time, while being far away in terms of physical distance. But no matter how far away we are physically, we still feel *closer* to a story told through social media because we have some interaction with it that the teller can respond to. So the distance is only a relative or a *perceived* thing. It does change with literal physical distance, but through technology, we can achieve a figuratively close distance while being across the continent.

This idea of distance is important because it makes you feel very removed from the story, as in watching a television show like *Law and Order*, or you can feel like a participant in the story, like when people watch contest television shows where they can vote on the outcome, just like *American Idol*. This is a growing sector of importance in terms of marketing, advertising, and entertainment because the technology has been organically growing to reach a point where we can now interact with our entertainment and stories in some way. How we intertwine the two together is entirely up to the future, but we can see some marriage between them in the form of narrative-based game entertainment as well as newer forms of advertising and marketing, where the user can choose their ad experience or somehow interact with a commercial by making a choice that affects the outcome in some way.

CHAPTER 3

How Do We Tell Stories? Formats of Storytelling

HUMANS, AS A SPECIES, have been telling stories for as long as we have recorded history and probably as long as we have had some form of language. It's simply a part of our nature (and we'll get to that down the road!). But the *how* is what we really want to concentrate here. Because the methods of storytelling have shifted and evolved over the past 100,000 years along with technology, one interesting thing to think about is the fact that the original methods of storytelling have never really gone away—we just keep adding new ones. We need to explore the many different ways we can communicate stories to one another and how they influence the nature of the relationship between storyteller and audience and permanence vs mutability.

3.1 ARCHAIC FORMS OF STORYTELLING

Archaic forms of storytelling are just that—*ancient*. They've existed in some form since the dawn of humanity. The fundamental characteristic of these forms of storytelling is that they must by definition happen at a very close range. There is no way to communicate further than the voice can carry and the eye can see. There is no way to record the story and view it later. These forms of storytelling must be viewed live and in person. This generates a huge amount of bidirectional interactivity between the teller and the audience, as we have previously discussed.

3.1.1 Oral Traditions

Oral traditions are the very first form of storytelling in terms of technology. Oral traditions are stories that are passed down, from person to person, and told in front of people in an egalitarian manner. Some famous examples of oral traditions are *The Epic of Gilgamesh*, *The Iliad and the Odyssey*, and *Beowulf*. All these stories are early forms of storytelling, which were memorized in verses and told to others around a campfire at night, which would be the equivalent of Paleolithic Netflix.

Oral traditions, in terms of technology, only require one thing (and it's a massively important thing): a spoken language. As long as we can communicate complex thoughts and concepts to others through making sounds and gestures, we can tell a story! The human mind will fit all the pieces together into an imaginative puzzle, fitting together anything left out by the teller. In this way, human beings first began to craft the art of storytelling, often delegating these tasks to specific people as a specific skill, which involved memorizing thousands of lines of poetry, characters and names, and then dramatically reenacting it in front of an audience, which frequently involved themselves in the telling by creating sound effects and responding to the parts of the story. This is the earliest form of "interactive multimedia." And although this is considered an antiquated form of storytelling, it is still considered a living folk art practiced and celebrated across the world. Oral traditions and folk storytellers are still attending festivals and telling their tall tales to this very day. And if you consider this antiquated, or old fashioned, you should think long and hard about the nature of modern stand-up comedy. If you watch stand-up comedians, you will see a reformatting of this oral storytelling tradition in a modern setting. They may be telling jokes, but what are jokes but miniature stories? Stand-up comedy is really the ancestory of the original format of storytelling.

One of the most important aspects of this form of storytelling is the fact that despite the memorization of the story by the teller, there was no written form of language at that time. The story lived entirely in the teller's head, and for that reason, the story itself was a mutable thing—it could change depending on who was telling it. The names might be similar, the events may basically be congruent, but the total content of the story was not written in stone! That means that the teller could alter minute things, make one character more significant, downplay another, and ultimately come up with a significantly different tale than he or she started with.

Why would the teller change the story? Oftentimes, the storytellers, or the travelling bards, would find themselves in varying tribes or cultural climates. In one place, a certain name would make more sense. In another place, a particular character would be far more popular. Sociocultural differences, the teller's own preferences, and multiple other influences could play a part in altering the original story, which of course was altered from the preceding, and so forth. After three generations of storytellers, you can imagine that it was like an incredibly long game of telephone, where the result barely resembled the original.

Another aspect of oral traditions is the egalitarian or the equal footing of the audience and the teller! The teller was right there, in close physical proximity, interacting with the crowd as they approved or disapproved, applauding, booing, shouting, and reacting to the story as it happened. The teller was on the same level, interacting and drawing the story from the crowd as much as the crowd was drawing from the story. In this instance, the distance between the teller and the audience is at its closest—there is a direct line of communication between them.

Let's explore the height of the teller against the audience. The teller, being on the same physical level as the audience, should feel very much equal—they are not yet on a pedestal of sorts, but existing inside the same physical space as the audience. Of course, the teller could tell a story from a metaphysical position of authority *or* be a goofball and make people laugh. The style of telling is very much up to the individual teller—which makes the performance of the story mutable as well.

So we can see here, at the dawn of humankind, that we were already engaging in frequent storytelling and that those stories were completely fluid in both content *and* performance, but came from a course that was tangible and close to the audience.

3.1.2 Stage Plays

The first enormous leap in technology in terms of storytelling was the advent of writing. Once things could be recorded on some sort of medium, the stories could be set down in stone, both literally and figuratively! A story that had previously been memorized and performed by the storyteller could now have its characters, events, drama, and historical significance become permanent! Once this was permanent, the story stopped being mutable. Once there is a source, you can always check things against that source, and if you deviated from it, people would know. Written language provided a good way to make things permanent, especially when it came to stories (Figure 3.1).

But the idea of a *book*, where that story is recorded and you walk around with it everywhere you go, was a long way off. Most early writing was on clay or stone, or even sometimes on scrolls and parchment. It wasn't something you took with you. It was usually something held in a library or in a protected place, where only scribes (usually the only literate people), priests, and academic sorts pored over their contents, stooped and covered in dust.

The rest of the world was busy with mundane daily tasks such as farming and soldiering and bartering and commerce. The most common everyday use of writing and recording was actually for those tasks—recording how many sheep, bales of hay, goats, or gold coins a person owned, owed, or spent. There wasn't a lot of use for recording of stories for the purpose of reading. So where did they get our entertainment?

They got them from plays. Why plays? You'll have to ask the ancient Greeks that question—they started performing them in the sixth or the seventh century BC, but the earliest surviving one we have is *The Persians* by Aeschylus, in 472 BC. The first plays had two important components—a single actor, who performed the main dramatic parts, and a chorus, or group of others who sang the narration as the part the oral storyteller used to assume. As the evolution of the play continued, the actors grew in number and the chorus was reduced, eventually becoming what we now know as a *staged theater*, with no actual narrator but multiple actors

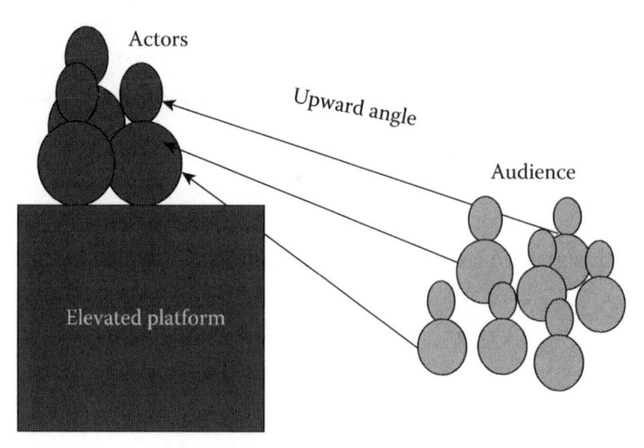

FIGURE 3.1 Elevated platform stage in the Elizabethan era model of productions and storytelling. Notice how the audience must look up at the actors.

telling the story through conversations. Most likely, the initial format of a Greek staged play evolved from the old oral traditions, where the teller would tell the story and the rest of the audience would be a part of the action, only the roles were inverted as a single actor played the main role while a multitude of singers acted the narration.

Eventually, the Shakespearean stage from the sixteenth century is what we now think of as theater—with the actors elevated onto a stage and the audience watching from below.

What are the important considerations and attributes for a staged performance? The biggest change from the oral tradition is the permanence of the script. The story, no matter what, is now set in stone. The storyteller can no longer arbitrarily change parts of the story at will, because there is a central authority to the story. The performance, however, *can* (and often does) change, evolve, and shift as do the actors and the director/producer. A live performance can always change, sometimes night to night, and this provides a total mutability to the story as it is told, despite the fact that the dialogue should always remain exactly the same. In this way, the concept of storyteller or story maker and performer became separated, and the two could exist in entirely separate time periods, as we often see Shakespeare or Becket or Checkov or other famous playwrights' work performed again and again. The play and story have become eternal, while the performance can always be refreshed and adapted to modern considerations.

It may be interesting to note here that radio shows from the 1920s to the 1940s and indeed much of the first years of television were thought of in stage performance terms. Most television shows were filmed in front of a live studio audience, and some still are today (*The Daily Show*, game shows, many morning talk shows). Why would we choose to film shows in front of a live studio audience when there's no real need for it anymore? Why indeed would the early television shows, such as *The Honeymooners* or *I Love Lucy*, choose to perform live when they could have easily been recorded in front of cameras (once the technology became available) without the need for an audience?

The answer comes in the form of our old friend, *perceived distance*. When the distance between the teller and the audience is near, there is feedback between the performers and the audience—they hear the laughter, the catcalls, and the murmuring and derive energy from the performance, which in turn drives the timing and the pacing of the events unfolding. As television became more and more distant and film-like, the need for a live audience decreased and television became much more like mini-films with commercial breaks and less like staged performances.

3.1.3 Books and Literature

The modern age of storytelling begins with the printing press. For the first time in the history of humankind, we could all become the audience of a story when we chose to and wherever we were, and all have identical content. Although writing is much older than the printing press, it was always done by hand and never mass produced. So although we were able to record stories, they were never created for mass distribution. As soon as we could do this, the advent of the novel and the journal for mass consumption followed quickly, using this new powerful tool of communication available.

The modern age of storytelling is also a very important shift in the paradigm of the bi-directionality of the story. With information that is recorded and mass distributed, it is no longer possible to have any input from the audience. The audience suddenly becomes incredibly passive, and for the next several hundred years, the passivity of the audience in these format of storytelling absolutely became the norm.

With the advent of the printing press came the ability of individuals to possess their own, portable copy of a story that would be the same as everyone else's (Figure 3.2). Mass production of media meant that, for the

FIGURE 3.2 An early printing press; the first machine that could mass-produce text and disseminate it out into the world.

first time, the exact same printed media could be distributed to millions of people and they would all have the exact same frame of reference (including images).

3.2 POSTINDUSTRIAL FORMATS OF STORYTELLING

3.2.1 Radio

Radio broadcasting deserves special attention here because it was the hallmark of a new age in communication. For the very first time, live performances (albeit only audio) were able to be broadcasted to a huge audience simultaneously (Figure 3.3). The technology, unlike printed books, could not yet be recorded (like a podcast), so synchronicity was absolutely necessary. It was the dawn of the family-gathering phenomenon of storytelling, where a certain time and place was marked for listening to the radio shows

FIGURE 3.3 An early radio set, from 1923. The radio was the first media able to broadcast at large distances.

being broadcast. Once again, like a printed book, this audience was completely passive and did not interact with the storyteller at all.

3.2.2 Television

With the advent of motion pictures came the final (or so we thought) blow to the idea of mutability. Once we could film a performance and record it, everything became permanent. The performance is always the same—Clint Eastwood will always squint like a badass and blow away the exact same street punks with an enormous .44 Magnum in San Francisco as Dirty Harry, forever. Unless you're George Lucas rereleasing *Star Wars* (again) with new effects, the film is always going to be exactly as it was the first time you saw it.

This permanence changes a lot about the nature of the story. We tend to watch films on huge screens, where the actors are physically and metaphysically larger than life. We also have no input to them at all—we know that what we are watching was filmed a million miles away, years ago, and that we have no visceral connection to the performers or the story. This creates a tremendous sense of distance from us to the story, and it also creates a high level of passivity while engaging in the story. Instead of interacting in some way, we are simply receivers of the information on the screen (or earphones if it's a podcast). We don't have any input into it at all. Film and television have now become passive entertainment, vessels of unidirectional content. The technology reached a static point and stayed there for more than a full generation without really changing.

3.2.2.1 Reality Television

Reality television presents a fairly unique sector of what would normally be in the category of film or filmed television. The reason reality television is particularly unique is how the format is presented.

Reality television, and by this I mean *real* reality television, where the participants are not actors and the events have not been scripted, is unique because although the performance is completely permanent and eternal, on a per-episode basis, the story is completely mutable. Since there's no actual script, the story is completely unplanned every week, with mostly conflict between the personalities driving the events or perceived narrative through the episodes. There are some who would say that there's not really a transformative narrative at all in reality television, but I personally believe it to be more subtle than that; reality television is a reflection of the bigger picture. It rearranges our relationship to the elements of storytelling by putting it into a format that mirrors the advent of social media and nonlinear information.

Formatting of information, even if it *is* a story, is very important. In a film, or a traditional narrative television series, the narrative and information are shown to you through the lens of a moving (if not always linear) timeline, with the individual actors or cast acting unaware of the filming of the events. The story is told to you in a format as if you were a passive observer somewhere in the background, watching the story unfold. Reality television, in its most common form, is giving you the third-person perspective of events, *but* you get the added feature of the cast giving their personal commentary over the classic third-person narrative. This is the most vital component of the reality television format—you get to hear the future version of the character talking about the *present* events happening in front of you. It's like a chronic commentary from the future about the present from multiple perspectives all at once!

Let's really break this down into logistics. The sequencing of a standard episode of *Jersey Shore* shows short clips of certain interactions or events surrounding a central cast of characters. While these short clips are being showed to the viewer, ostensibly showing something that happened in the past, the individual cast members are giving their own interpretation of the playing events, from an interview chair, sometime in the future (but yet still in your past). Talk about messing with sequencing and the multiple perspectives! You almost get all views of a situation from a personal perspective at once, with two alternating timelines. It's essentially entertainment cubism. The amazing thing is that your brain can stitch *all* this together without batting a proverbial eyelash! Your brain, as we will continue to see throughout this book, is a pattern-recognition machine and bases its observations or perceptions upon associations and not through data crunching or numbers. The brain knows things because it makes associations between multiple elements that appear to have meaning (even if they don't), and this is how it forms reinforcement about commonalities. The point of this discussion is that it's easily able to take multiple perspectives from multiple timelines and put them all together into one meaningful narrative, even if the pieces are scattered all over the place! This is the great and difficult-to-reproduce part of the human mind—it can make sense out of things that computers simply can't, or at least not without a lot of programming.

Now the real question here, about *Jersey Shore*, and the rest of popular reality television, is *why* they suddenly made such a tremendous impact on the formatting of popular entertainment. In the course of about 15 years, reality television went from a single show on MTV (*The Real World*) to the majority format on some cable networks. The format was so popular that it even inspired successful comedic mockumentary shows such as *The Office*, in which the same format was used in a sitcom based on a paper sales office in Scranton, Pennsylvania for comedic purposes.

The advent of these reality shows seem to coincide with the increasing popularity of social media, which in itself was a revolution in interpersonal communication. For the first time ever, we were able to see, hear, and communicate in short blurbs to people across the world, sharing concepts, trends, ideas, baby pictures, or images of our food (which are still inexplicably popular on Instagram). As we were able to share all this and personally comment on current events as they happened, the formatting of the popular entertainment mutated to reflect the shift in pace and focus of storytelling. The focus on the narrative, the plot, and the subtlety were slowly warped to focus mainly on the characters and the conflict between those characters. This mirrors the forms of Internet social media focus on the individual and the conflict with other individuals.

3.3 THE INFORMATION AGE OF STORYTELLING

I have chosen to separate the new forms of storytelling from the archaic by way of technology; the classic forms are based on technology that was fairly well cemented from 1950 up until about 2008, at which point the iPhone and mobile technology became popular, prevalent, and feasible for at least half the world. This advent of technology, while not necessarily an absolute influence on every form of media technology, was an important shift from the passive entertainment of the latter half of the twentieth century into the new interactive entertainment of the twenty-first century. It's not that we don't still enjoy our television and film content! We just supplement them heavily with second-screen content, or even constant social chatter about the content. The most important aspect of the following new forms of storytelling is their level of interactivity with the story; the audience has some level of influence on the direction the narrative will take or which characters will continue to be in the story.

3.3.1 Contest Television

Contest television presents a separate category from reality television, despite the fact that it often mimics the format, because of one single important factor: interactivity with the audience! True contest television uses audience participation to actively engage the viewers and allow them to participate (albeit very little) in the story itself. The story can move forward based on the collective voice of the audience. *American Idol* is the most classic and, at the time of this writing, the most influential of all contest television shows in American culture. Even though the audience only has some limited control over the direction of the show, that tiny amount of control is a tremendous draw for an audience! There is a reason that *American Idol* has become one of the most successful shows in American television history! It created, once again, some level of audience participation and control over the outcome.

American Idol is not entirely democratic. The first several rounds are decided by panels of judges. But from the semifinals onward, the fate of the show's contestants is decided by public vote. During the contestants' performance as well as the recap at the end, a toll-free telephone number for each contestant is displayed on the screen. For a two-hour period after the episode ends (up to four hours for the finale) in each US time zone, viewers may call or send a text message to their preferred contestant's telephone number, and each call or text message is registered as a vote for that contestant. Viewers are allowed to vote as many times as they can within the two-hour voting window. Over 110 million votes were cast in the first season, and by season 10, the seasonal total had increased to nearly 750 million. Voting via text was made available in the second season, and 7.5 million text messages were sent to *American Idol* that season. The number of text messages rapidly increased, reaching 178 million texts by season 8 (Figure 3.4). Online voting was offered for the first time in season 10 (Figure 3.5).

Now let's analyze the level of interactivity of this show. You may think of it as minor, with millions of people having a tiny say in the forward narrative, but it's set up incredibly cleverly. Do you remember the concept of *distance* when it comes to the storyteller and the audience? Interactivity is one of the things that can shrink that distance down intensely, and digital media technology is able to shrink our perceived distance between the audience and the story by offering them a direct line of influence, even if it is crowdsourced with millions of other viewers. But the timing on the influence is crucial—you must watch the show and vote within the small window after the show to have that influence. This limited-timed level of interactivity is vital because it must happen inside a small window. This is the concept of *synchronicity* and how fast any form of interaction can occur along with the feedback from that interaction. Think about synchronous

All 15 years of season premiere ratings for Fox's flagship singing competition

Season	Live 18–49 rating	Total viewers (Millions)	
1	4.8	9.9	*(Premiere low in total viewers, although unknown commodity and the summer date)*
2	11.9	25.1	
3	12.9	29.0	
4	14.0	33.6	
5	15.3	35.5	
6	15.8	37.4	*(A season premiere high, per both metrics)*
7	13.8	33.5	
8	11.7	30.4	
9	11.8	29.9	*(First season without Paula Abdul; Ellen DeGeneres joined on Feb. 9)*
10	9.8	26.3	
11	7.4	21.9	*(First season without Simon Cowell; Steven Tyler and Jennifer Lopez joined)*
12	6.0	17.9	
13	4.7	15.2	
14	3.2	11.2	
15	2.9	10.9	*(Demo low, through one million more total viewers than series' summer premiere)*

Source: Nielsen

WRAP

FIGURE 3.4 *American Idol* ratings for season premieres.

and asynchronous communications with your mobile phone. If I call you on the phone and talk to you, you are expected to have a synchronous conversation with me; therefore, I say something and I expect a pretty quick response. This is a synchronous conversation. If, however, I text you a question, I don't necessarily expect an immediate response. You could be driving, or walking your dog, or just taking your time thinking about responding. This is asynchronous. In terms of interactivity, the level of synchronicity has a huge impact on the perceived level of control over a story, with the more synchronous the control, the less distance between

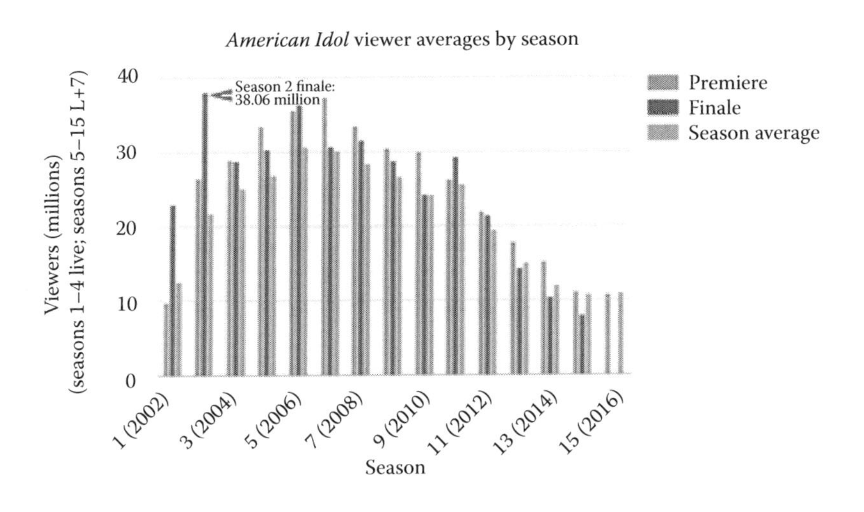

FIGURE 3.5 *American Idol* total viewership statistics.

you and the story. So when *American Idol* created a brief window of time to vote on the contestants, they deliberately created a high sense of control on the part of the audience, despite the very small level of influence an individual vote will have. If you see the results of your vote within hours, you have a much higher level of connection *to* that vote.

3.3.2 Social Fiction

What is a *social media story*? How does it differ from a regular story? Social media, such as Twitter, YouTube, Facebook, Snapchat, Vine, and Instagram, not only have unique and differing formats that allow one to tell a story, but also get interaction from fans, audience members, critics, and just random people. It's almost as if social media recaptures the essence of the stage-based performance and turns it global and asynchronous! The storytellers have a limited, asynchronous, bidirectional conversation with the audience, but one they can choose to shut off, limit, filter, or just plain ignore any time they choose.

Each individual social media type has its own set of methodology and formatting, which are too numerous to go into in the scope of this book, *but* the parameters of interaction here are very similar. Audience interaction happens by way of comments, which are a mishmash of likes, hates, psychotic ramblings, and trolling that go on as optional entertainment with each posted video, baby picture, or wall posting. We may choose to scan over this information or dismiss it, but it's really an important part of the social media storytelling experience because it allows us to express our opinions in a general way, interacting with the other audience members and sometimes just throwing our personal opinions at an invisible wall just to watch them stick. And in a way, it's that invisible wall that matters so much, the feeling that you are a part of a bigger experience. It's not so dissimilar from the voting that goes on in *American Idol*! You get instant feedback in the form of a conversation with another living, breathing human being. In this way, we are able to sneak in multiple forms of interaction into certain types of storytelling.

It's also important to note here that social media storytelling can be an effective tool in developing *and* distributing narrative-based story material. Social media is no longer just about posting baby pictures and random cat videos. It's slowly becoming a genuine medium for legitimate entertainment. *DadBoner* is a comedic Twitter story from Mike Burns, who portrays the world of Karl Weitzin, a soon-to-be-divorced husband and father, as he plays out his pathetic midlife crisis in typical American buffoonery. The important thing to note about this story is that it was entirely Twitter-based, playing out its drama in 140 characters or less each time. The Twitter feed became such a runaway success that the contents were purchased and sold as a television series, which should be in production at the time of the writing of this book. Whether or not the format of Twitter can be successfully turned into an episodic sitcom and retain the same comedic appeal remains to be seen; however, it's a sign that social media is maturing and turning into a genuine storytelling medium unto its own.

3.3.3 Game-Based Storytelling

Games are at the highest level of interactivity and synchronicity in terms of storytelling. A video-based game, whether mobile, personal computer, or console, is an object in constant flux and, as such, requires a constant flow of input from the user. In fact, unlike all other formats of storytelling cited in this book, the game is the only one that requires input from the user—all other formats are interactive only if the audience chooses such. You don't have to vote for *American Idol* and you don't have to leave comments on somebody's YouTube animation; however, in order to move the story forward in a game, you absolutely must be an active participant. This means that it requires a very high level of mental activity, and indeed, we can see (based on multiple MRI studies) that the brain activity lights up in an entirely different area when playing a game as opposed to watching an episode of a sitcom on television.

Now, of course we know that not all games are stories or even contain the essential building blocks for a story, but a surprising amount of them not only have complex stories, but also allow the player to participate and even shape that story into something unique. One of the things about a game is that you have multiple possible measures of interaction with the story that the game is based upon, and those different amounts can be quite variable. At its simplest, the story and the game run in parallel, where the player really only watches the story as it progresses, in between gameplay. You can read much more about all this in Section III, titled "Interactivity."

CHAPTER 4

What Are Stories About? The Content of Stories

YOU MIGHT THINK, READING the title of this chapter, that I'm being deliberately obtuse. "Wait a minute," you might say, "Can't a story be just about anything?"

The answer to that question is *yes*, but also *no*. What I mean by this is that, of course, you can tell or create a story about any person, subject, event, lifestyle, or plot characteristic you want to; however, there will be some commonalities that tie all stories together in some form. One of the most important things about stories and storytelling is that they are primarily a form of *communication*, and in that communication between humans, we will always be able to identify common behavior, psychology, symbology, ideas, and emotions. We're all human, after all, unless you're an alien, and *then* you probably wouldn't understand the story at all.

But let's now explore what it's like to have a human commonality behind all our stories. It means that our psychology drives the content of our stories, and that psychology is derived from feelings, emotions, mysteries, and circumstances that surround all our lives. The heart of the human being beats with a complex set of fears, jubilations, and reverence for the world in which they find themselves both a helpless subject of *and* a simultaneous master.

In his book *The Power of Myth*, Joseph Campbell identifies very specific common mythologies and exposes their commonality with aspects of the human psyche, explaining how they derive not from actual events so much as a shared *human experience*, which is seated deep in our subconscious mind. In his writing, he postulates that there are many shared experiences that all humans connect with on a deep emotional level. These shared experiences and emotional constructs weave their way into our stories and mythology and reflect some of the inner working of the mind.

For your convenience, I have pulled three specific categories of stories and further broke them down into subcategories which explain the commonalities between different stories, both mundane and epic. I have done this in order to illustrate the generalities of stories and storytelling and what these types of stories are constructed from as well as the role they have in human communication. I separate these into the human experience, the mythological experience, and the learning experience.

4.1 THE HUMAN EXPERIENCE

Can we have any experience other than the human kind? If you're reading this book, chances are you're a human being, and that you and I have experienced incredibly similar events in our life. Those major events leave a lasting impression on each individual that experiences them—and all of us will have to undergo two of these experiences just in order to qualify as human! Human experiences define us as human; therefore, we tend to form stories around them. Not only do we form stories around these experiences, but we also know that other humans will identify with them simply because they are human. It is in this manner that we can connect with others emotionally when we are telling a story. We know that they have had the same experience, and it will reverberate with their consciousness. Other than dogs and cats, I've never really tried to tell a story to a nonhuman, and if I did know any aliens, I'm pretty sure it would be hard to communicate to them through storytelling—they might not have any similar frame of reference to work from! Come to think of it, the dogs and the cats I was talking to didn't seem to be very interested in my stories either.

Joseph Campbell, in his book *The Hero with a Thousand Faces*, published in 1964, began his own personal exploration into the world of comparable mythology (Figure 4.1). In this, and his subsequent series of interviews with Bill Moyers, later published as *The Power of Myth*, he delves into the human psyche as it pertains to, and hence creates, the archetypes of mythology and the stories they entail. His thesis and body of work on the subject entailed deconstructing myths and stories, both modern and ancient, from a psychological perspective, which broke down the elements of the stories that we tell and retell into their primary human experiential

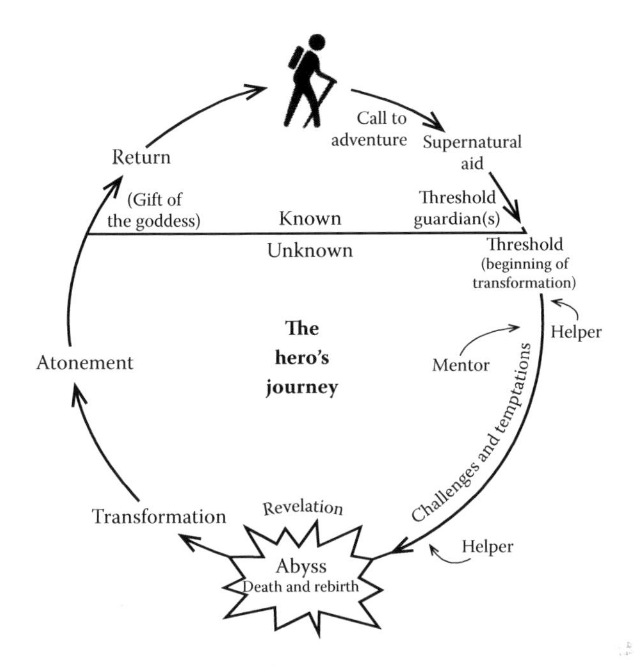

FIGURE 4.1 A diagram of the hero's journey, as explained in his first book *The Hero with a Thousand Faces.* George Lucas explained many times that his original inspirations for much of the original *Star Wars Trilogy* came from reading this book in college.

components. In this way, he could easily explain the entirety of storytelling and story content from our personal quest to ultimately understand ourselves and the mysteries within the human life.

The human stages of life are easy for us to create stories about, because they all dwell well within the range of our personal experience, or the experience of those who we are close to. Each stage of our life and subsequent lives we witness are subject to our desire to understand it and share our experiences with others through the creation and the telling of stories.

4.1.1 Birth

Everyone is born, right? And even if you are grown in a test tube and birthed by an evil robot baby farm 500 years in the future, you are still *born* so to speak. It's a beginning to life, an entry into the physical world in which you currently exist, a moment of creation. Birth is the ultimate genesis for the concept of humanity, because this is how we propagate the species. All of us are born with a *tabula rasa*, or a blank slate of consciousness and an empty state of morality. We have no preconceived notions or personal sense of ethics. We are, lacking all other words, new.

This sense of newness is reflected in our stories. The miracle or concept of birth in one way or another pervades our sense of innocence and helplessness. Think about the iconography of the baby Jesus or the child Krishna. The idea that the newborn child is a thing to be both protected and revered is deeply instinctual and of course provides a vital role in evolution as the relative time from birth to viable maturity in humans is the longest of the animal kingdom. Many other species are self-sustaining almost immediately after birth or hatching! This is not so for humans.

4.1.2 Childhood

Childhood is a distinct state from birth in that it represents a vital learning component to the human life. Although you can continue to learn your entire life, learning vital aspects about the world, your place in it, what to do in order to facilitate survival, morality, ethics, action/consequence, etc., is an important part of any normal human childhood. In fact, few children would survive into adulthood without guidance during this incredibly important part of a human life cycle.

Stories of childhood are especially rife with these influential circumstances, and many stories include or deliberately *exclude* the childhood (Zeus, Jesus, etc.) in order to generate the notion of a person (or Deity) who has never been young, foolish, or vulnerable in any sense, which is often what sets them apart from normal people..

The characteristics of childhood are very specific—generally (but not always), the child is physically and mentally vulnerable and requires an adult or a set of adults to protect and nurture it. In that situation, it is common for the child to have a differing or reduced set of responsibilities while it is learning how to be a member of the society in which it has been born. It is this combination of semi-innocence and lack of responsibility that generates later feelings of nostalgia, which is a positive connection to events, technology, or symbols of an earlier time period in which you were a child and had less emotional weight to bear. Childhood is a shared common experience with all adult humans, and the act and art of growing up is explored in multiple types of stories.

4.1.3 Transformation

Transformation is a tough category to pin down, because it occurs in so many different forms in many different societies and cultures, but the concept is nearly universal in humanity because at the very least, there must be a transition from child to adult at some point. This point of transition is celebrated and well defined in some cultures (such as a bar mitzvah) and not so well celebrated in others. Because the nature of the narrative in terms of storytelling must involve a transformation of some kind, these "coming-of-age" stories are often the most common and popular.

The transformation from one thing to another can come in the flavor of gender as it pertains to growing up. The man's transformation is often from child to warrior, child to hunter, or child to soldier. In effect, the boy child takes on the responsibility of violence, provision, protection, or aggression in his male-dominant society in order to become an adult in the adult world. In more modern storytelling, we can see adulthood be defined also as fatherhood, a point at which a man must learn to cope with the needs of other than his own.

The woman's transformation is also discussed often, but with a much different take, based on biology. The three-pronged aspect of the female journey is often characterized by the Virgin (child), the Mother (birth/parenthood), and the Crone/Witch (wisdom/magic). The biological imperative seems heavy handed in this instance, but the truth of the shared human experience is that women must be able to give birth in order to propagate the species! So their traditional transformation is often seen in those terms.

Joseph Campbell often refers to the *hero's journey* as part of the transformation mythology, in which an individual undergoes a strife-filled journey, returning a different person in the end. This transformative journey is always characterized by a series of difficulties and trials, after which the hero has transformed himself. The most common geneses of this concept is cited as *The Epic of Gilgamesh* and *Homer's Odyssey*, which both depict heroic but all-too-human men in the stages of their transformation and journey.

Transformation in a more modern sense may not come in the vestiges of literal growing up! *Breaking Bad*, by Vince Gilligan, is a great example of a modern transformation of a mild-mannered high school chemistry teacher into a homicidal criminal drug lord for the sake of money and protection of his family. In this modern tale of transformation, we can see the lines of psychology and morality being explored by the story creator. Transformation can be defined as any series of events or actions that dramatically and permanently alters the basic psychological makeup of a character.

4.1.4 Strife/War/Journey

Strife, war, and difficult circumstances are a part of most, if not all human experience. They are characterized by events larger than one individual can control, but must exist in or combat against in one form or another. They can take any form.

Reactions to these circumstances and the alterations to lives that result can be the focus of many stories. A great example of this would be *Gone with the Wind*, a biopic set against the backdrop of the Civil War, which in itself was an intensely transformative period of American history in every aspect of technology, culture, agriculture, economics, and personal lives. The strife and the war behind the individual stories gave it an engine with which to view the characters and their struggle.

4.1.5 Love/Sexual Passion

Do we need elucidate? Love stories abound in all corners of society. From *Romeo and Juliet* to *Kramer vs. Kramer*, we're all suckers for a good love story. The bonds of love and sexual passion are so strong, and the sensations and the life-altering emotions are so foundational that most humans can connect with the experience on an incredibly visceral level. We tell these stories because they evoke sympathetic emotions in the teller and the audience alike.

The stories of love are powerful, eternal, and bound to resurface from day to day because they are part of that incredibly natural and eternal human drive for emotional connection to another, and the potent instinctual sensations of the experience often override the most basic element of our evolutionary imperative: survival. Anything powerful enough to drive us to override the basic survival instinct has got to be something that resides so deep in our subconscious that we must need to relive it as often as possible through our stories.

4.1.6 Parenthood

Often portrayed as a transformation of some sort, and in brief, covered under modern male transformation or motherhood female transformation, nevertheless, the concept of parenthood can be elucidated here a little. Becoming a protector of an innocent brings up the concepts of the child, the childhood and the responsibility, which in itself is a transformative experience.

4.1.7 Death

Death is the big experience, the last experience, the impending doom at the end of the road. It's important to note here because we all see it coming, we all know it as an essential part of the human experience, but nobody really knows what's on the other side of it. We can't talk about it with somebody after the fact (not with any level of certainty anyway), and we can't relate the experience to any other we've had.

Stories about death are a huge focus for us as human beings. Our eternal focus on the supernatural is derived from this fear of death that pervades every step of our life as we focus (or not) on the end of it. Stories of supernatural entities are a vestige of our focus on trying to push the persistence of consciousness beyond death and believing that, like a vampire, we can outlive our own demise. The undead are reflections of our desire to remain in some corporeal form after the inevitable physical death in the physical world. Our focus on ghosts and post-life entities also illustrates a deep need for the conscious mind to survive the physical death.

Not all stories of death are supernatural, however. The death of friends, family members, and loved ones will play a transformative role in everyone's lives eventually, and the experience is so powerful that it is easy to connect with when engaging with a story related to it. Most stories based on the human experience have some tinge of death to them, if not in actuality, in terms of danger or fear. The specter of death, lingering off of the left shoulder somewhere in the background, as the heroic protagonist fights off hordes of Mongols or tromps through the wilderness or engages his or her mortal enemy in combat, will add a sharp cut of excitement to an otherwise boring and dull story. The fear of, and aversion to the concept of physical death is a major driving force in the narrative of many stories because it is a primal and pervasive mystery of biological life.

4.2 THE MYSTICAL EXPERIENCE

The mystical experience, or mythological experience, is a set of categories that encompasses all the things that are outside the fundamental human understanding. If the human experience is a set of concepts we are all bound to by commonality of knowledge, the mythological experience is a set of concepts we are bound to by commonality of ignorance. These are the things we *don't* know. These are the things we *don't* understand. These are the things that mystify us and boggle the mind, the things we must make sense out of. But every culture does it differently! This is what makes stories based on mythological experience so rich, creative, and variable. Since these are not shared experiences, they can be incredibly original and imaginative. This is the place where our creativity shines as human beings, and the ability to generate, remember, and manipulate concepts in our heads assists us in creating a world which does not exist in the empirical realm.

4.2.1 Creation

Figure 4.2 shows the famous Sistine Chapel rendition of the Christian creation myth, where the monotheistic God created the world and man along with it, giving him a wife (first Lilith, then later Eve) and a garden to hang out in (until they both screwed it up and got kicked out later).

Other creation myths involve primordial mounds (Egypt), dreaming Gods (Hindu), slain dragons (Babylon, Tiamat), and the amorous coupling of Sky and Earth (Greco/Roman). It is here where the true ingenuity and massive creativity can thrive in the human imagination, because there is no collective experience governing the narrative! It's basically whatever you can come up with.

4.2.2 Nature

What is more terrifying and encompassing in scope? We live inside the container of the natural world, and natural phenomenon can be incredibly spectacular. It is larger than life, a taker of life, and a giver of life. Volcanoes destroy entire civilizations; the Nile floods and provides life in the form of persistent agriculture. The natural world was once and always will be mystifying to the human mind. We are a slave to it at times and a master of it at others, and although we are a part of it, we also seek to understand, conquer, and re-create it as much as we possibly can. Nature and man's relationship to it is an essential part of storytelling, from *Moby Dick* to

FIGURE 4.2 The creation of Adam, on the Sistine Chapel. This is the Judeo–Christian creation legend and mythology.

The Old Man and The Sea, the struggle of the individual human against the ultimate power of the natural world is often the theme of the stories we are familiar with.

Prescientific societies often created deities, gods, demigods, and monsters in order to explain the natural world and the repeatable phenomenon which was a part of their environment. Why does the ground shake and heave sometimes? Perhaps a group of giants are trampling the earth, running down from their ice world and causing it to be so. Why does the volcano spew hot molten lava from its core? It's Hephaestus, the smithy god, forging weapons in his workshop. What is the origin of thunder and lightning? It's Thor, or Zeus, or a dozen other storm gods of the sky, striking down people and trees in anger as the lightning sears an oak to a crisp in seconds. Where does the ocean get its strength? It's Poseidon, lord of the deep, in control of all the seas and the oceans in the world. Why does the winter come and lay cold and death to the world? It's Persephone, the fertility goddess, weeping for her daughter while she is in the underworld. Where does the sun come from? It's the chariot of Helios or, better yet, the face of the god Amon-Ra, or a giant ball of fire set in the heavens by the gods, and so on. These myths were rationale for the natural phenomenon which one could often *see* but never grasp physically, and for this reason, they were relegated to explanation mythos which offered up some form of reasoning (no matter how fantastical) for the basic natural phenomenon of nature.

Of course, as science and technology have provided such reprieve from foolish notions in our modern understanding of the universe, we still refer to these mythologies and irrational explanations for the natural world. Any child who heard that "Jesus is bowling" when the thunder cracks has heard a modern version of the Thor myth. We still like to come up with fantastical explanations for natural phenomenon in the modern world.

4.2.3 Fate/Influence

Why do we need these gods and goddesses in the mythological pantheons? One reason is that we need channels of influence over the events we have no power to change. Things such as rainfall, river flooding, fertility, crop growth, illnesses, volcano eruption, or hunting bounty are all natural things that occur with or without our personal input. We have little to no power over many of these events and catastrophes, so we have invented stories of gods and goddesses and magic and incantations and even potions in order to change our individual fortunes. These stories collectively create a vessel through which we can channel our energies in order to influence the result of a desired wish. The modern form of this can be seen in the multiplicity of Christian tales of saints and their prayers or deeds of sacrifice, and how those deeds were rewarded; prayers, answered; enemies, defeated; or pious ascension to heaven, achieved! We as humans want to connect stories with our need for a way to change the mind of the gods, mostly by bribing, entreating, or bargaining with them in some form or another.

4.2.4 Purpose and Origin

Why are we here? Who made us? What does that maker want with us? These are questions that have been asked (and answered) many times over throughout the history of the human species. We have a burning and vociferous need for validation of our basic existence, which is apparently unique to the species. We ask these questions often, and with just as many postulative theories as individuals asking the question! Ultimately, we don't know why we are here, what our purpose is, or who made us, and despite ~80,000 years of different answers to that question, it remains a mystery.

But the lack of certainty only allows the human mind to generate a million fragments of curiosity and imagination-driven worlds with entities and characters and motivations. Our purpose and origin are explained through a thousand creation myths, with accidents and deliberation at an equal level, which is to say that it's just as common for humanity to spring forth through a random occurrence or to be purposely crafted by a creator deity. In either case, the purpose, or the lack thereof, provides the central narrative of any creation myth. And these myths provide the glue that stitches the delicate human ego together, ensuring that at some point they believe in a greater purpose, a usefulness to their existence beyond the mundane life of picking berries and figs to survive another day. We love to create these stories, and indeed our active imagination appears to re-create new stories fulfilling the same role every so many years, as evidenced in the proliferation of religions and cults through the past decade alone.

4.2.5 Mystery

What's life without a little bit of mystery? The mystical experience contains all the elements of life that can't be explained by us, which mystify and fill us with a sense of wonderment. Most modern and ancient religions contain some aspect of these elements because without the mystical experience, life can be mundane, boring, and tiresome. The human mind craves mystery and discovery—it's one of the natural hallmarks of our species. Why else would there be so many mystery novels? What else would drive the need to create fictionalized mysteries and mystery-solving characters? From modern television detectives to Sherlock Holmes, the chronic need for our species to engage in and solve mysteries is a fundamental need for our psyche. These mysteries are spun into stories for us to indulge our own creative problem-solving skills, which need to be exercised and flexed just like our physical muscles in order to feel healthy and fulfilled. The mythological experience allows us to weave the mysteries of life such as birth, purpose, and death into a tantalizing set of answers that we feel may be out there, but ever slightly beyond the reach of our frail, human minds. Like the Holy Grail, the mysterious is predicated upon a quest for answers that can never truly be achieved. These stories of explanation which are devoid of explanation represent the element of mystery itself, its elusiveness, and the paradox with which we are always somehow fascinated.

4.2.6 Explanation of Death

One of the biggest and most imperative drives of the human psyche is to make sense of the most looming and universal elements of humanity: death. Death is the ultimate truth which we all understand and know will eventually occur to ourselves, but the mystery of what lies beyond the physical death is the progenitor and indeed the inspiration for a large amount of our story content. From demons to angels to vampires to *The Tibetan Book of the Dead*, we constantly seek to understand, make sense of, and in some way comfort ourselves that beyond that physical death, our conscious mind persists and becomes something else. Stories, therefore, often deal with this explanation and categorization of post-death experiences for the very reason that we are universally terrified of the concept of our own impending doom. The psychological fear that drives us also inspires our internal creativity, which becomes the genesis of our stories involving religion and the divine as it pertains to humanity. So every time you read a ghost story, hear somebody talk about angels interacting with humanity, or watch a movie that involves reincarnation, you can see the origins of the desire for such content.

Valhalla was the heaven of Nordic mythology, where the warriors slain in battle would go and feast with the Valkryies for all eternity. The heaven of the Christian mythology is a wonderful place where everything is at peace for all eternity. The underworld of Hades in Greek mythology is a dark and dismal place, where humans are sent to tasks that work in equal retribution for all their sins (which explains why the Greeks were very married to earthly pleasures!). In Egypt, a person had to be prepared and mummified to face the gods in the trials which would determine the quality of afterlife one would have, if indeed it would happen at all! What do all these stories have in common? As you can see, the only commonality is that there *is* an afterlife, and at the very least, your mind and personal perceptive consciousness will survive the cessation of your body to support it. In essence, all cultures believe in the device of the soul, which is a nonphysical imbuement of your mind as it exists outside of the corporeal structure (the body). And why is this important? It's important because it allows for continuity, the unbroken ability to continue to exist, in this world or in another. The stories that are based upon this continuity are there as a rational explanation as to not only *why* we do finally pass from physical life, but also what happens afterwards. It is this desperate need to understand the most vital and impending aspect of life that drives a huge amount of storytelling content.

4.3 THE LEARNING EXPERIENCE

Do we need stories to educate? Couldn't we just read each other facts and figures and memorize them? It works in certain areas of education, such as mathematics, quantum physics, and chemistry.

Learning the Fibonacci sequence by way of a math book may be a great resource because it is inherently *objective* knowledge, but when it comes to learning the aspects of communication and the things that are *subjective*, we require a much more pattern-based context. For this purpose, we as human beings often tend to gravitate toward our storytelling skills in order to impart pieces of knowledge into those who do not possess it. And this is the important part of the learning experience—we tell stories about people who are learning lessons. Our pattern-recognition machines, also known as the *brain*, don't have as much use for numbers, math, and statistics when it comes to behaviors and subjective information. What we need is a story to connect behaviors to.

This may sound odd when you hear it in an objectified statement, but I'll try to put it to you in terms that any western-educated person will understand. The purpose behind a large portion of the stories we are told when we are young come in the form of fables and parables. Let's take the most common examples and analyze them.

Remember the *Little Boy Who Cried Wolf*? It was a story, with ancient origins, about a boy in a village who cried "Wolf!" as loudly as he could to see all the people from the village run around in a panic with axes and picks (ostensibly to kill the wolf in question), but when they ran around looking for the wolf, the little boy laughed at them for his own personal amusement. This act continued and annoyed the townspeople so much that they stopped believing anything the little boy said, and one day when a real wolf showed up, he cried out at the top of his lungs but nobody came running. And then the wolf ate him because nobody would save him from it, believing that they would just fall prey to his ruse once again.

FIGURE 4.3 An illustration from *Uncle Remus' tales of Bre'r Rabbit*, a children's fable from the Deep South in America. Fables and education experiences often use animals and allegorical tales to teach children the wisdom of cause and effect.

Why are we told this story, and often repeat it to our own children, time and time again? What purpose does this folk tale or parable serve? It's a story designed to impart an element of *wisdom* or a simple formula of cause and effect, to the uninitiated. There are few ways to impart a sensation of cause and effect to an individual who has never experienced it first hand; the generally accepted way of doing this is to use one of the thousand fables and folk tales available to impart certain types of knowledge into a young or otherwise inexperienced mind (which is why they are usually told to children). The concept of the folk tale, the fairy tale, and the fable is to manufacture a story designed to insert an element of truth or wisdom into a young mind. When the pattern then repeats itself in real life—for instance, a little boy telling lies that suddenly nobody believes any more—that pattern will be reinforced by the application of the fable principles to the real-life situation. This can only occur if there is a pattern to compare the events to—which is the essential purpose of the fable! We all know the *Little Boy Who Cried Wolf* and can all therefore compare the cause and the effect of telling lies to the cause and the effect of crying wolf. Eventually, if there's never a real emergency, people will begin to ignore you. And when a real disaster occurs, you will be far less likely to find help.

The formats of fables and folk tales are incredibly similar, across multiple cultures. The characters populating these tales are often anthropomorphized animals, like Winnie the Pooh, Br'er Rabbit, and others (Figure 4.3). These characters are simplified versions of adult humans, resonating on a more childlike level and removing them from complex responsibilities and motivations, allowing the child mind to connect with them more easily. Aesop's fables are commonly known versions of these educational tales devised to impart wisdom, ethics, or morality.

CHAPTER 5

Why Do We Tell Stories? Functional Storytelling

So now that we know the *what* and the *how*, we need to focus on the *why*. You might say that we tell stories strictly for entertainment, and I wouldn't disagree with you completely, but stories have all kinds of important uses that we as endless consumers of entertainment simply overlook. We are often fed with stories that serve very specific purposes without being fully aware of it. They come in the form of political speeches, commercial advertising, educational television shows, public service campaigns, and all kinds of things in between. They come at us from print ads, streaming devices, mobile phones, billboard displays, and even on the backs of matchbooks. You could say that we are awash in a sea of stories, constantly raining down upon our heads, and most of the time, we only really pay attention to the ones we deliberately pursue for entertainment purposes.

In this chapter, we are going to look over the reasons why stories are told and some basic examples of each. I have identified several categories and subcategories of targeted, purposeful storytelling that can be derived from a simple observation of our culture.

5.1 BEHAVIOR MODIFICATION

Behavior modification is changing what someone does based on storytelling. This may not seem like a usual purpose of storytelling, but I and a million marketing/advertising executives would absolutely beg to differ with you

FIGURE 5.1 An old tobacco advertisement. Getting a person to *do* something is the foundation advertising.

upon that point. Stories are devised every day that are designed to get you to buy a product (Figure 5.1), vote for a candidate, prevent you from drinking and driving, or possibly do a multitude of other things that you might not be inclined to do otherwise. If some person just walked onto a stage in a commercial break, stuck a big box of some product into the camera, and said "buy this now", would you do it? Probably not, or at least you might be less *inclined* to do so. So in order to get you to do something, I have to figure out how to influence your behavior with some sort of associative reference. Remember, our brain is a pattern-recognition machine that eats up associations like candy! So if I can tell you a story that increases the positive associations between one thing and another, I can get you to do something you might otherwise not be inclined to do. The following subcategories are examples of targeted behavior modification that are frequently employed.

5.1.1 Choosing Something

How many times do you see the same laundry detergent commercial? How long have the makers of Tide and Gain or Pepsi and Coke been battling it out for your dollars? The important thing here is that everybody is going to be doing laundry, right? Assuming that you are an English-speaking citizen of a reasonably affluent economy (and even if you aren't), chances are you're going to wash your clothes at some point! And when you do, you'll have to *choose* a laundry detergent to buy at the store (unless you make it yourself). So when you go to the store and look at the aisle with all the different laundry detergents, chances are you're going to make a choice about which one to purchase. And that choice is heavily influenced by advertising—because advertising is there to tell you a story you can *relate to*, a story that somehow makes you more interested in their product than any other.

There are a few ways that a company can make you more interested in their product than the other. They can make their product cheaper than the competition. This makes you more likely to buy it, especially if the products are similar in quality. Tide and Gain are pretty similar in quality—I don't think one of them is made with better ingredients than the other. So if one is cheaper than the other is, you might be more likely to purchase that one. On the other hand, if you make a product better or of higher quality than the other, you can charge more for it than a competitor based on the quality or the perceived value—such as cars. A Porsche and a Ford are two brands with high levels of disparity in quality and perceived value. But the thing about creative storytelling in advertising in terms of choice is that you're really working with similar products, at similar price points, with similar quality. So what can you do to distinguish one from another?

This is where creative advertising is best applied. You see, you need to generate a story, or a campaign, aimed at distinguishing your product over another similar one. What is your goal? Who is your intended audience? How can you create a story or series of stories that can speak to them about making a choice for your product? All the classic elements of storytelling are applied here! You'll need characters who will appeal to the intended audience, and with whom they can identify. You need a sequence and a perspective. You can use *setting* to create associations with your targeted audience. You also need a focused narrative, in which the point of it is to not only communicate certain objective facts to the audience, but also make personal emotional connections with. And this is really the power of advertising as it pertains to storytelling: making a personal emotional association! Advertisers are smart; they've been working for years with surveys and focus groups and statistics in order to find out just what interests you and just how much. From the color of the packaging, to the name on the box, to the actors that work in the commercials.

If you want a good example of creative storytelling for advertising in terms of choosing a product over another, a great place to look is television ads. I would suggest any competing product ads that target similar products (hair products and soft drinks are always a good choice). In one television ad for Pepsi vs Coca-Cola, there are two men in a grocery store depicted, who are building display stands for the competing products. The display guys are competing for best or most elaborate display stacks of the two products, each one trying to outdo the other. In the end, the Pepsi guy builds a stage where Snoop Dogg appears and takes the microphone. Of course, the Pepsi guy display wins, and the Coca-Cola guy accepts his loss to the choice of *The Next Generation*, which Pepsi has consistently branded itself with (and reinforced by hip-hop icon Snoop Dogg's appearance on behalf of the product). So in this ad story, we have a simple but powerful message that somehow Pepsi is just more cool than Coke, if for nothing else than the celebrity association. But the important thing here is that one product has been chosen over another by Snoop Dogg, and in that choice, he will influence other individual choices between two products that are almost chemically identical in their major ingredients. So the choice has to be completely arbitrary on behalf of the consumer. This is a great place for targeted advertising, and a great place to see how the power of storytelling works in conjunction with behavior modification. Because you are more influenced emotionally and associatively by storytelling than factual information (such as statistics on hip-hop stars and their nonalcoholic cola beverage of choice), the advertisers used a short but targeted story on behalf of their product.

5.1.2 Buy Something

Like choosing something, buying something is a very similar methodology of targeted storytelling. What's the difference? At first glance, these two things might be very similar, as in they both involved a purchase of some kind (Figure 5.2)—*but* buying something new indicates that you

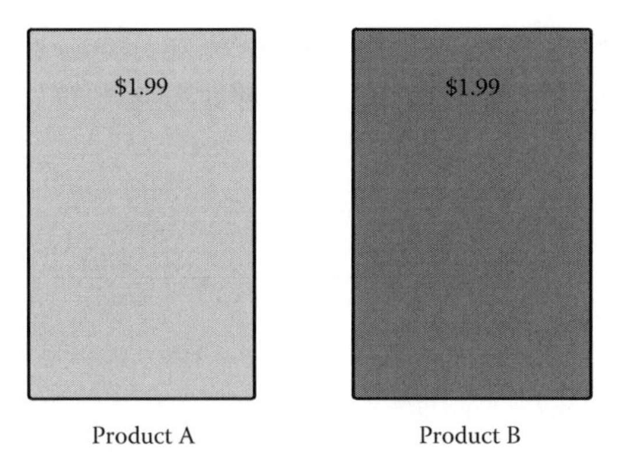

FIGURE 5.2 Choosing one product from two competing, similarly priced options often boils down to how the storytellers make you *feel* about it.

don't already *have* this thing and may have never *owned* this thing. The difference here is in how you frame the message to the intended audience. Instead of influencing your choice in a product you're going to buy anyway, influencing somebody to purchase a new product requires that you convince them that they actually need this product. Unlike Tide, a new top-of-the-line barbecue grill or a Foreman Grill are things you don't necessarily need—they're luxury items. So the dialogue for devising a story to sell you a Foreman Grill might be vastly different than getting you to switch from Tide to Gain laundry detergent.

How do we devise a way to sell somebody something they don't necessarily need, but definitely want? The best way is definitely targeted storytelling. You can tell somebody a story about how a person got lost driving and eaten by cannibalistic headhunters because he or she didn't have a Garmin global positioning system (GPS) installed in his or her car. In this (fictional) Garmin commercial, the person can't find the right turn, ends up running out of gas in a jungle, and is suddenly surrounded by vicious, angry, headhunting cannibals intent on eating him or her. Maybe the chief of the cannibals scans the inside of the car and says (translated with subtitles), "Maybe you should get a Garmin." So here we have devised a story that tells the audience how bad the circumstances could be *without* that GPS installed in your car, despite the fact that people have been driving cars for over a century now without GPS and manage to get where they are going without being killed and eaten by headhunter cannibals. The point is that we have created (albeit absurdly) a terrible circumstance for *not* buying the product.

On the contrary, we can definitely contrive a story that creates fabulous (and unrealistic) circumstances in the event of you buying a product. Axe body spray commercials are a stellar example of this use. Body sprays and colognes are not necessarily products you *need*, but they are definitely products that you might be interested in. The Axe body spray commercials consistently market their product to young, single men, predicated upon the premise that if you wear the Axe products, women will literally throw themselves at you in a sexual manner. Although the products have created multiple ministories from this single premise, they never really alter the essential narrative, perspective, or characters in their commercials. The male characters are almost always young, single, and white (which is a good clue as to who they're intending to market the products to), and the female characters are universally young, fit, and attractive. The male characters are often *not* extremely fit or attractive but instead more often than not of average height or attractiveness level, some being even on the lower end of the attractiveness scale (in subjective terms). The important thing about this is that it frames the narrative to the specific audience. Men who aren't seen as inherently attractive can somehow imagine that by buying the Axe body spray product, they will become incredibly attractive to women who wouldn't feel that way *otherwise*. And there's the targeted storytelling! You need to convince someone to buy your product by telling them a story of how a similar person to themselves reaped benefits from that same product they wouldn't have otherwise.

5.1.3 Do Something

Doing something is a separate function from buying or choosing something because it assumes that at the end of the action, the individual will be left without any tangible element. This sounds confusing, but let's use the example of politics. You are constantly being fed information about people and stories in order to get you to vote for a candidate. At the end of the vote, you may or may not get to see your candidate win. Even if they *do* win, you probably won't see anything tangible occur as a result (unless you're a lobbyist or a corporation, but then we can say you're purchasing the vote and hence buying something or choosing something). Voting is an act that you can perform but, in the end, not receive a direct result of doing. So in getting you to vote for a candidate, or vote on an issue, or even just plain vote period (as voter drive campaigns urge you to do), the advertising or the message can be put to you in the form of a story.

Doing something based on targeted storytelling can also involve watching a television show, going to a website, giving money to charity, or pledging time to a volunteer service. Basically anything that you have to perform but do not purchase as a product can fall under this category. The lack of the take-home aspect, or the ability to hold the tangible result, changes the nature of the story that you can tell in order to get the person to do what you want them to do.

5.1.4 Preventing Something

Not doing something is a hard thing to get your head around. When would we need to generate a creative story that influences somebody *not* to do something? The most obvious and prolific examples of this are the so-called public service campaigns that we often see as advertisements in print, online ads, and television commercials. Most prevalent are anti-drinking and driving commercials and antismoking campaigns. I use the term *so-called* in relation to public service campaigns because, often, there are influences behind these entities that stand to benefit from your improved health or draconian DUI laws and negative consequences. What is often overlooked in these instances is that insurance companies, often the most liberal of donators to the ad campaigns, can certainly stand to financially benefit from lower instances of lung cancer, emphysema, and drunk drivers. This is not to say that that's not a better result for our society as a whole! But it's definitely a good thing to keep in mind the concept of cause and effect when observing the creative storytelling that goes on in the public service ads—it's no different in many aspects than the targeted commercials of Axe body spray. There is a definitive cause and effect, often in the negative, in order to prevent an individual, or at the very least make them more aware of the negative consequences of their actions.

Using the anti-tobacco advertisements as a great example, we can see multiple storytelling techniques used in order to influence people to stop smoking, or to prevent people from taking up the habit. The earlier advertisements had a dark, sinister tone, where the ravages of lung cancer and tracheotomies were clearly shown, often cancer patients smoking cigarettes from stomas in their neck, clearly caused by throat cancer. These ads were dark, gruesome, and often horrific in their approach to illustrate the many medical pitfalls of smoking or continuing to smoke. But more modern approaches have shifted the tone of the ads, making them much more bright, cheerful, and inclined to appeal to the humorous side of the issue. In these ads, comedically inclined young actors are often depicted as casual smokers who are being "suckered" by Big Tobacco as they bathe in giant pools of cash money, which is coming from the pockets of unwitting or foolish consumers who are paying for the highly addictive product. These commercials are clearly appealing to the desire not to be a fool or a sucker over the desire not to have a hole in one's throat and be on a respirator for the rest of one's life. Of course, I'll take being a sucker or a fool over a stoma and respirator any day, but the principle here is that there is a positive and humorous way to get the point across, just as there is a negative and bleak way! What's the difference in the two appeals? The tone, as identified earlier as a secondary aspect of a story, is the important thing that is tweaked in these examples. By altering the tone, you can alter the raw emotional effect on the audience and create a different association. In this case, the intended goal is to get people to stop smoking (or not to start). But the humorous, light-hearted tone can do so with a positive association against a negative association. In both cases, you can see a clear use of associative storytelling to create the influence. Once again, reading a statistics report on smoking and cancer incidence in order to get people to stop smoking is not very effective, because it doesn't have the emotional significance to the audience. If there is no emotional significance, there is far less impact on the human mind.

5.1.5 Change Opinion

When would somebody want you to change their opinion about something? Public relations campaigns are generally prevalent for the sake of increasing awareness and/or sympathy for corporate entities (such as BP oil), large-scale product ingredients (such as corn syrup or pork), and public figures (such as politicians and judges). The opinion-based campaigns often use storytelling in order to change how you feel about a certain thing.

Changing how you feel is predicated on the fact that you feel anything at all—so the major intent here is to reverse or alter your perspective about certain things. In the early nineties, there were a series of public opinion campaigns on pork, similar to the campaigns on corn sugar (formerly known as *high-fructose corn syrup*) today. The idea was to reverse or alter a commonly held perception that pork was somehow bad for you or high in cholesterol and saturated fats and that it wasn't as healthy of a choice of meat. The purpose behind the commercial ad campaigns was specifically to get people to become aware of the healthy benefits and low-fat elements of pork as a healthy alternative to chicken or fish, which at the time was considered white meat, and hence somehow less unhealthy.

BP oil also had a recent slew of public opinion-altering commercials focused on the cleanup effort after the Gulf oil spill, when an off-shore drilling platform exploded and unleashed an oil spill from the ocean floor that caused massive devastation to the entire Gulf Coast ecosystem, destroying the fishing, shrimping, and vacation/boating industries for several years. BP was held responsible for the damage, and public opinion of the brand became rapidly sour. Despite eventually capping the oil spill and cleaning up the region, the company was continuing to reap the negative consequences of the incident in terms of public opinion. The interesting thing about this example is the complete lack of financial liability in terms of consumer purchasing! Although the oil company reaped significant loss in terms of public opinion and billions in cleanup cost and government fines, the incident and poor public opinion resulted in very little negative consequence at the pump. People bought relatively the same amount of fuel at the same amount of BP-owned or BP-supplied gas stations all over the world, for the obvious reason that you buy gas where and when it's convenient, not based on public opinion of the owning company. Why then did BP go to the trouble to try to create a public opinion-altering campaign that cost a significant amount of advertising dollars? In general, the act of goodwill toward a company or a brand, despite that company selling a product you'll buy anyway, has been considered to be a good thing. Public image is important to any large, international entity, and hence, they spent time and effort developing a story in order to sell the altering or the reversing of public opinion. They did it by showing the cleanup effort and the people involved who were working hard and earnestly to restore the Gulf Coast to economic and environmental viability.

The important thing here about generating a story to change public opinion is that it generally only moves in one direction, from bad to good! It's hard to see why anyone would want to change an opinion about their product from good to bad, but of course, enlisting some negativity could be a good way to change the opinion of your competing product. That kind of issue, however, I would relegate to the *choosing something* concept over the concept of public opinion. Public opinion is reserved for more general concepts, products, and ideas.

5.2 ENTERTAINMENT

What is *entertainment*? It's interesting to note here that although it's a huge part of the human experience, it's incredibly loosely defined. Entertainment is, in many ways, the essential undefinable need of the human mind. We need things to fill up idle time in a social manner that we can identify with. We, of course, like to watch and participate in all kinds of entertainment all the time.

While things such as sports, games, and competitive activities occupy a large amount of the Western culture's percentage of entertainment, the lion's share of the leisure time we spend is based on storytelling. Television, digital streaming content, podcasts, and even old-fashioned radio are all centered around the advent of creative storytelling. We *really* like our stories! From soap operas (originally sponsored by soap advertisements) to the latest spin-off of *CSI*, storytelling is clearly the hemoglobin in the bloodstream of modern-day entertainment.

But this once again begs the question: what exactly *makes* it entertaining? What makes the content of a story compelling to watch, again and again? There has to be some takeaway or inherent reward system in watching a soap opera or a sitcom in order for us to be so compelled to sit through the soap commercials and the body spray ads for 30–60 minutes at a time. Just what is it about these stories that make them entertaining? This is where we get deeper into the human mind and what makes it tick. I have identified seven distinct reward systems that we get from interacting with stories in some form or another. Not all these are completely passive, you will notice, and many of them only really take on value when fully interacting with entertainment, such as an Xbox game.

5.2.1 Reward Systems

Reward systems are naturally occurring elements of human behavior, often supported and supplemented by chemical systems that provide a chemical incentive. A reward system can be intrinsic or extrinsic, or a combination of both. Intrinsic reward systems are only rewarding *while* engaging in the activity; while extrinsic reward systems continue to provide the effect *after* engagement has occurred. Thusly, an extrinsic reward system offers the advantage of moving with the audience even when they are not participating in viewing or interacting with the story. I have identified the following distinct reward systems: *collection*, *achievement*, *competition*, *catharsis*, *role-playing*, *social interaction*, and *discovery*. Most of these are used in the interactive aspects of storytelling and will be covered in Section III, but the most important aspect of a reward system in terms of storytelling as it pertains to passive storytelling (as in television, podcasts, or film) is *catharsis*.

5.2.2 Catharsis

Catharsis is defined by *Merriam-Webster* as follows:

> **1:** purgation
>
> **2a:** purification or purgation of the emotions (as pity and fear) primarily through art
>
> **2b:** a purification or purgation that brings about spiritual renewal or release from tension
>
> **3:** elimination of a complex by bringing it to consciousness and affording it expression

But it deserves treatment here strictly in the context of creative storytelling. *Cartharsis* is the act of purging emotional stress or releasing of pent-up emotions vicariously through watching others perform it inside of a narrative. Think about it. When was the last time you saw a sad movie? Why would anyone watch a sad or a depressing film? What is the purpose of telling a story that is sad, depressing, or makes you feel bad? In absolute terms, we should avoid that which makes us feel bad and move toward that which makes us feel good. So in some way, we must reap a reward or a benefit from watching stories about sad or depressing things. This is the principle of catharsis. Catharsis through creative storytelling allows us to feel bad about something terrible happening to someone who isn't *us*. So if you see a depressing film about a depressing subject, the moment you walk away, you feel better because you aren't the people in the film. Watching bad things happen to people somehow makes you feel slightly better about your own circumstances, which allows for a release of pent-up feelings.

But depressing, sad catharsis isn't the only aspect of the principle that we can discuss! Anger and extreme violence in stories are another way that we can engage emotionally and vicariously through our emotional connections to the characters in that story by momentarily placing us in the situation and allowing us to release pent-up hostile or violent emotions that are characteristic of human nature. By acting out violence or playing violent games, we exhume that part of our nature for a temporary amount of time. It also allows us to act out, whether vicariously through characters, or directly through gameplay, deep-seated primitive violent feelings that we all harbor as member of the species.

Laughter, of course, is the simplest form of catharsis, in the sense that it allows us to momentarily feel the emotion of joy, despite any other problems in our life. Laughter and humor are extremely common forms of storytelling-based catharses in our society, as witnessed by the extreme amount of sitcom (short for *situational comedy*) and romantic comedy films that we eat up like pancake batter at the box office.

So in essence, when we talk about stories for entertainment, we're really talking about stories for catharsis. The better the catharsis, the better entertainment we consider it. And of course, cathartic feelings are always relative to the individual; that is to say that some people find some kinds of stories and cathartic mechanisms far more compelling than others. This is why some like only comedies and some like violence, and some like mysteries or period drama. Everyone has their own favorite flavor of catharsis, which is why our story-based entertainment is so rich and varied in the forms of books, plays, television, film and now podcasts.

One thing that is essential in understanding about the principle of catharsis and the feelings that it creates is that it is strictly intrinsic. You can't take it with you! Catharsis is the immediate release of pent-up emotions, similar to crying or yelling, but it is not a concept or a reward system that can be carried outside of the immediate release. So if catharsis cannot happen continuously, we will have a need for continued indulgence in it. This means more stories, in more forms, with more characters, and more novelty, and different settings, and different circumstances, with different tones. The idea of the constant onslaught of story-based content in graphic novels, podcasts, streaming channels, television, and games is almost mind boggling and appears to have a weight of its own. This is why any medium for communication humans invent, it will always be used for telling stories in some manner. We need catharsis to occur, especially in modern society, in order for us to function properly within the confines it presents.

5.3 LEARNING/EDUCATION

The third and final use of storytelling is for education. Education is the imparting of specific knowledge from one individual to another, which the receiving individual did not already possess. That's a very structured pedagogical definition of education, but it's important to separate storytelling from behavior modification and education. One makes you *do* something; the other makes you *know* something.

The most important aspect of education and storytelling is why you need it at all. Can't you just memorize facts and equations in education? Can't you just read a list of cause and effect or historical dates like chemical compounds and periodic element charts?

Maybe you can. But would it be the best method of conveying complex emotional information? It certainly works for physics—but physics, like most sciences, is based entirely on objective facts and figures, which can be checked against mathematical equations and empirical tests. Much of history, literature, communication, and humanities is based on pattern recognition and emotional referencing and hence not really transmittable through lists and memorized tables alone. The education of morals, principles, and cause/effect relationships can be approached in a much more associative manner than algebra. You certainly don't *have* to use creative storytelling to educate people, but it's a proven and effective manner in doing so. If you aren't still convinced, just go as the creators of *Sesame Street* or *Barney the Dinosaur*. They might tend to agree with me.

How to go about developing educational creative storytelling is beyond the scope of this book, but it's important to mention here that interactivity seems to be a key part of success in educational stories. If we look at the bidirectional role of the storyteller and the audience from ancient forms of storytelling, such as the oral tradition, we can clearly see the model that *Sesame Street* and offshoots used. *Sesame Street* was able to create a sense of interaction with the audience by having them say things out loud or follow along an action, thereby making the (albeit naive) audience believe that they had direct input into the story they are observing. Most children's shows, which are exemplary in the use of storytelling and education, employ this method to some extent. Therefore, the perceived distance between storyteller and audience is shortened, and a more direct causality can be entertained. This means that the children believe themselves to be a participant in the story, or at least to have some direct input into the story, and, when combined with specific targeted learning objectives, can have a powerful effect on imprinting the information into the audience. Remember that the emotional associative elements of the brain are *far* more powerful than the rote memorization elements, and the pattern-based knowledge gained from interactive storytelling can far outstrip a memorization-based technique for certain key objectives. Learning some things is far easier to do by interactive storytelling than it is by militant memorization, testing, and repetition.

CHAPTER 6

Activities for Storytellers

6.1 ACTIVITY 1: FUNCTIONAL STORYTELLING

Being a good functional storyteller means that you can take a set of objective parameters and devise a story that can fulfill that function. Objective-based storytelling occurs all the time in the world of marketing and advertising, where behavior modification for a very targeted demographic is the desired result. The following are three targeted exercises, with directions to test out your storytelling skills in this arena. When going over them, remember to structure your story based on the seven elements of storytelling and answer the following questions while you are constructing the story:

- *Perspective*
    - From whose viewpoint are we seeing this story? How does that change the nature of the story?
    - How does this perspective positively affect your outcome?
- *Narrative*
    - Can you encapsulate the transformation that occurs in the narrative in a single sentence?
    - How does your narrative positively affect your objective goal?

- *Sequence*
    - Is the sequencing of your story temporally linear or nonlinear?
    - How does the sequence change the story and work toward the objective goal?
- *Characters*
    - Who are the characters in your story? What are their attributes and motivators?
    - How do your characters appeal to your targeted audience? Can they be identified with?
- *Setting*
    - What's the specific setting of your story?
    - What does your setting communicate to the targeted audience?
    - How does the setting work toward your objective goals?
- *Tone*
    - Describe the tone of your story. What's the gut-level emotional feeling?
    - How does your tone influence the objective goal of the story?
- *Intended audience*
    - Describe your targeted audience in detail. What are their characteristics? What are their goals? What are their primary motivators?
    - How do you intend to connect with your targeted audience?

6.1.1 Behavior Modification Task 1: Choosing a Product

You work in the marketing division for a brand new soda company, intent on competing with the likes of Sprite, Pepsi, and Coca-Cola. You want to target the market of this new soda to affluent, middle-class teenagers, from ages 11 to 15 years. Your challenge is that you are competing for market share in a heavily populated field. How will you design an ad campaign that will compete with the heavy hitters and distinguish your product from theirs for your targeted demographic? Make sure to consider your market, what they like, what they want, and what will make them desire your product over the others.

6.1.2 Behavior Modification Task 2: Changing Opinion

You run the marketing division of a small ad company that has only one client, which is the top national pizza delivery chain. The execs at the company are concerned that they are losing market share to new start-up health-oriented food delivery services popping up around the country, which are running constant ads and marketing ploys to portray pizza as the food choice of unhealthy, unattractive, obese people. The company refuses to change anything about the ingredients of the pizza *or* the pizza offerings themselves. They are solely intent on changing the perception of their potential customers from thinking that pizza is bad for you to thinking that it is part of a healthy, active lifestyle. They want a series of commercials and social media ads that tell this story. It's your job to come up with a way to change the perception of public opinion *without* offering any new product or choices! Your challenge is to get people to think differently about a product they already are familiar with.

6.1.3 Behavior Modification Task 3: Negative Influence

You are working for an ad company that caters to Latino and Hispanic markets, products, and campaigns. You have a local city government client trying to push a public service campaign that reduces the rate of high school pregnancies among the Latino population in the area, *without* offending or transgressing religious or cultural lines. Your challenge is to generate a television ad, with accompanying social media tie-ins that influences the behavior of the intended audience (Latino teens) into preventing teen pregnancy but to absolutely not mention contraception or abortion. You will have to find creative ways to negatively influence behavior.

6.2 ACTIVITY 2: EPISODIC DIGITAL STORYTELLING

In the past decade, there has been a tremendous push from the viewing of a single, self-contained film, to a multitiered, multiepisodic format of storytelling. Stories are chopped up into small, bite-sized pieces and serialized into 15–50 minute segments. Story-based podcasts are becoming extremely popular, based on the original podcast Serial, in which the format became popularized. Some of the features of this format include the ability to create segues in between the episodes, almost like cliff-hangers in order to increase viewer interest for the next episode. Another feature of these episodic stories is their individual, self-contained stories that are told inside an umbrella of the big narrative, which is generally moved forward through parts of the little stories that are in the episodes. While some people may find this approach novel or innovative, it's really nothing of the sort, and it's been going on since comic books, old-time radio broadcasts, and soap operas! Your task is to design your very own serial, narrative-based podcast for public entertainment consumption.

Constructing an episodic series requires that you lay out the pieces of your story like blocks, describing each asset as an individual piece that can be reassembled at any moment to make a new narrative, episode, or segue (cliff-hanger). Pay special attention to the characters, the big narrative, and the perspective as it pertains to the audio formatting (since you don't have visuals to use).

- *Characters—List them in detail as building blocks*
    - Who are your characters?
    - What are their primary motivators?
    - What is their relationship with the other characters?
- *The big story*
    - What is the summary narrative of the entire series?
    - How do the individual episodes move this narrative along?
- *Episodes*
    - List each episode and give a synopsis of the narrative (including the transition from the previous segue if not the first episode).
    - Include which characters will be in which episodes.
    - Include how each episode will move the big picture forward.
    - Explain the cliff-hanger or the segue ending.
- *Perspective/audio formatting*
    - Is there a narrator? If so, who is it?
    - Are the characters aware of the podcast?
    - Will you have interviews?
    - Will you include stealth recordings?

6.3 ACTIVITY 3: INTERACTIVE EDUCATIONAL STORYTELLING

In the fine tradition of *Howdy Doody*, *Sesame Street*, and *Barney the Dinosaur*, you have a child's television show that is responsible for teaching primary elements of ethics, morality, values, and common sense to children aged 3–9 years. Construct a story to address the following lessons. Make sure that you use the setting, the tone, and the targeted audience carefully in deciding what to say and how best to impart the lesson into the child's mind by making specific emotional associative connections.

6.3.1 Lesson 1: Prudence

Construct a story for children with the intended objective goal to impart unto them the wisdom of saving for a rainy day, or keeping things in reserve for some future date at which point they might need it. The intended goal here is to make them understand the principle of prudence and that forgoing immediate gratification can improve some future point in time for them when they are in need. Pay careful attention to the characters, the setting, and the sequence in order to best make the point you are trying to make.

6.3.2 Lesson 2: Honesty

Construct a story for children with the intended objective goal to impart unto them the important lesson that they should be honest and that people will believe them. You may choose to go with the negative lesson here, as in *The Boy Who Cried Wolf*, in order to teach them the disadvantage to dishonesty, *or* you could show them a positive effect of honesty, as in George Washington's "I Chopped Down the Cherry Tree" fable (although nobody really rewarded him for chopping down that tree after all). The important thing here is not only to illustrate the importance of honesty as a moral imperative (which is debatable) *but also* to impart a solid sense of cause and effect into their minds, which hopefully will carry forward as a model unto future behavior.

CHAPTER 7

Conclusion

IN CONCLUSION OF THIS section, let's follow up with a brief synopsis of all that we've learned. This section was all about the fundamental mechanics of the story and the storytelling. This means that we first had to define what a story *is* and *isn't* and then understand all the subelements that a story contains. Remember, a story isn't something that's so easy to define—rather, it's the *lack* of certain things that can tell us whether something is truly a story or not! But I think we've got a pretty good feel of just what is a story and what isn't, which is the first element of understanding this complex but prevalent subject.

- *Key elements*
  - Characters
  - Narrative
  - Perspective
  - Sequence
- *Secondary elements (not necessary but generally present)*
  - Setting
  - Tone
- *Tertiary elements (may or may not be present)*
  - Intended audience

Next, we really needed to understand *who* is telling the story, who is *listening* to the story, and what kind of relationship these two individuals have with one another. This is where we explored the *distance* and the *height*, and the *interaction* between these two elements. Because you always have a teller and an audience, but the perception between those two participants can vary greatly depending on multiple factors.

We also had to understand *how* we tell stories, what our communication methods are! And, of course, those have evolved as our technology has evolved! This influences all kinds of things, such as distance, height, and levels of interaction. The further we go back in time, the more interaction we have with the audience because the technology had not been developed for us to disseminate stories to multiple people at once. So as the people we told the stories to were close in literal distance, the more interaction and bidirectional amount of feedback existed. As we looked forward into technology, we reached a point where we could reach large amounts of people at once with the same story content (books, magazines, radio, television) but lost the bidirectional elements on interactivity between teller and audience. The technology could send, but not yet receive. As we now look into the future, we are seeing the technology evolve again, allowing us to send and receive simultaneously, reinvigorating the elements of interactivity in stories and changing the landscape once again.

- *Level I of technology (direct audience participation and feedback)*
  - Oral traditions
  - Staged plays
- *Level II of technology (no audience participation and feedback)*
  - Print (books, magazines, pamphlets)
  - Radio
  - Television
  - Film
- *Level III of technology (variable audience participation and feedback)*
  - Games
  - Contest television

- Social media
- Mobile media

Once we understood *how* the content was presented, we had to delve into *what* the content was all about! In this case, we saw that there were only three basic types of stories and that we can fit all current stories into those categories, with an infinite amount of variation between. We saw how those stories were essential in creating personal emotional connections to the content, based on human psychology derived from our personal and collective experiences.

- *The human experience*
    - Birth
    - Childhood
    - Transformation
    - Sex/love
    - Parenthood
    - Death
- *The mythological experience*
    - Nature
    - Influence/fate
    - Purpose and origin
    - Mystery
    - Explanation of death
- *The learning experience*
    - Ethics
    - Morality
    - Cause and effect

Once we learned all about the different types of stories, we then finally explored just exactly *why* we tell stories in the first place! Stories have a specific and very necessary function in our culture, as evidenced by their universality. As many stories as we can see, across all cultures and history, it all came down to a very brief set of purposes:

1. Communication
2. Behavior modification
3. Education

To wrap things up, we've got all this information now about the fundamental components of stories and storytelling. What do we do with it? Well, that's all up to you; the most important thing about breaking *down* the story as a theoretical structure is that now you can reassemble the pieces and create something of your own! In the Activities section, you will find a host of specific, targeted needs for creative storytelling that put you in the driver's seat.

II

Media

CHAPTER 8

The Still Image

WHAT PUTS THE *MULTI* in *multimedia*? For that matter, what exactly does *media* mean? We know that *multi* means "many," and *Merriam-Webster*'s definition of *media* is as follows:

> **1:** [Late Latin, from Latin, feminine of *medius;* from the voiced stops' being regarded as intermediate between the tenues and the aspirates]: a voiced stop
>
> **2:** [New Latin, from Latin]: the middle coat of the wall of a blood or lymph vessel consisting chiefly of circular muscle fibers

Whoa, that's pretty strange! It doesn't say anything about Instagram pictures of your dinner anywhere in that definition (unless you eat the middle coat of a lymph vessel for dinner)! All jokes aside, the actual term *media* is a plural form of *medium*, which is defined by *Merriam-Webster* as

> **1a:** something that is sold in a medium size: something that is the middle size when compared with things that are larger and smaller
>
> **2a:** particular form or system of communication (such as newspapers, radio, or television)
>
> **3a:** the materials or methods used by an artist

So we really want to look at the word *medium*. And since we're talking about communication, you can see that the word (in some contexts) is defined by communication, or as a means through which we communicate. So the *medium* isn't really the communication itself but, in reality, the form in which it takes.

I'm not trying to overcomplicate the subject, but it's important to understand what we are even discussing when we use the word because it has become a catch-all definition that scoops up anything we *feel* like dumping into it. If I tell you I work in multimedia today, it usually means some kind of Internet/web/video/service that involves the delivery or the creation of content in some form or fashion. And that's not incorrect—most of the time, it means exactly that!

But what *are* the various media we're involved in creating and delivering? As you can see in the definition, an artist uses some type of medium to bring you his/her vision. Now that media will always directly correspond to some kind of human sensory input. We, as humans, have certain ways of inputting information into our central processing unit (called "the brain") and making sense of it. And if all of yours are working perfectly (or imperfectly, as the case may be), then you're pretty used to getting tons of sensory data flooding into that neural cortex every second! If your brain weren't really good at processing all those data, you'd be in some serious trouble. You would walk out into the street and get hit by a car, fall down the stairs, and drink paint instead of water.

We have five primary senses: taste, touch, sight, hearing, and smell. There are some secondary senses as well, such as the relationship of your body parts and a natural sense of motion, kind of like the accelerometer in your phone. When we discuss media through which information is transferred to our brain, we pretty much have to rely on these senses to *get* that information. Unlike a computer, we can't just read a series of zeros and ones as information. It all has to be processed by the organic components of our body and brain, such as the eyes, the ears, the nose, the mouth, and the skin.

So far we have only mastered two of those forms, in the sense that we are able to record and transmit information that can be processed by others in a portable form over distance. Those two forms, of course, are sight and sound, which we can record and transmit relatively anywhere synchronously between two people. It would be really interesting to wonder why we never created an ability to transfer tastes and smells instantly across the world … no "tele-smell" or "tastel-vision." Probably because those senses are often associated with eating which is impossible to do at a distance (so far). I'm pretty sure that if dogs had evolved to become the dominant technological species on Earth, they would have invented and mastered a way to record and transmit smells instantly across the world because they rely much more heavily on their sense of smell than we do for information. That's not to say that we don't use smell to process data as humans; it is just that our eyes and hearing are so much more important to us in order to get information about the world around us.

Touch, interestingly enough, *is* being developed as a remote media, but the intimacy of it requires some delicacy on the part of the designers (and there are plenty of developers interested in the carnal side of this type of input as well). Aldous Huxley, in his extremely prescient book *Brave New World* (written in 1931), depicted an antiutopian future in which technology had advanced to the point where people went to the "feelies," or films that included tactile information on top of audiovisual entertainment. The mechanism was never really described, but it was part of his futuristic musings on how the tactile data would provide an added depth to the level of entertainment in a carnal society. But for now, we're pretty much left with the two types of media that we involved in storytelling—images and sounds.

Sights and sounds are the least carnal of the senses and, hence, the most likely for incorporation into the modern era of instant transfer! Perhaps I am being deliberately obtuse here, but of course, I'm talking about instant transfer of images and audio, which have been a constant part of your life since the day you were born through the technology of television and radio. And even if you only had three channels to watch when you were a kid (like me) and you had to actually remove yourself from the sofa, walk 15 feet over to your 30 inch tube-based television and crank that heavy plastic knob in a circle until it landed on something, you were still getting infinitely more information transferred through the vacuum of empty space than some cave dweller was 100,000 years ago. But would he/she have noticed a difference between the outside world and the television world?

I think not. You see, watching things move at normal speed on television with normal sound wouldn't be all that impressive, since even a Neanderthal brain was pretty used to seeing things happen in the real world, in real time. But hand that person a photograph, and it would probably have freaked him/her out a little bit. Why? Because in that photograph you have effectively become a master of time, in the sense that this is the only one of our senses that we can freeze time. That doesn't count those scratch and sniff stickers from the eighties, of course, which was a slightly "grosser" version of the same principle. The point is that our modern forms of media can manipulate time and space in a way that makes them extremely powerful tools in telling stories and communication.

So what are we doing with all this media and how does that help or hinder us in this art known as *storytelling*? Media (and we will limit the scope of the definition here to sight and sound) allows us to convey emotional information as well as words, either in substitution or in supplement. Images, video, animation, sound effects, and music are all methods of conveying information from one person to another. Sometimes this can convey emotional feeling and emphasis that words simply fail to do. Sometimes the mimicking of our sensual reality in image and sound can create within us powerful feelings tied to our instinctual emotions and reactions that words alone cannot. I love Shakespeare, but he can't make me jump out of my seat like a 30 feet high Tyrannosaurus rex in *Jurassic Park* popping out from behind a computer-generated fern in a movie theater! The film used my instinctual reptilian brain to trick me into an adrenaline-filled state that activated my central nervous system (CNS) before my conscious brain could figure out what was happening. That kind of power in communication is only possible with sights and sounds! These are our instinctual methods of gathering information about our surroundings, which, in a primitive state, is information that might keep us from getting killed; so you can bet that they will evoke powerful sensations that are far deeper than a sonnet could ever do.

Because of its powerful effect on our CNS, we mostly tell our stories *through* some kind of vessel (which is why *media* and *middle* are from the same etymological construct), and that vessel tends to be audible and visual. These are our primary conscious forms of communication with one another. Interestingly enough, if a dog could tell a story, would that story be told in smells? Since dogs receive exponentially more information through smell, they might evolve one day and be perfectly fine with "telesmell," which would be a primary way to communicate with one another. But human stories are formulated through our mind in terms of concepts and words and then transmitted to other humans through sound and visual information. The only exception to this media construct is straight literature, which consists of *only* words. But let's not forget the human talent for imagination! Without audio/visual cues, we will create them in our head from the words we are reading, forming powerful images, sounds, smells, and even tactile input completely on our own from constructs and memory. We can't really create stories *without* media of some kind, whether or not it's completely constructed out of our own imagination or up on a screen in front of us!

In this section we are going to explore those forms of media and how they can enhance, detract from, or replace the words of a story altogether. Images, video, animation, sound, and music are used prolifically in *all* forms of storytelling and communication and have been since the dawn of our species. We must communicate in terms of images and sounds; therefore, we use these media as a constant stream of information transmitted from one individual to another, sometimes in synchronicity and sometimes recorded for posterity and review. Without media, we would be rendered almost unable to communicate at all.

8.1 DEFINING THE IMAGE

When was the very first time a member of our species (or offshoot species such as a Neanderthal) created a representative image? Just what does a representative image entail? In this case, we must separate the images of the real world that we see every day as a normal course of height and a representative image. At some point, somewhere far back in the misty corners of time, one of our ancestors took a stick and drew a little figure in some dirt or loose sand on a beach. It might have looked something like Figure 8.1. What is that an image of?

If you said a wooly mammoth, then my art skills are better than I thought! Or maybe not. The interesting question here is how did you *know* that this was a drawing of a mammoth? After all, you've never actually seen one in real life (unless you're older than I thought). And although you've probably seen a bunch of images or reproductions or fossils of a

FIGURE 8.1 A loosely based figure drawn clumsily on the modern equivalent of some sand (a Wacom tablet).

mammoth somewhere, this hardly looks like a million-dollar museum reproduction! It's mostly just a bunch of lines on white background. But somehow, you *recognize* those lines as a depiction of a species that went extinct long before anyone we know was born.

So how did you recognize this picture? It's all due to the marvel of the human mind. Once again, our pattern-recognition machine is fast at work, analyzing the pattern of lines against all similar patterns in our memory and nearly instantly recognizing the key features of the drawing as it relates to the multiple pictures of elephants, mastodons, mammoth and other related species. So you deconstructed these squiggly lines on a background and *reconstructed* an entire extinct species, roaming around in the ice age, looking for shrubs and avoiding saber-toothed tigers. Can you see how amazing your brain is? The important thing here is to start understanding exactly what an image *is*. It's a physical representation of an object (or just random abstract patterns), frozen in time. It's a recording of sorts. It's a way to visually represent something from your mind. Since our mind is incredibly visual, I would be willing to bet that the origins of art go as far back as the origins of our species. Our brains are hardwired to communicate through the creation and the manipulation of images, and we can do it either by *describing* those images with words from a spoken language or creating a physical construction that merely resembles the thing we are communicating, like what I did in Figure 8.1. Once again, it doesn't have to be a perfect representation! Your brain will immediately construct the actual thing in place of a few clumsy lines as soon as it recognizes it. In this way, you can start to see how our mind works and why stories are the more complex equivalent of the mammoth in Figure 8.1.

8.1.1 History of Images

The earliest known images created by humans that we have any record of date to the Stone Age, in the form of cave paintings. The mechanism of painting is not completely known, although the current speculations are simple animal- and plant-derived pigments that were put in the mouth and spit painted or brushed on by hand (Figure 8.2). It's less important as to *how* they were drawn than *what* they were drawing! In Figure 8.3, you can see that the majority of these Paleolithic cave paintings were depicting animals, and not just any animals. What the now-famous cave paintings in Altimera, Spain, and Lascaux, France, were mostly depicting were big-game animals, such as deer, stags, and

FIGURE 8.2 An actual Paleolithic bone-carving and depiction of a horse's head in simple lines.

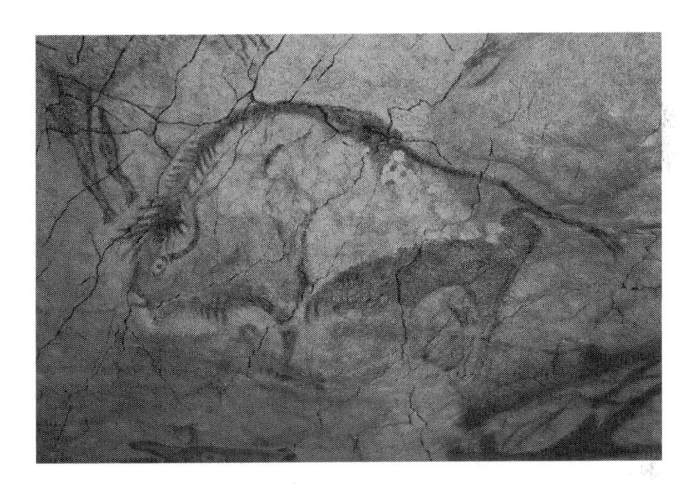

FIGURE 8.3 The famous Altimeria prehistoric cave paintings. This one is of a bison.

bison. These were large, herd-based animals that populated the plains of Europe at the time in great abundance. What is noticeably lacking in the paintings is the depiction of *humans*, a mystery that has baffled many paleontologists over the centuries since the first discovery of the mysterious artwork.

Since these are the first real recorded depictions of art from a human (although I would doubt the earliest), it's important to analyze them. While art may indeed be subject to the eye of the beholder, there is little doubt as to what these images are depicting. The herds of big-game animals have a beauty that transcends time and, despite the flat perspective, impart a sense of *life* and *movement*, frozen in time for over 40,000 years. What drove man to create them? There are many theories. In the documentary *Prehistoric Astronomers* by Stephane Begoin and Vincent Tardieu, a radical new theory was presented that the animals were actually in correspondence to constellations and stars. Traditional theories suggest that the earliest humans were big-game hunters and that they were depicting their food on the wall as they imagined the hunt. Other theories place these animals at the center of a mystical cult with psychoactive hallucinogenic drugs ingested and communication with nature allowed the humans to take on the qualities of the animals. It's way beyond the scope of this book to theorize about the impetus behind the creation of the images, but of the images themselves, there can be no doubt. They were created by a human's hand, as a recorded interpretation of what he/she saw that was important enough to spend hours on his/her back in a cramped cave with little illumination making the images.

It should be no surprise then that the cave paintings were not a singular phenomenon! Using images to communicate information that words are not enough to get the point across was immediately recognized as a powerful tool. There are multiple examples from the Paleolithic period of cave paintings and individual pieces of art that started to define the ability of humans to record what we saw into the world around us. Long before the advent of writing, we were still able to record in some fashion information we could convey to another human being, without having to be in the same place at the same time. Information could be transferred from generation to generation now with some level of retention.

The still image has gone through multitudes of technological innovations since those first cave paintings were created. When assessing the still image as a tool in visual communication, we must evaluate certain things about the delivery of that information! We live in an age where visual media is near ubiquitous, but this was not always the case. Each step of the way on the technological stairway from cave painting to Instagram has carried with it a certain alteration in the way that we perceive, value, and react to still images. A still image can be assessed based on certain criteria I have developed to make it easier to understand it as a communication tool. An image, or a type of image, can be assessed based upon its *portability*, *accessibility*, *subject matter*, *medium*, and *level of realism*. These are the essential characteristics of an image as they pertain to visual communication tools.

8.1.2 Portability

Portability is the ability to take the image with you. This may seem silly in terms of today's technology, but there was a certain time that images were carved on gigantic rock walls and couldn't exactly fit in your pocket. Of course, we have giant monuments today, such as the Statue of Liberty, but since we can't stick that in our pocket, we can surely take a photo of it with our phone and look at it later. Portability is very important with a still image because it allows us to look at it whenever we desire. Otherwise, seeing the actual thing would only be possible when it was in our direct presence. So you can take a picture with you of a loved one and be reminded of them when you look at it. The very first portable art or human-made depictions were bone carvings and fertility goddess dolls, generally female busts with voluptuous features that were small enough to fit in a knapsack or a bag and be carried with the individual (Figure 8.4). In that way, you could bring the gods with you if so desired!

Eventually, portability became more frequent, allowing a simple image to be carried with an individual person. Things such as coins and parchments were able to be transported and exchanged with other people (Figure 8.5). The portability of things such as coins made them perfect for putting important images on them, such the representation of an emperor or an empress or a king or a queen (Figure 8.6). In this way, the image of your ruler could propagate itself across an entire population. So the more portable a still image or a piece of artwork is, the more people are able to view it. Portability is the speed at which a still image can communicate.

8.1.3 Accessibility

Accessibility is the ease of access to a particular still image. It determines if a person can see it, how often they can see it, and in what context they see the image. The access to images in our modern technological age is near universal, but once again, this was not always the case. A piece of artwork or a depicted image of a scene was often times only seen in certain contexts, in certain places. We can go way back to the example of the cave paintings at Altimera to see how this works, or fast forward in time to the medieval period in Europe, where the only time you would see any representational image at all would be in the church, in the form of giant stained-glass windows and the crucifix, balefully hanging over the podium. An image with limited accessibility becomes rare and therefore much more valuable to the audience. It's

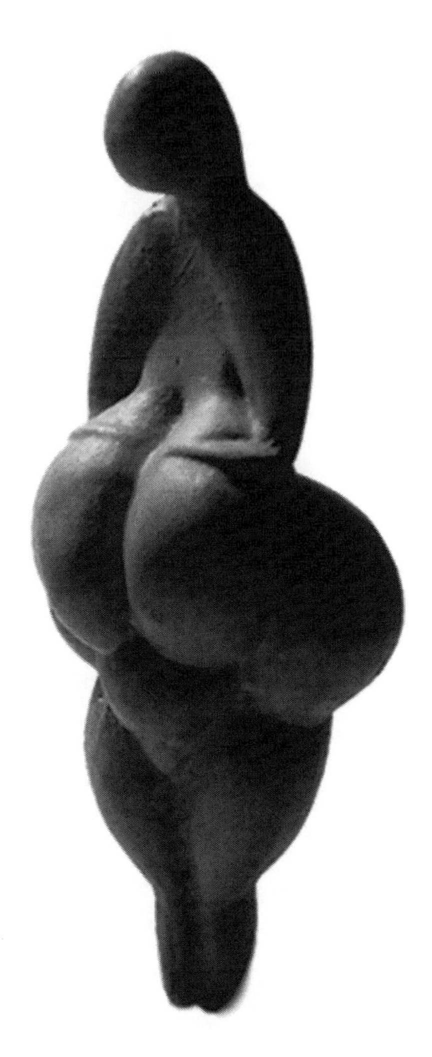

FIGURE 8.4 These feminine goddess fertility symbols were some of the first portable art known to exist. Although their purpose is not entirely clear, the supposition is that they were symbols of birth and used symbolically.

important to understand that value as we learn how to use media in creative storytelling, because it's easy to *over*-proliferate images in modern digital forms of storytelling, but never forget that the rarer a depiction is, the more impact it has on the viewer. Limiting access to an image can vastly increase its value, such as a Leonardo da Vinci painting. You

FIGURE 8.5 Pottery was perhaps the first canvas of portable goods upon which humans could paint imagery and move it rapidly from place to place. With more space, you had more room to paint more elaborate scenes.

FIGURE 8.6 Finally, a picture you can put into your pocket and carry around! Coins represent the ultimate in portability and indeed have changed little in layout, design, and concept since the Roman Empire.

may only see one in your entire life, if that, but of course, you now have an infinite amount of reproductions in the form of photographs and digital images. Nothing would compare to the real thing, of course, but the proliferation of the digital content has made that experience less valuable nonetheless.

8.1.4 Subject Matter

What is the image depicting? That's an important aspect of the characteristic of an image because it can put it into some sort of context. Images usually (although not always) have a real-world depictive equivalent. That is to say that they are generally pictures of something in the real world. The subject matter is important because it provides some context as to what we are communicating or being communicated to. Religious subject matter often depicts representations of scenes from mythology and stories pertaining to religion, and political/economic images are relegated to the representations of state or the head of state (such as the picture of Caesar on your coin). This is the targeted storytelling aspect of the still image—it's there to speak to you about one thing or another. Images aren't just decorative. They provide a story unto themselves based on visual information. When looking at an image in its context, always pay attention to the subject matter being depicted.

8.1.5 Medium

Here's that *media* word again. What do we mean by the medium of the media (no pun intended)? The medium is the physical nature of the still image. It could be on a digital screen (most common today), on a piece of photo paper, on a rock wall, sculpted with bronze, or painted onto a canvas. The medium changes the nature of the image class. A giant marble sculpture, such as Michelangelo's *David* (Figure 8.7), has a vastly different impact than a 4 ft × 4 ft wood panel by Hieronymous Bosch (Figure 8.8). The medium can be three-dimensional or two-dimensional, colored or not colored, metallic or painterly, etc. The medium is the vessel through which the visual communication is made.

8.1.6 Level of Realism

Realism is the similarity to the way in which it is received by the human eye. Abstraction is removing the image away from realism and more toward exaggeration of color, perspective, and form. A realistic example would be a photograph, which is a flattened representation of almost exactly what our eyes see. Abstraction can be seen in Figure 8.9, where the artist Henri Matisse has drawn, in a few pen lines, the outline of a female nude. The Matisse Nude in Figure 8.9 is extremely abstracted from the actual image it depicts, but we can tell exactly what it is without

FIGURE 8.7 Michelangelo's *David*, nearly twice the size of life, is an imposing piece of artwork.

hesitation. The important thing about abstraction is that it creates the freedom for your mind to fill in the blanks and the spaces between the lines. As we have learned, the brain is an incredible pattern-recognition and creative machine, and if it sees a pattern it recognizes, it won't hesitate to fill in the blanks and shade in the colors if there aren't any there. So abstract depictions of things can fire up your imaginative juices, allowing your brain to fill in those blanks or ramp up the emotional impact of a scene or an image. Conversely, the photograph, or the hyper-realistic depiction, can close down multiple interpretations of the scene and add a layer of grit or empiricism to an image.

FIGURE 8.8 A wood panel painting from the fourteenth century. Do you notice how small the scale is? The medium changes the message of the artwork in some form.

FIGURE 8.9 Matisse Nude, drawn in beautiful sparseness.

Figure 8.10 shows an equestrian art piece by Peter Paul Rubens. If you look at the depiction of the horse, it conveys a strong sense of movement, action, and liveliness, despite the fact that it is a still image. Compare this to the cave painting in Figure 8.2, and you will see strong similarities in the outlines and the sensation of movement. This should imbue a sense of continuity in the depiction of movement, action, and intention on the part of the artist. From the Paleolithic era to our current time, the ability to physically render and comprehend visual information recorded in a still image has not changed.

The level of abstraction here makes a big difference when we look at pictures. A cartoon face might work great for a child's comic book, but it would seem out of place on a dollar bill! In there, we want a higher level of realism, for the reason that we are using a depiction of our first president George Washington, and displaying something with a sense of reverence requires a high level of realism (Figure 8.11).

FIGURE 8.10 Equestrian Portrait by Peter Paul Rubens, depicting movement and action in a still image.

FIGURE 8.11 A modern, 1-dollar bill, with a highly realistic depiction off George Washington's face.

8.2 IMAGE FORMS THROUGH THE AGES

8.2.1 Cave Paintings

As mentioned earlier, cave paintings are non-portable and extremely limited in terms of accessibility. Most of them were depicting big-game animals such stag, bison, and bulls, which were created with organic pigments and stylistically depicted. Other more abstract elements were also found along with the image in Figure 8.12, such as handprints.

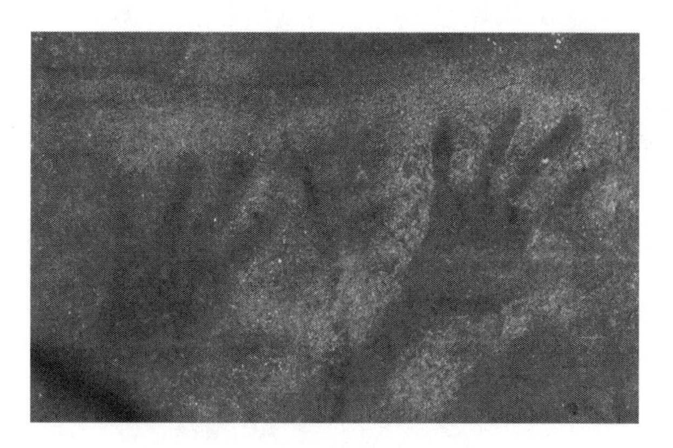

FIGURE 8.12 Aboriginal cave art with handprints.

8.2.2 Portable Sculpture

Bone carvings are very primitive forms of images, but they are characterized by the ability to transport and exchange them. This, in a sense, was the first form of Instagram! Small carvings that had representative imagery on them could be seen by hundreds of individuals over several generations. You can see the horse head carving in Figure 8.2.

8.2.2.1 Pottery

Painted pottery, with depictions of representational art (instead of just patterns or grooves), began showing up in during the early Bronze Age, with the most spectacular examples being from the Mediterranean and Asia. Pottery was like a miniature canvas, where scenes from mythology and hero stories could be easily depicted. Gods and goddesses, heroes, hunters, and monsters could all be depicted in a semi-realistic (but lacking 3D perspective) style. Pottery is also highly portable and easy to produce, so the proliferation of images could flood an entire population easily. Often, there would be centers of production of art for these vessels, mass-producing them for distribution. In this way, the still image, which previously had been less available and less accessible, suddenly became very common. In this way, we were able to communicate visual information across vast distances, bonding together common cultural concepts such as religion, politics, and of course myths, legends, and stories that underpinned entire societies. See Figure 8.5 for a depiction of pottery imagery from Greece.

8.2.2.2 Coins

What better place to stamp the picture of your king or queen/emperor or empress/president/resident god or goddess? Coins have always been based on currency, which is backed by a geopolitical structure, which is usually owned by the person whose face is *on* the coins. Highly portable and accessible, coins are a perfect place to proliferate an image across a large population and generate a cohesive economic and political structure. The image of the king or the queen, the emperor or the empress, or otherwise provides a powerful form of stability in the medium of gold, silver, brass, or copper and communicates the information. Figure 8.6 has a depiction of a Roman coin, replete with a bust of the emperor.

8.2.2.3 Rock Carvings

When the Egyptians, Babylonians, Assyrians, or Mayans wanted to depict stories in a format that everyone could see, they chose gigantic stone walls to carve them into. The advantage of this medium is that its size can be imposing and provide enough real estate to put down huge amounts of information that would otherwise be terribly difficult to transmit in a piece of pottery or something smaller. Great victories by the resident ruler or important cosmological events could be depicted in huge rock wall reliefs, visible to all who were in the vicinity. These gigantic images were characterized by their near universal accessibility, but they completely lacked portability. You had to see them in person. Their presence was predicated by the location, usually in the heart of or the entrance of a major focus of political power or religious worship. Giant stone reliefs are a way to make events and rulers seem larger than life. Even our own Mt. Rushmore has the faces of our former great presidents chiseled into the rock face in tremendous proportions. Rock is a medium through which we can create a sense of permanence and grandiosity that a little photograph cannot do justice to.

8.2.3 Statues

Statues have the advantage of being 3D. They obviously come in all sizes, from the miniature gods and goddesses that a typical household possessed and paid homage to the gigantic, overwhelming statue in the temple of Zeus. The medium produced a more lifelike entity, one that took up 3D space, and although they were not real in the true sense of the word, they were seen as far more real than a two-dimensional representation. Statues of the gods were often worshipped as physical entities, with offerings of blood, food, and wine frequently given as homage by worshippers, despite it being well know that they weren't actually going to eat or drink literally. The fact that the medium was 3D made them seem far more real than if they had only been paintings.

8.2.4 Paintings

Paintings come in many forms, shapes, and sizes, but the portability factor for them as an image would be relatively small. Even though you can walk around with a painting, it would generally not be considered an image you took with you or were able to move from place to place as easily or frequently as a piece of pottery or a photograph. Paintings were fairly stationary items, hung in places such as homes or churches and looked at only in those spaces. The accessibility of an actual painting has always been variable, but fundamentally limited to those who could afford it. Now, of course, you can buy a painting at a yard sale for 10 bucks, but you have to have a home and a place to hang it! So the idea of the painting was always relegated to certain people who could both afford it and have a place to put it.

Another aspect of the painting as an image is its medium (Figure 8.13). The canvas is (generally) square in shape and somewhere between 1 and 100 feet in size. The dimensions of the medium somehow drive the subject matter, the subject being encapsulated within the confines of the walls that define it. This means that the concept of a still image being a square, with certain preconceived boundaries in shape and size, was actually a novel concept. This is the point at which our idea of an image started to conform to this format, despite having multitudes of other ways to create it. Our notions of the still image have now been boxed into a square, and this is how you would often imagine something if I said I had a picture or

FIGURE 8.13 Typical portrait style painting by Rembrandt.

a drawing or a depiction of some kind. You would imagine a square, and that image somehow encapsulated within that square. Certainly, some enterprising artist could use only circular canvases or non-square shapes (and many do), but the majority of our notions of art as a painting come in square form. What does this mean? I'm not really sure—but the idea that the medium can have some influence on the perception shouldn't be lost here. If we see images in rectangular terms, we might be far more likely to think in this manner, rather than seeing things from other perspectives. Of course, the convenience of the square canvas means that it might take some doing to stretch our brain around something different, but the interesting thing here is that we don't actually see in rectangles. We just tend to frame it as such in both art and technology. How would a round computer monitor or an ellipsoid computer monitor change our perspective?

8.2.5 Tapestries

Tapestries were often used in medieval Europe to depict daily events, political events, religious stories, and local mythology (like some saint killing some dragon or serpent) (Figure 8.14). In terms of the format, the portability, and the shape, they don't differ much from a painting except that they are woven from fabric, which changes the look and the feel of the art in some way. The real question is why would somebody want to hang a giant rug with pictures on it in the hallway? The answer is the same reason we wanted to paint a piece of pottery or put images on a cave wall.

FIGURE 8.14 Medieval Beyeaux tapestry. Tapestries were large enough to depict historical events such as great battles, victories, or political events.

The desire to create art is universally human, whether you're making stick figures with a Crayola in kindergarten art class or just doodling on that napkin while you talk on the phone. It's a deep-seated fundamental drive that connects us as humans. Not only do we *like* making art, but we also love to display it.

8.2.6 Reliefs/Frescoes

These are like paintings on steroids! Basically, reliefs and frescoes are decorations for buildings, but certain societies such as the ancient Romans, and later the Renaissance artists of Europe in homage, loved to paint collage scenes on the walls of public buildings like bathhouses and forums. These pieces of art were highly accessible but, of course, not portable and thus could only be seen when the person was in the location. Most of these paintings were of life and humanity, sometimes even sensual or sexual in nature in regards to the ancient Romans, and often depicted men and women in the act of sex or at the very least in the nude. Even the great Renaissance artist's work such the famous Sistine Chapel of Michelangelo depicted the human nude in a certain level of sensual glory and with some level of 3D perspective that had a much more realistic style than abstract.

8.2.7 Printing Press/Woodcuts

The principal characteristic of woodcuts and lithographs was their reproducibility. Before photographs and digital media, there was no way to reproduce an image exactly. One had to copy the original and copy the copy, to the extent where the filter of the multiple artists making copies eventually became a shadow of the primary artist's intent. But the printing press not only made it possible to reproduce words identically, but also images! In this way, a single image, drawn by an artist, could be faithfully reproduced *over* and *over* again and everyone would be able to see it, in a far-spreading area of distribution. So that means that people across an entire area could see the same exact image in a very short period, which was something not possible previously. In Figure 8.15, you can see one of the earliest and most evocative of wood print mass-distributed images of the Boston Massacre, which served as an instrumental incitation for the early stages of the American Revolution. The woodcut, just like a modern image in a newspaper, was highly portable, highly accessible, and extremely good at communicating visual information about current events! The subject

FIGURE 8.15 Early printing of the Boston Massacre. Note the British redcoats firing into the crown of innocent civilians. Even if this weren't the truth of the incident, this image was in the hands of colonials all over American, causing feelings of anger and resentment against the British government. Only with mass distribution could this single image have made its way across the length of the country so quickly. We still use this same image in History textbooks today!

matter was often something about current politics, religion, or cultural (such as sports).

8.2.8 Photographs

The photograph was a milestone paradigm shift in the advent of still images. For the first time in the history of the human race, we were able to record visual data without human interpolation. That is to say that we could freeze a moment in time and put it into a portable form which would display exactly like the human eye perceived it. No longer was an artist needed to create a depiction of visual reality. You could simply snap a button on a device and result in a small piece of paper with an extremely realistic image on it. The advent of photographic technology was a tremendous change in the way we perceived the world. We could record, exchange, and transmit accurate visual information incredibly quickly.

8.2.9 Digital Media

Digital imagery was the next step in the paradigm shift that began with the photograph. Naturally, if we could turn visual information into a recorded rectangular version of it, we would eventually find a way to transmit those data across the air, onto a screen! It started with television, which was the transmission of live video being filmed, and eventually it has become the ability to have portable image-viewing machines in our pockets, able to instantly capture, transmit, and share images with anyone in the world. This proliferation of images into our lives has made the accessibility and the portability of them almost infinite and thus forever changed our valuation of them. Where once the intrinsic value of a still image was high because it was so rare, we now live in a modern world in which we are so saturated with them that they often lose their gravity. It's easy to see, however, that the image still affects us despite its ubiquity; it just affects us in much larger waves. Instead of seeing or receiving information from a single image at a time, in which we are able to view it often and review it, imagery often floods our input sensors and influences us in terms of trends and not single individual instances. For instance, if you look on Instagram and suddenly everyone starts posting pictures of an event, or a fashion, or a piece of news happening, the trend toward that particular thing will influence how you think or what you do. But the individual images, existing outside this context, will mean little to you on their own. They require the bigger context in order to influence you in any way.

8.3 COMPONENTS OF THE STILL IMAGE (BREAKING DOWN THE STILL IMAGE)

Now that we're more familiar with the aspects of still images as they applied in a global sense, we need to really analyze them in an individual sense. Regardless of portability, subject matter, accessibility, medium, and level of realism, each image can have very distinct characteristics that apply to it individually. A still image has a purpose, an intent, and it is used as such universally throughout the human existence. Each image can be broken down into components that characterize its primary attributes. Every image possesses the properties of subject, shading, color, and composition.

These are what embody all the visual information that we would need to analyze and assess an image for what its intention is.

8.3.1 Subject

The subject of an image is basically what its main focus is. It could be an object. It could be a person. It could be a body part. But every image you have ever seen, whether a crayon drawing or the *Mona Lisa*, has a specific subject matter depicted. The subject matter is the instrumental vessel of the story being told, the subject and the circumstances and the emotional feel. The subject is the hub around which all these other properties revolve.

8.3.2 Shading

Shading involves the play of light and shadow in the image. Without light, there is no such thing as vision, and without vision, there is no way to record visual data. But light comes in many different forms, at many times of day and night. Light and dark create mood in an emotional manner, because the bright ambient lights of the daytime juxtapose distinctly with the dark, spooky shadows of the night. Light without shadow can appear happy, or lacking in darkness, while high-contrast areas of light and dark can create a sensation of high drama. The manipulation of these levels of light and dark can dramatically change how an image or a film (more on film in the following) affects the viewer on a fundamental emotional level. Light and shadow can have a strong effect upon the sensation of high or low emotional states, and given a strong contrast, it would indicate a roller coaster of intensity.

For instance, an image of a happy woman (Figure 8.16) in a normal, bright color range can be easily rendered into an entirely different emotional state by adjusting the lighting of it (Figure 8.17). As you can clearly see, changing the tones of the colors from one image to another will make the image have different emotional connotations, which can be useful in generating gut-level feelings that would otherwise be difficult to produce.

8.3.3 Color

Color, as it pertains to the still image, is a deep and complex thing. Evaluating an image for what it conveys in emotional terms can often times be interpreted from the color combinations and the brightness. But colors have multiple emotional connections, and they can be learned or are inherent. Color adds exponential depth to any image, and the combination of color can completely alter the perception of an image.

FIGURE 8.16 Original image, without alterations.

FIGURE 8.17 Image with extreme alterations using image editing software. Notice how much less friendly and more disturbing the extremes of color make the image?

Solid colors and color schemes that are monochromatic are easier to extrapolate emotional states from. With solid or monochromatic color ranges, the similarity of color shading has a much more unified feeling, and although the color associations can be arbitrary, or at least *subjective*, there is an associated mean or a statistical average with colors and emotions across culture.

In 1809, Goethe, the German author, wrote a treatise called *The Theory of Colors*, in which he theorized upon the emotional impact of colors with nothing more than intuition and anecdotal evidence. Since that first study, many others have been conducted to get a grasp over just what connection there is in color and human emotion. Very little conclusive evidence has been procured over those past 200 years, but a consensus of opinion has been formed over certain colors and color combinations that seem to fit the most common use of them. Interestingly enough, in nature, these colors *all* exist at some point or another in the form of flowers, designed to stand out from the green tints to attract pollinators to them. So nature itself is rife with color and color combinations designed to be appealing to the animal eye.

1. *Blues*—An overall bluish tint generally emotes sadness or depression, as can be seen in Picasso's so-called Blue Period, where the artist used mostly blue tints to generate a sensation of deep melancholy and depression.

2. *Greens*—Dark greens and bright greens are the color of grass and tree foliage, which are inclined to depict the sensation of well-being and physical health and vibrancy. Greens are associated with fertility, spring, and nature.

3. *Reds*—Mars is the red planet, named after Ares or the god of war, with his sanguine nature and violent tendencies. Red is the color of blood, and the skin takes on reddish hues when pumped full of vigor and muscular effort. Therefore, red is seen as an angry, warlike color, often used in depicting violent acts or thoughts. The color red is visible over large distances and easily distinguished from other colors, which makes it naturally draw the eye toward it when used in any image.

4. *Yellows*—Yellow, and ochre, is often the color of flowers in the natural world, but in the world of art and imagery it is often avoided, especially in the darker hues, due to its suggestion of illness, bile, and natural danger warning (as in the yellow jacket or the bee). With the exception of the pastel variety (often used in Easter colors), yellow often evokes the sensation of being ill or out of sorts.

5. *Orange*—Orange and orange-red combinations are the color of fire, and hence, they evoke deep-seated primal feelings of both excitement

and simultaneously danger—which is the most likely reason that we use orange cones to depict danger zones and orange signs to warn people of impending danger! It's also easily visible against the blue of the sky, which makes it highly noticeable for a person in motion. Any still image with bright oranges (such as the Tide packaging) is going to have a high level of visibility.

6. *Violet*—The colors of twilight and some parts of the sky when the far away nebulae appear in the night are always somewhat mysterious colors, and it may not be coincidental that the priestly Catholic robes are in this family.
7. *White*—White is the absence of color, or the absence of darkness, and is thus associated with a sense of cleanliness, wholesomeness, and purity.
8. *Browns*—Brown is simultaneously the color of dirt, clay, and fecal matter. It's a sludge or a slurry of multiple colors that create the spectrum of brown. It's an earthy color, however, and despite its fecal waste association, it is also the color of fertility and nature. Bark is brown, and the deeper shades of brown for the damp soil with which we associate it means fertile soil for agriculture.
9. *Pink/rose*—This is the color of skin, flesh, sensuality, and youth. It often provides sensations of love, lust, femininity, and fertility.
10. *Black*—The absence of color and light, it evokes deep fear and darkness and mystery. Black is the color behind our eyes at night, and as such, it is almost universally depicted as a vessel of fear or austerity in cultures.

8.3.3.1 Common Color Combinations

A few colors can be drastically altered by simply adding another color to them.

1. *Blue and yellow*—While each of these colors may not be indicative of health independent of one another, together they invoke the appearance of a bright, sunny day, and are often used as backgrounds for children's cartoons.
2. *Blue and white*—This combination is clinical, in the sense that pharmaceutical companies, healthcare companies, and similar entities often use it for logos, commercials, and advertising. Blue with a light

tint has a cleansing effect on the mind in contrast with the white, which always invokes a sense of cleanliness and wholesomeness.

3. *Green and blue*—The color of water and the ocean, green and blue are often used to depict water and provide a sensation of depth, fear, and sometimes a floating sensation.

8.3.3.2 Unnatural/Emissive Color Tones

Neons and techno-colors with extremely high levels of saturation are often used in our modern chemical-based culture to indicate a conquering or an overstep of the natural in favor of the technical. These are almost universally *post*modern color types, usually favored in liquid crystal display and digital formats for the almost emissive quality of the screen, where it can bleed out the glowing hot red, greens, and blues. This is the color of fluorescence, the colors that seem to glow and pulse of their own accord. It is the color of the light saber, and the color of technological progress as it pushes us past the natural colors and into the human designed. These colors are used to depict the lasers and the ray guns and the energy-based weapons and tools we imagine ourselves building as our level of technology grows.

8.3.4 Composition

If we look at the most mundane of photographs or images on Instagram, we can find within them an entire story told from a single perspective, frozen in time. The thing about the rectangular format of the modern image is that it often obfuscates what it's re-creating. The perspective of the camera, or the image of the artist, must be interpreted by our brains as visual data, which means that it will be interpolating it as if it was seen from the eye of the viewers themselves. Composition is the re-creation of that perspective. If the subject or the focus of the image is filling the frame, then it *must* be happening very close to us. If the contents of the image appear to be small and are completely inside the frame, they must be far away from us (and therefore much less likely to pose an immediate threat). The rectangular frame of the image provides a canvas which is *re*interpreted by your brain as your field of vision. In this way, the size and the composition of the image can evoke very strong feelings from the viewer.

Figure 8.18 shows an image of a man smiling from a long distance. A man, smiling at you, from that distance should pose little threat or interest

FIGURE 8.18 A man, standing far away, smiling at us.

to you (unless he has a gun). In this instance, the composition has made you far less interested in the subject, because it's depicted from fairly far away.

Figure 8.19 shows the same man smiling from mid-distance. This man, if we were to do the math, would be mostly framed in your view as such if he was 4–6 feet away, enough to be important, even a potential threat to your reptilian brain, and definitely enough to be the focus of your attention.

Figure 8.20 shows that man again, but now his face is filling the frame. In this instance, you should feel very uncomfortable. You should feel this way because this composition of extreme close-up is entering into your personal distance safety zone, and this raises your danger flags. Despite the fact that your higher brain knows this is just an image, and that there

FIGURE 8.19 A little closer but still not threatening and remaining friendly.

is no man near you, the part of your brain responding to visual stimuli and fear reacts much faster than your higher reasoning, which is the reason you feel alarmed at the image despite the fact that it's not actually physically present. Why is this? If you think about it, there are only two reasons this person is so close to your physical space: either they are going to kiss you or bite you. I call this the *kiss me/kill me phenomenon*. Extremely close-up images are naturally disturbing, especially if the person doesn't have sultry eyebrows and puckered lips. In Figure 8.21, we can see a Hollywood glam shot of an actress close-up, with pursed lips and a dreamy look in her eye. Now that's somebody I'd definitely want in my personal space! Your fear buttons are much less likely to be triggered with the difference in facial expression.

FIGURE 8.20 Now that the composition of the man is in our personal space, he suddenly seems a lot creepier and less friendly, almost threatening in some way. It's exactly the same picture! Only the composition has changed. This is how the still image can be manipulated to generate primal emotions like fear.

8.4 TARGETED IMAGE ANALYSIS

You can see that even in a single image, there is a dense thickness of visual information. Large amounts of information can be stored visually and told back to the viewer as a story, with all the requisite pieces of the puzzle which are *missing* (that being sequence and narrative) assembled by your brain into a format that is comprehensible. The old adage "a picture is worth a thousand words" is not so cliché after all, if we understand that visual information encodes many layers of data into it, much of which is being processed by your lower level brain simultaneously with your higher level brain, which leads to subtle nuances in emotional and conceptual impressions of the same image.

FIGURE 8.21 Now this photo looks a lot less threatening when seen close up. It's the come-hither look on her face and the slightly puckered lips that say "Lust for me" instead of "Fear me."

These unique aspects of still image media all work fabulously for advertising and have, hence, been used vociferously over the past century in the form of magazines, newspapers, comic book, and now, of course, the Internet and social media. They work so well for advertising because they allow your brain the flexibility of assembling the pieces of the puzzle itself while still appealing to that lower-tier of mental process which is generating raw emotion and gut-level appeal based on lighting, color, and composition. In Figure 8.22, we can see a traditional cigarette ad from the classic American period of 1950, circa 1951. I personally love cigarette ads from this period because they are so transparently blatant in their drive to sell smoking cigarettes as a healthy, sophisticated part of an all-American lifestyle despite the current trend in the exact opposite direction. Since we all now know how incredibly damaging and foolish smoking cigarettes is, the classic 50s and 60s cigarette ads can peel back

FIGURE 8.22 Sherman Billingsley, in a Fatima Cigarette ad, circa 1951. Notice the muted colors, friendly composition, and smiling face.

the man behind the curtain and show us just how insidious and deliberate advertising is.

The Fatima cigarette ad in Figure 8.22 tells us a simple story, encoded into a seemingly innocuous image of a man, at a table, smoking a cigarette (it's actually Sherman Billingsley at the Stork Club). But if we really analyze the image in greater detail, we can clearly see the multiple visual cues being handed to us. The man is smiling, well dressed, and apparently successful because he is wearing a business suit, has all of his teeth, and he looks happy. Why is he happy? He's happy because he just lit a delicious Fatima cigarette and is enjoying the fresh tobacco taste. Notice the cigarette is freshly lit, omitting the nasty ashes or the smoke trails in the air. All cigarette ads will show you the first puff, which mimics the first rush of nicotine into the system upon lighting the cigarette, which most smokers will say is the most pleasurable. The advertisers do this on purpose, because your pleasure-seeking synapses have already fired the moment you see a pattern which reminds you of a similar pleasurable sensation (such as watching somebody take the first bite of a cookie). We certainly don't want an advertisement showing a dirty ashtray with multiple cigarette butts and smoke filling the air. His ashtray is *empty.*

Even the composition of the image is nonthreatening. From the perspective of the print ad, this man is sitting far enough away from us not to pose a direct threat, and he is smiling in a friendly manner. The perspective from the viewer's standpoint is inferior—meaning that you're actually looking down at him from a standing position. He's almost inviting you to sit down and share a delicious Fatima cigarette with him at the table! The inferior perspective, based on the composition, makes the viewer feel less threatened by the subject. If he was standing over you, thrusting a cigarette in your face, this image might take on an entirely different meaning.

CHAPTER 9

The Moving Image

IN TERMS OF MEDIA and format of media, images, frozen in time, are only the tip of the iceberg. Although moving pictures as a common media form haven't been around all that long, they've become an integral part of our daily lives over the past century. The moving image, as opposed to the still image, contains the extra dimension of time to add to the layers of information. But that extra dimension of time can add to or detract from the act of telling a story with it. While you get to re-create movement as it pertains to the perspective of the eye, you *lose* the flexibility of allowing the brain to create its own individual narrative and sequence based on the removal of time. When you remove time from the visual cortex, it has much more time to create an imprint and a creative narrative of the story unfolding in the visual data. Now that you add multiple images, over time, you detract from the brain's creativity because it has to process all the information it is receiving. For this reason, television and streamed content is somewhat passive by nature. It depends on feeding the audience reams of visual data, engaging those reptilian brain sensors without engaging the conscious mind. Passivity is the hallmark of twentieth-century entertainment in the form of storytelling. That's not necessarily a bad thing; it's just a side effect of the communication medium.

9.1 ANIMATION

It may surprise some that I begin with animation, especially when many people imagine animation to be the *newer* format of moving visual information. But animation, in its raw form, has been around since at least the fifteenth century, in which illuminated manuscripts had wheels of images that could be spun around an axis, causing the images to alter their position and create simple movement. Even the original animation of the twentieth century was a flipbook of images with a dinosaur as the primary subject. So animation, and the concept of such, is extremely old and much more than the moving pictures we are used to.

To put in simplest terms, animation is art/time or the manipulation of a sequence of drawings that are shown to the human eye at a rate fast enough to produce the illusion of motion. The human perception range is about 24 images per second, a number which has become the standard for what we now know as *real time. Real time* means that the images being shown to us happen at the same speed as they are processed by our senses. This may seem to be something trivial, but in fact, it has been the subject of a long scientific study over the past century. It is vital in animation, moving pictures, film, and most recently interactive 3D media. In order for things to happen at the same rate on a screen as they would in normal observation, a simple experiment can be conducted. For example, I capture a film of a person walking across the room, let's say on a film camera that has an adjustable capture rate, and I tweak the values to capture and play back at the same rate. Now if I capture the film at 24 frames per second and play it back at 24 frames per second, the speeds at which the person on film walks and the person in the room walks should be exactly the same amount of time for him/her to walk from one side to the other as his/her image on the film does exactly the same thing. If the capture rate and the playback rate are at 24 frames per second, you should have an exact match.

Now here's the interesting thing. What happens if we capture at 100 frames per second but play back at 24? This is called *slow motion.* The interesting thing about slow motion is that it isn't slow because it's being played back at a slower rate; it's slow because it was played back at a slower rate than it was captured. The inverse is true with *fast motion.* If you capture the film at a faster rate than you play it back, the movement will seem jerky and faster than normal (just like those old Charlie Chaplain films).

This affects animation in the sense that the closer you are to 24 frames per seconds or, in this case, 24 drawings per second, the smoother and the more lifelike the movement will be. Conversely, if you only have 12 drawings and you play them at 24 frames per second, it will seem less smooth and more jerky. Sometimes this is a good thing—animation can be surreal in movement without the human eye noticing as much, and you will see a lot of animation deliberately scaled down to 12 or 15 frames per second for this exact reason. But also, it's difficult to do animation and very time consuming, because drawn images (unlike captured images) require a human being to sit down and *draw* 24 frames per second! That's a lot of time drawing. But most animation houses, even Disney, practice some sort of doubling, where they only draw 12 frames per second and then double each frame. This provides a level of smoothness while cutting down on the actual time drawing, without noticeable lack in quality.

If animation is art/time, then it stands to reason that all of the elements of art apply. Each frame is drawn or computer generated (more on that later) and therefore filtered through the human mind instead of captured with a lens. This means that animation can possess qualities far more abstract and surreal than a film could ever do. We are able to piece together aspects of the images being displayed and formulate the pieces in our mind, with the brain filling in those gaps between missing visual information. We are willing to accept tremendous amounts of play on time, space, and physics because of this level of abstraction from visual information that more closely mimics the real world. Cartoons are a great example of this, because the exaggeration of time and space most often occurs in these types of animation. Classic twentieth-century animators, including Disney, Warner Brothers, and Hannah Barbera, often used these principles of abstract physics to depict time, motion, and action through a distorted lens for the purpose of projecting exaggerated movement.

Animation, such art, is not an exact mirror of the world around it. As such, certain principles were discovered about the implementation of time and movement to the still image. Although these principles are mutable, due the highly subjective nature of art, they still hold some level of cohesive fundamental rules that are generally followed by animators. Early animators such Disney were credited with discovering these rules or developing certain techniques to utilize the human brain's pattern-filling tendencies to trick it into seeing certain things. Whether he created or discovered these principles is a subject of debate, but their effectiveness is certainly not! They definitely work well, despite the surreal aspects of the art.

9.1.1 Exaggeration

Exaggeration is the hallmark of *all* animation. It's vital to impart intention of movement and enhance the action. What would be normal movement in the real world often appears to be stale and lifeless in animation. Therefore, it's vital to have highly exaggerated movements in the world of animation, which then appear to be normal or read better to the human eye. There are a lot of reasons for this, but the important thing to know about animation is that movement is highly exaggerated, in terms of screen space and character action.

9.1.2 Squash and Stretch

Squash and stretch can refer to one of two things. It can be used to describe the manipulation of *time*, or it can be used to describe the manipulation of volume as it pertains to the character or the object shape. Since squash and stretch of time is always present in animation, we will discuss this first.

Using time like a rubber band adds the lifelike movement and the dynamic tension to cartoons that are necessary to be understood by the human eye. In animation, certain actions slow down time as they are performed by the characters, and certain other actions speed up rapidly or accelerate. By manipulating the acceleration and the deceleration of time, the action of the animation can be exaggerated enough to be read dynamically by the human eye. Without this acceleration and deceleration, we wouldn't get that sense of physical action. Imagine a baseball pitcher, winding up for the pitch. If he winds up from his start position to the ready-to-fire position at the same exact rate, it would look bland and boring in a cartoon animation. *But* if he decelerates the rate at which he cranks back his arm, and then *accelerates* rapidly into the firing position where the ball leaves his hand, the stretching of time will provide a much more dynamic action. This is where the real world and the cartoon/animation world vastly differ. Most of the time, we don't have visible stretching of time in our physical actions! As humans, we tend to move rapidly or slowly and deliberately. There is some natural acceleration when doing things that require it, such as throwing balls or spears or rocks. This is how we are able to throw things, because we create a pendulum with the mechanics of our arm. But it's rare that we decelerate any movement naturally. However, in animation, this slow stretch and snapping of time is like pulling on a bowstring and letting go of an arrow. It builds dynamic tension, which is rapidly released, making a much more effective visual imprinting of action. What seems appropriate here for action in animation is ludicrously overstated compared to real life (another aspect of exaggeration).

The second aspect of squash and stretch, commonly (but not always) deployed in traditional animation is the technique of making objects and characters seem rubbery or squishy. While this is not *always* the case, it occurs often enough to merit it as a technique in its own right. The rubbery appearance of characters is often a method to reinforce the squash and the stretch of time, as the expansion and the contraction of movement will be

FIGURE 9.1 An early cartoon, depicting Betty Boop. The style of rubbery and stretchy bodies was an early technique to create a dynamic sense of motion.

visible not only in the acceleration and the deceleration of time, but also in the volume of the characters. The character's body and limbs will actually squash and stretch *with* the action, using the same principles as the squash and the stretch of time but applying it to the volume of the character. As long as the appearance of volume is maintained, it will often look like the characters are made of a rubbery or a pliant substance. This is most obvious in the earliest cartoons, from Disney to *Betty Boop* (Figure 9.1) to Warner Brothers (Figure 9.2).

9.1.3 Anticipation

When a person in real life moves, there is very rarely any preceding indication. Sometimes, however, as in the case of our fictional baseball pitcher, a person needs to charge up kinetic energy by moving in the opposite direction of the intended action. In the case of the pitcher, he/she is winding up or charging his/her arm to throw the ball, which is the main action of the movement. In order to charge up kinetic energy, he/she brings his/her arm all the way back before slinging it forward, rocketing that baseball toward the strike zone at 100 mph. When you watch a baseball game, you know when the pitcher is about to throw the ball, because he/she winds up his/her arm first.

When a character in a cartoon or an animation moves, it needs to be anticipated, just like our pitcher in real life. Now, in the real world, we don't always wind up in anticipation, but the in the cartoon world, it tends

FIGURE 9.2 A Warner Brothers cartoon. Bugs Bunny and Porky Pig with an unnamed dog.

to read better because it prepares the eye and, hence, the brain, for what comes next. This is why all the characters in Scooby Doo run in place *before* they shoot forward (in a cloud of dust to further emphasize rapid movement). This prepares the viewer for their action. This also occurs when the characters in cartoons step back or prepare for a forward movement. In Figure 9.3, you can see the character's anticipation before springing forward in motion. If there is no anticipation frame or position, the movement will happen faster than the eye can register, and the action will not read as well. Cartoon anticipation is extremely common and a fairly universal aspect of animation.

9.1.4 Constant Movement

Another principle of animation and art/time is the need for constant movement. It's an interesting trick of the human mind to feel the need for a constant amount of movement in moving images. While we may not need this in captured film, we seem to require a constant state of movement in an animation or our eye quickly reverts to still image mode, which makes it begin to lose the illusion of movement required to make any animation work. Unfortunately, there are many places in animation where a certain level of stillness is *needed* for the character to hold a position in anticipation or in the process of follow through. If the animator leaves too many frames of the same action without changing the background or some

FIGURE 9.3 Cartoon anticipation. This character is preparing to run forward, hence the exaggerating winding up effect, as if he were a baseball pitcher, winding up for the throw. This exaggerated sense of motion creates a more readable action when played back as a cartoon.

other element of the scene, the action will often read as totally flat and boring. Therefore, the need for constant movement is often met by some sort of static or noise in the background images, resulting in an interesting appearance for the eye. Don Hertzfeldt, a modern animator, is often known for using a somewhat crinkled background that constantly shifts, even when his characters are in a static position. This wrinkled effect adds layers of visual interest to the animation, even when no other action on the screen is occurring. Traditional, hand-drawn animation often compensates for this naturally by having constant irregularities in the drawn images; however, 3D animation, in which a screen is constantly rendered by a computer and each frame can be exactly the same, often suffers from this lack of irregularity and hence can suddenly seem frozen on the screen if no movement occurs.

9.1.5 Three-Dimensional Animation

Three-dimensional animation deserves its own category for the reason of being computer generated. Three-dimensional animation, as a general rule, was originally created to strive for the re-creation of the real world of physical lighting and computer-generated objects that act and behave as if they were in real space. Three-dimensional geometry and objects take up virtual space and volume in a computer-generated simulation and take on characteristics of the real world, with far less resolution or roundness. Three-dimensional simulations were originally for the purpose of physics more than art, but over time, the community of animators and game developers quickly adopted them as both the hot new emerging art form of the twenty-first century as well as a way to make games more immersive by making them more realistic. Despite the push for hyperrealism in game-based 3D art, many filmmakers (such as the famous Pixar Studios) quickly gravitated to it and rapidly conformed the technology to their creative vision. Soon *Toy Story* was produced and became a huge success; 3D animation became seen as a viable art form that coexists with traditional forms of animation.

But 3D animation is drastically different from hand-drawn animation in the final product. When traditional art is created, by a drawing or a painting, the imagery is filtered through a human mind, which oftentimes strips down the visual information and resets it to make it representative in some way. This removes a certain amount of visual data from the image. Figure 9.4 shows the *Mona Lisa*, the original painting by Leonardo da Vinci, while Figure 9.5 shows a digital 3D rendering of the same exact thing. Although the 3D version is artistically rendered, it has a much more artificial feel than the original painting. The reason for this is that the interpretation of a thing in real life as filtered through the lens of the human mind and transformed through the medium of paintbrush or pencil is drastically different from the ordered rendering of pixels to a screen. A computer tends to generate *too* much information, and even when it's filtered or blurred in some form, it happens in too orderly of a format for us to see it as real or human. We need some form of human-created randomness in the shading and the color in order to be reinterpreted by our human brain. Even though the composition and the subject are exactly the same in both images, the hand-painted image looks real and aesthetically pleasing, while the computer-generated one looks plastic, artificial, and dull. These traits are all incredibly *subjective* but appear to share common necessities for proper human-like quality.

But where 3D really shines in terms of performance for artistic creation is interactive entertainment. Real-time 3D is a staple of the game development industry because the movement and the rendering can be incredibly lifelike and immersive when done correctly. Modern 3D gaming often goes for a hyperrealistic style that can read to the player as more real than a hand-drawn animation. Of course, two-dimensional (2D) cell animation

FIGURE 9.4 The original *Mona Lisa* painting, by Renaissance master Leonardo Da Vinci.

FIGURE 9.5 A 3D rendition of the *Mona Lisa*. Notice how flat, lifeless, and uninspired the 3D rendering is? Computer-generated still images often lack the soft, interpreted lines of human influence and appear artificial.

FIGURE 9.6 Real-time 3D games are designed to look and feel real in order to make the experience more exciting. This is a frame from a mobile zombie shooter in progress.

games exist but are still mostly designed, drawn, and developed on a computer. To my knowledge, no truly hand-drawn game exists because of the need for constant action based on human input, which would require a tremendous amount of hand-drawn frames in order to compensate for a full control scheme. But the difference here is in the *movement*, and not in the rendered image, which we can see is often not as pleasing as some kind of hand-drawn art. But movement, when rendered in three dimensions, is much more immersive because it more closely mimics the perspective of the human eye than 2D cell-based animation (Figure 9.6). The movement happening from the camera representing the human eye makes the content much more lifelike, which in turn synthetically stimulates all the triggers that a real experience might, such as adrenaline, testosterone, serotonin, and dopaminergic reactions. That deep reptilian brain is tuned to react to movement, which often means that the realistic movement of a 3D shooter will be far more effective than a pastel-rendered artistic equivalent might be.

9.2 DIGITAL MEDIA DEVICES

The last vestige of shift in the availability and the portability of still images has most recently come in the form of digital media devices such as personal computers, the Internet, and mobile phones with high-resolution capability. Just as the printing press once completely shifted the paradigm of storytelling and imagery, the computer and now mobile device have completely shifted the meaning, the intention, and the proliferation of images. Digital imagery is now instantly available to anyone, anywhere, as long as they have an Internet connection and a device that will read it. Now that these images are highly available and portable, they have taken on a new meaning, or lack thereof, to our mind. When the portability and the accessibility have become nearly universal, it detracts from the *value* of the image to the individual. Each independent image that we see exists in a sea of millions of others, which we are inundated with every minute of every day. This constant influx of readily available images will reduce the emotional impact of them, and even now in the age of digital manipulation of photography, we might have a reduction in the legitimacy of the information itself. Anyone who has ever been tricked by an Internet photo hoax now knows to be extremely leery of getting too excited when watching a gigantic shark about to eat a person on a helicopter ladder. The important thing here is to note that with the increase of availability and portability, we become somewhat desensitized to the content but, at the same time, have a massive increase of ability to communicate through the medium of imagery, which in turn increases our sense of social and cultural connection. We may not *believe* that the shark is real, but we've all *seen* it (and maybe gotten fooled by it). That means that visual information is moving incredibly rapidly through our culture, allowing us all to connect with it rapidly and with more homogeneity in our understanding of it.

9.2.1 Film

What the photograph brought to the creation, the sharing, and the distribution of images, film and motion pictures took another leap forward in technology. Not only could the perspective lens of real life be captured and frozen into a still image, but now, the actual real-world movement of these images could be captured and replayed. For the first time in the history of humans, we could record *movement* and action and play it back whenever we wanted. The advent of film recording was a hallmark of the twentieth-century form of communication, where we could suddenly go to a theater and watch the performance of a story and see exactly the same thing time after time. It was like the printing press was to the distribution of images. Movies and television were watched by multitudes of people all over the world, who suddenly had a common frame of cultural reference because they'd all seen the same thing. Cultural ideas, stories, and news were now global and not just tied to the local community.

Most of the aspects of photography, in the attributes of lighting, color, composition, and subject can be applied to motion pictures and television, but the one *added* component to this form of media is *time*. The time and the passing of time in capturing and playing back the movement is an essential element and tool in producing content that has certain emotional impact. Often early films, devoid of color, used high-contrast lighting to convey drama and mood. Many early German films, such as the still from *Der Golem* in Figure 9.7, were created with high-contrast lighting and developing techniques to provide a stark and spooky appearance.

Films, as they were produced and distributed, were much different in their inception than they are in their current state. Films were distributed to theaters, which were often converted from dramatic live-action play venues, and treated as such. A film, when created beginning to end, was much more like a book than a television show. The stories were told as a one-off element, from beginning to end, and the running time could be anywhere from 90 to 200 minutes, often with intermissions in between to rest and socialize (Figure 9.8). A film was often a self-contained story that would not be revisited or a sequel made (although many films did eventually become so popular that sequels were produced). So the film was

FIGURE 9.7 A still frame from German film *Der Golem*, about a fictional monster created by a wizard, in the vein of *Frankenstein*.

FIGURE 9.8 Charlie Chaplain, playing his loveable tramp in early silent films.

considered a self-contained story that had a certain element of glamour to it. The screens and the stars were larger than life, literally being projected onto a large cinematic screen with high resolution.

9.2.2 Television

The advent of television in the late 1940s and 1950s was another landmark method of media distribution where, for the price of a television set, you could suddenly have moving pictures transmitted directly into your home. The commonality between cultural references and information became even more universal, because instead of the audience physically going to congregate at a theater, they could stay at home and have the stories, the information, and the news delivered right to them in the form of moving pictures.

The resolution and quality of film were much, much higher in the early days of television, and would remain so for the entirety of the twentieth century. This disparity between film and television resolution was due to both the capturing equipment and the technology used to transmit the signal to the television sets, which would remain at 720 pixels by 480 pixels as defined by the National Television System Committee in America (and similar standards in Europe under Phase Alternating Line). This, combined with the basically lousy reception and cathode ray tube technology in the delivery of the media, made the medium drastically different from a film. Figure 9.9 shows a television set, circa 1978, and how small and low resolution they were before the advent of the digital age.

The formatting of programming for television came from its previous incarnation: radio. Radio was part of broadcasting, which was fundamentally a different entity from film. Since people paid to go see a film, there was no need for advertising inside the film itself (although that certainly doesn't stop them anymore in the previews). But broadcasting was *free.* You could watch television or listen to the radio for only the cost of the reception device. Of course, with the advent of cable television in the late 1980s, you had to pay for programming *and* watch commercials, but you paid for the better reception and the larger array of options for programming. So if early television was free, just like its previous counterpart in radio, it had to have commercial advertisements pay for the programming that you were watching, whether it be a game show, a news broadcast, or an episode of *The Honeymooners* (Figure 9.10). That's why announcers always said things such as "This episode brought to you by so and so...." Being a child of the radio broadcast, television formatting and programming was drastically different from film. Television had to have *variety,* and since the programming had to fill about 12–18 hours a day, there were different types of shows for different times of day. Homemakers might like to watch soap operas or game shows, while men (who were the large percentage of

FIGURE 9.9 A Sony television set, circa 1978–1988.

FIGURE 9.10 Jackie Gleason as Ralph Cramden and cast in the background in one of the most successful and original sitcoms to air on early television.

the workforce from 1940 to 1970) might want to watch sports or news at night. Stories were told in a much shorter, episodic format, often revolving around a cast with situational comedic characters or dramatic elements. There were kids' shows, and superheroes, and all the requisite elements of traditional storytelling, but they were usually much shorter and broken up into segments, usually between 30- and 60-minute blocks (which include the commercial time). This formatting is still used in modern storytelling, especially in the advent of podcasts, which is an audio-only format.

9.2.3 Streaming Content

As the resolution and the technology of television increased over the years, the line between film and television became more and more blurred. The quality of resolution with high-definition (HD) television and streaming technology quickly changed the availability paradigm of content for the audience. HD quality in capture, distribution, and display has made television or episodic content as good as film in this regard. Films are often released onto streaming services, available for viewing on personal devices such as laptops, tablets, and phones. So if films are available on your personal device, why go to the theater?

Availability, or accessibility, is a major feature of current content. An important attribute of any content is *when* you can see it. Films are generally available for first preview in the theater only, prompting people to see them as they become available, in a single location. This is a limited accessibility and nonportable format. But now that you can see this content in an immediately accessible, portable format, the only thing that divides the two are when you can see it and how high the resolution is (the theater experience).

Streaming services such as Netflix, Amazon, Hulu, and multiple others have now fully embraced the concept of full season availability as opposed to the former one-episode per week release of traditional network television. This new formatting and level of availability has completely changed viewing habits, which used to be spread out by choice but now is often done in large chunks of time, often called *binge-watching*. The really interesting thing here is the fundamental paradigm shift that has occurred because of those two important aspects of media: accessibility and portability. Technology, once again, was the driver of the paradigm shift. Technology, in the form of high-resolution streaming, increased accessibility and portability, just like the printing press or the smartphone did for the still image. As soon as we had available content anywhere, anytime, there wasn't much interest in going back.

9.3 MOVEMENT, TIME, AND EFFECT

If we use time and speed of time to create effect in animation, we use it to a lesser degree in live film and video for the same purpose. Slow motion and fast motion are both used to change the tone or the emotional content of the action. Slow motion is a technique often used in film and television to create a more dramatic effect. When the frame rate of capture is much higher than the frame rate of playback, the effect results in slower motion without loss of resolution. The slow-motion effect is a way of making people appear to be more dramatic, more important, and in some ways cooler than the opposite. Slow motion is often used to make action cinematography more dramatic, easier to read, and increase the visual novelty in some way. One ironic use of slow motion is to make a comedy film in which the technique of slow motion is used to overemphasize the overuse of the technique in films.

Inversely proportional to making things look a lot cooler in slow motion, things look a lot more comedic in sped-up motion. Speeding up the motion in playback creates a halting, jerky style of action that is often used in comedic chase scenes and elements of humor. Films such as *The Pink Panther* and shows such as the *Benny Hill Show* would often use a silly, comedic, sped-up playback of certain chase scenes (often to the point of exhaustion) in order to generate humor. Somehow, sped-up action appears to be more comedic than slowed-down action. Although there are no hard data on psychological reasoning for this phenomenon, it's a generalized but well-known constant in the art of filmmaking.

CHAPTER 10

Memes and Symbols

SYMBOLS AND MEMES ARE two highly important, emergent forms of media that deserve attention. They are images, to be sure, but this category of images is highly abstract and representational terms, and often encodes complex messages into a simple mix of image and text.

What is a *symbol*? The simple definition from the *Merriam-Webster's Dictionary* is as follows:

> **1:** an action, object, event, etc., that expresses or represents a particular idea or quality
>
> **2:** a letter, group of letters, character, or picture that is used instead of a word or group of words

In this, we can look at definition 2, which concerns a letter or a picture that *represents* a word or a group of words. In terms of media, a symbol is an image, or a set of images, which is representative of some idea, concept, or set of ideas that would be far longer to describe. Symbols are often culturally sensitive, in the sense that they are only representative of certain things if you are familiar with that reference. For instance, in Figure 10.1, you can see a road sign for a restaurant or a place to eat. Even though this sign is from France, which has a completely different language than English, this is something that anyone from the Western/European culture would understand as a symbol for food or restaurant. Why is that? Because we all eat with forks, knives, and spoons! If you are in Japan or Vietnam, it might not make so much sense to you (they eat

FIGURE 10.1 A symbol from a French road sign. Even though this symbol is from France, we have a commonality that makes us understand it means "food served near here."

with chopsticks). These images are *symbolic* or abstract representations that say, "There is a restaurant nearby," without having to spell it out in type. Figure 10.2 is a road sign for a Norwegian highway. If you aren't Norwegian, you probably don't know what this sign is telling you. Neither do I! That's one of the pitfalls of symbology; it doesn't necessarily mean

FIGURE 10.2 A Norwegian road sign. If you're American, you probably don't know what it means! Neither do I. We lack the commonality of culture that would clue us in.

anything if you don't have a reference for the representation on the image. The Norwegian image in Figure 10.2 doesn't have any frame of reference for a non-Norwegian!

Symbols are actually complex things. Some of the earliest written languages, such as Egyptian and Mayan, were hieroglyphic languages, which means that they recorded information into symbols that had multiple and contextual meanings (Figure 10.3). Each symbol had not only a phonetic, or an audible, equivalent, but also a conceptual one as well. By combining the different symbols together, different meanings could be put together from the contextual connection of the symbols and the order they were placed in. In this way, complex information could be encoded into various symbols with multiple meanings based on sequential order. Eventually, most of these symbols were converted into phonetic symbols, which represented the sounds a human could make when speaking, also known as *phonemes*. Because we have a certain limit on sounds we can make, the alphabet or the total number of symbols could be drastically reduced and become much easier to learn.

Where do symbols fit in to modern multimedia and interactive experiences? They fit everywhere. We can find the common digital realm rife with symbols and symbology. The use of symbols is actually on the increase, due to the limited screen space of tablets and mobile devices, which are quickly becoming the most-used tools for Internet browsing and social media. With limited screen space for all those apps, developers and designers

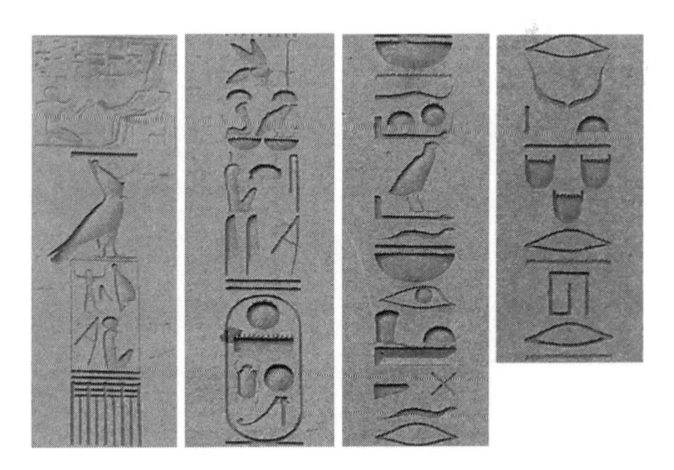

FIGURE 10.3 Egyptian hieroglyphics. These are multilevel symbols which stand for both words *and* concepts.

oftentimes need to condense wordy data or information into simple, square symbols that encode multiple pieces of information into it. This is how we understand not only what app or option we are choosing, but also what kind of function it will perform. Symbols are often used by companies for branding or establishing a personal relationship between you and the product they offer. By familiarizing you with a certain symbol in the logo, they can create a positive personal connection between you and their product. Popular social media sites such as Facebook, Instagram, and Twitter all use symbology to familiarize you with their product and access their features or share information from other sites. Instagram has my favorite symbol as its main icon, as you can see in Figure 10.4. The symbol itself is reminiscent of early instant cameras, which were self-contained units that processed the film in bulky boxes behind the main camera mechanism. The images that were produced from these instant cameras were often heavily processed and artificial-looking, which gave them a certain style of appearance. Instagram originally was just a set of filters for your digital images that were intended to reproduce the look of these old, instant camera images, as a kind of hip, retro appearance. Eventually, it morphed into the behemoth of image sharing on social media, but the symbol remained the same. Figure 10.5 shows the original Polaroid camera.

As we can see in the example of the Polaroid camera, symbols often represent something in the real world, or at one time intended to do so.

FIGURE 10.4 Instagram icon.

FIGURE 10.5 Original Polaroid camera.

The connection is made with the original intent and eventually becomes a recognized element unto itself. Symbology is vital to digital interaction because of the small size of the screens and the flat interface. If everything were completely done in text (and at one time, it *was* only text), it would not only be boring but also incredibly verbose! GUIs, or graphical user interfaces, are what evolved computers from specialist tasks to global common user prominence (Figure 10.6)! Without the first GUI for performing computer tasks, there would be no digital media. It would just be a bunch of text. We operate in a graphical world, and those graphics are

FIGURE 10.6 If computers all had interfaces like this, most of us wouldn't want to use them! End users require a GUI, and a GUI requires heavy use of symbols.

FIGURE 10.7 Popular Twitter emoji depicting the act of laughing so hard you cry. This is vastly different than tears of sorrow, so an emoji must be used to indicate a smiling face combined with tears.

oftentimes highly abstract or representative of something in the real world without actually looking like it.

Texting, a popular form of mobile communication, uses symbols often with emoticons and emoji icons, which are often used to convey emotional information or verbal emphasis to text that simple punctuation is not able to infer. Figure 10.7 show an example of this, with a simple emoji or symbol conveying emotional content. The emoji in Figure 10.7 is conveying the fact that the sender found something so funny they laughed hard enough to shed tears. Try sending that in text! The emoticon adds a simple but powerful visual message that has emotional content connected to it.

10.1 MEMES

What is a *meme*? That's a good question. The term *meme*, coined by Richard Dawkins in his book *The Selfish Gene*, is defined by him as "a unit of cultural transmission." The concept of this still stands today, including the exact identical meaning. The term itself quickly spread from person to person and has been assimilated by us into the modern definition as occurring or coming from the Internet. A meme is a single entity, saying, or image that contains complex cultural information encoded into it. It's a lot like a symbol, but often combines text and certain images in order to convey a culturally bound piece of information. Many memes are stories unto themselves or tell stories with components mishmashed from popular cultural iconography or images, such as a still frame from a popular movie, cartoon, or television show. Internet memes are often used to convey emotional information that only people initiated into the common culture would understand, thus making them an exclusive form of communication for those in the know. They are essentially standing inside jokes, and getting the joke will mark you as a person with certain cultural commonalities to another.

Figure 10.8 shows a common meme, converted from a moment in a popular film, called *300* (Warner Bros., 2007), when the leading character kicks a negotiating dignitary from Xerxes, leader of the invading Persian forces, into a ditch while yelling the key phrase. The moment, captured here in a stick-figure mock-up, is simultaneously expressing personal and filial pride along with an absurd amount of overdramatic subterfuge. The meme therefore carries with it an ironic message sense of overdramatic self-importance taken to absurd levels of indulgence. The layers of information contained inside the meme are sophisticated, complex, and completely dependent on not only *seeing* the film in question, but also understanding the context of the absurdity in the reproduction of it in stick figures, which also carry with them some level of ironic messaging, due to the fact that stick figures are usually used to simplify an overcomplicated concept or idea and convert it into a sign. So as you can see here,

FIGURE 10.8 A simple stick figure illustration with a specific piece of text can exist as an ultracomplex, layered entity.

a simple still image can convey a high density of information with it on multiple contextual levels, provided the context is *understood*. And that is the key to the meme; if you don't get the full context, you will miss out on the subtleties of the information conveyed. What we get from memes is the ability to cascade cultural information and use it as a social sticking point. If you *get it*, then you are in my culturally homogenous group. If you don't get it, we can assume that you are not in the same group and are therefore naive to our commonality of cultural understanding.

REFERENCE

Warner Bros. *300* [Motion Picture]. Canton, M., Goldman, B., Nunnari, G., Silver, J. (Producers), and Snyder, Z. (Director). (2007). Burbank, CA: Warner Brothers.

CHAPTER 11

Audio

IF VISION IS OUR primary tool for analyzing information about the world around us, then hearing is a close second. Hearing has the advantage of operating when our vision does not, as in the case of the darkness of night or things that are out of our range of sight. Things that are behind us can often alert us of their presence through the use of sound, and if anyone has ever had someone sneak up and whisper in their ear, they can attest to the hairs rising on the back of their neck! Or if someone shouts in your ear from behind, you might literally jump out of your seat. Audible information alerts us to danger because it allows us to hear things we aren't able to see, and so, it fills the gaps of sensory information. In terms of media and storytelling, audio is such an important component, but it often gets ignored or sidestepped when creating multimedia. But audio and sound, however, are incredibly vital aspects of media that convey multitudes of information to the audience or the player, often times occurring on a subliminal rather than conscious level.

How does sounds actually work? Mechanically, sounds are waves formed from any vibrating object, which could be a twig snapping or the movement of air through your larynx and vocal chords. Those vibrations carry across the air, forming waves (much like waves in the ocean), which are in turn picked up by the ear, which is shaped like a cupped radar dish in order to amplify the sound into your cochlea and eardrum, which is a tiny membrane responsible for turning those airborne vibrations into discernible audible information, which your brain processes and becomes familiarized with through pattern recognition. Your brain creates a 3D map of the sound by using the disparity of amplitude between the two sides of your body, which, in turn, is why if somebody tries to creep up on your left and you hear them, you will quickly turn to your left. Your brain interprets the sound as if it is coming from your left because it's able to process the amplitude and the subtle offsets of the sound as it comes in from both sides slightly differently. This is why stereo, and now surround sound, have been such a big part of improving the cinematic experience. The added ability to change the angles from which the sound occurs greatly enhances the dimensional experience of any audiovisual presentation by making it seem as if the viewer is actually there in the film. Your hearing is highly tuned in to the dimensionality of the sound, especially on a subtle evolutionary level. It alerts you of danger that you can't see with your eyes and keeps you aware of your surroundings at all times, no matter which way you are standing. Hearing is an incredibly important sense of ours as it pertains to multimedia development, because it's the only thing other than sight that we get to manipulate, and it's the one that is able to sense things not directly in your line of sight.

11.1 TO SOUND OR NOT TO SOUND

With the proliferation of mobile media, games, and mobile development, the use of audio has become much more optional for certain types of formatting. And in some cases, such as the podcast, it is often the *only* form of media. So it's very important to know where to put the sound and where not to put the sound. And even if you *do* use sound with your interactive media, it may never be heard because the user is playing the game in line at Starbucks. So the use of audible media has to be carefully considered when developing.

For passive, streaming content, you can be pretty much sure that audio will always be needed. Very few people, if any, watch streaming video content without wanting to *hear* it as well. It's possible to watch television using only the subtitles, but it's never the preferred state. Subtitles are often used in gyms where there are television monitors in front of the cardio equipment, but anyone wanting to stay on them for any extended period will almost always use headphones. So you can guarantee that audio is going to be an important part of any type of passive media content or one-way broadcast in the form of a television show, a radio broadcast, or now a podcast.

But for games and interactive entertainment elements, sound is often optional. Especially for people in public areas, who are receiving or interacting with your content in a crowded area where sound may not be appropriate.

On the subway or the airport or when walking down the street, people often interact visually with the screens on their devices but not with headphones or the audio on. In this case, the audio you are using absolutely can't be crucial to the intention of the game or the content. If it is, then you will actually need to inform the user or the player in some way beforehand that this is the case. This represents a shift from the former living room format of content access since the place and the time you are choosing to engage with content is now highly personal and subject to individual choice. So you might make a game with great audio, but few people would know about it if they only engage through a mobile device with the sound turned off.

11.2 PODCASTS

Audio podcasts represent the most interesting development in media distribution today. Although the podcast has been widely available since 2008, the format has until recently been relegated to a talk show style of format, mostly with geeky, tech-centric content, conspiracy theorists, Bigfoot hunters, and rambling political extremists. But the advent of the investigative journalistic episodic podcast *Serial*, coproduced by Sarah Koenig and Julie Snyder as a spinoff of Ira Glass's *This American Life* in 2014, quickly evolved the format into a serious storytelling venue, also winning a Peabody Award in 2015 for its innovative telling of a long-form nonfiction story. This represents a hallmark paradigm shift for the audio-based format, spinning off multiple fictionalized versions of the same format, with varying levels of success. *Limetown*, *The Black Tapes*, and *The Message* are all good examples of the format used in fictional, serialized creative storytelling.

The current demographics show a rapidly increasing listenership in story-based podcasts. According to an article by Maximize Social Business, 46 million American tuned in to podcasts in 2015, or roughly 17% of the population over 12, which is up from 12% in 2013 (Geil-Neufeld, 2015). It's a rapidly growing format.

The unique thing about podcasts is that they rely on only audio, which is in itself somewhat of a throwback to the old radio broadcast formatting from pre-television production. You *only* have audio to stream; thus, the content must be completely devoid of visual information. The story must be constructed around audible information, which is why the investigative journalism style (where the actors speak to the audience) is such an effective format for this audio-only form of entertainment. Not only do you have to remove the content from visual information, but you also have to be creative about constructing the formatting to make the audio information a much bigger player in the narrative and other storytelling elements. A good example of this is in *The Message*, a podcast that begins with the premise of an alien transmission discovered by the US government in the early 1950s. The unusual audio recording is given to a national security team in order to crack the code and figure out just what it means. The message is entirely fabricated from audio effects, from which the rest of the story is structured. This is a good way to involve your audience in the story, since your media palette is somewhat limited without video. Keep in mind that this is absolutely *not* a new phenomenon! Radio broadcasting for entertainment and storytelling has been going on since the 1930s and never really went away, although it did lose popularity to television as a living room entertainment center. Pre-television radio show broadcasts used audio to tell stories just as creatively as podcasts today. An hour-long variety show on Lake Wobegon has been continuously broadcast since 1974, with segments that have continuity of characters like Guy Noir, a fictional detective based comedically off the gruff gumshoe detective from films and book series in the late 1940s and 1950s.

Where do people listen to podcasts? Usually in their cars and other places where it would be visually distracting to watch video or film. The podcasts often follow a short time format (15–25 minutes) broken into multiple episodes. In this way, they are little different from a primetime television show, but often times slightly less lengthy. Once again, none of this is new, but more of a reemerging art form due to the shift in technology and the ease of access.

The interesting aspect of formatting in podcasting, and thus the design of a series, is how to address the audience. The relationship between the storyteller and the audience can be defined in many different ways. We are generally used to a third-person perspective in the form of television and film, as in our perspective seems to float around as a non-active person mostly present during all the action (from the film camera perspective), present but not directly involved. With the audio-only format, however, we lose that ability to participate as a silent third-party through optical camera placement, and something must be addressed to let the listener (audience) know exactly what their role is as a passive member of the story. How does this happen?

Most of the popular podcasts series, borrowing from *Serial*, have been using the format of investigative journalism, whether genuine or fictionalized. In this format, the storyteller, personified by the person recording and managing the podcast, is the vessel through which the audience experiences the story. The storyteller in this instance is aware of the audience, and hence, the audience understands that they are being addressed directly by the storyteller. The storyteller is telling the story *to* the audience and recognizing that there is an audience to tell the story to. This is often called *breaking the fourth wall* in filmmaking (which is a popularized technique for specific effect), but in podcasting, it's often used far more in lieu of a third-person perspective. Other techniques, such as hidden recordings and overheard conversations are just as effective with the audio-only format. The limitations of the format make it necessary for the audience to find some sort of root relationship with the storyteller in order to anchor the relationship between teller and listener.

11.3 TYPES OF AUDIO

When working with audio, there are multiple types and purposes that one can have. Audio has many different layers and levels of information encoded into it, and when working with or developing audio content, the media developer must be hyper-aware of how each of these falls into the specificity of purpose.

11.3.1 The Human Voice

Obviously, dialogue is vital to convey information between humans (but not absolutely necessary). Without words spoken by human beings, the palette of audible information would seem a little bland. We, as humans, communicate mainly by talking; therefore, we must have dialogue in our methods of storytelling! Even if the story is told primarily with words, as soon as we put quotes around a paragraph in a novel, "it feels like somebody is speaking." In fact, those quotes are there to spark the audio cortex of your brain to perk up, imagining the sound of a human voice speaking.

The human voice is an incredibly complex sound generator. If we look at the size and shape of the throat, vocal chord structure, and larynx, it doesn't look all that impressive compared to say, a grand piano. But a professional singer might have the capacity to sing every note perfectly on that piano and just as loud, if not louder. (Figure 11.1 shows the structure and anatomy of the human throat.) But it's not only the musical quality or the vocal range that defines the unique characteristics of the human voice. It's also the variety of sounds we can make combined with the ability to convey subtle emotional information through the nuance of tone. Forget the meme as an encoder of emotional information! The human voice is a marvel of subtlety. For instance, imagine I just spoke the following sentence out loud:

And how are we this morning?

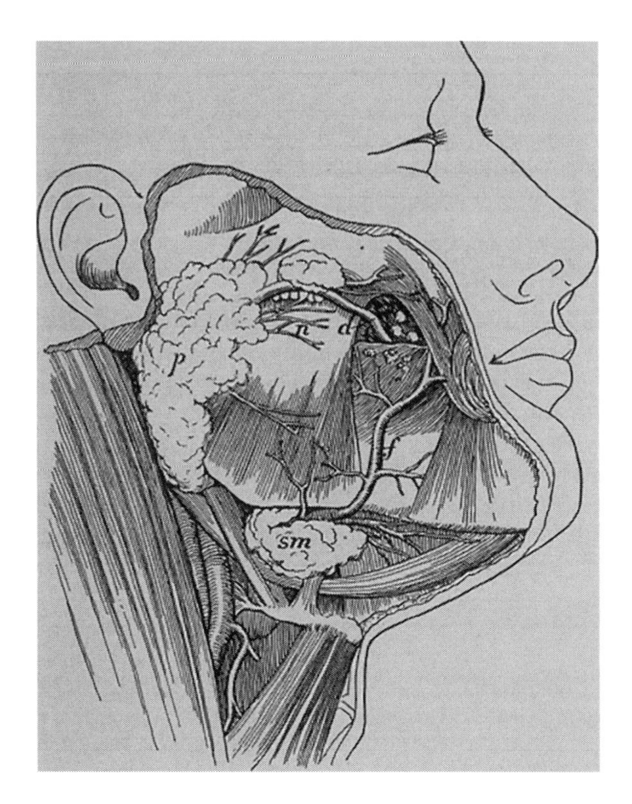

FIGURE 11.1 The anatomy of the sound-making mechanisms of our throat and mouth. For such a compact piece of anatomy it's a pretty phenomenal instrument!

You could probably guess if I were feeling sad, happy, frustrated, cheerful, or even feigning fatigue. Or perhaps I was being slightly sarcastic. If I change the emphasis of the word, it will completely change the meaning of the statement:

And *how* are we this morning?

When the emphasis is on the *how*, it infers that the *how* is the most important part of the question. As if your condition, or *how* you are, is the focus of my thought.

And how *are* we this morning?

Now I emphasize *are*, and it slightly changes the intention. In this instance, I am still interested more in the state, but the subtle shift has occurred because of the change in emphasis.

And how are *we* this morning?

The emphasis on *we* completely changes the question, focusing more on the person or persons, as if they are the main point of address and not their condition. Perhaps I am notifying you that I am shifting intent from one person to another or that I am focusing on one person after having focused on somebody else.

And how are we *this* morning?

Now the emphasis is on *this*, which notifies the intention and focus is on the *when* and not the *how* or *who*. As if perhaps I had asked you this very question a day ago. Or perhaps I ask it every day, and now the condition of time has changed and I expect a possible different answer.

And how are we this *morning*?

The emphasis here is still on the time, but instead of previously (which indicates that I asked you on a previous morning), now the emphasis on *morning* indicates that I might have asked you the question before, but not in the morning. Perhaps I asked you in the afternoon or evening.

As you can see, even without the tonal quality and pitch shift, I can ask you the exact same question with the exact same words and convey something different each time. Add on to it the ability to sound tired, whiny, annoyed, bitchy, irritable, loving, excited, or robotic using the exact combination of words with the exact emphasis, and you start to wonder how the same six words in the same sequence can have any real meaning at all! But remember, our brains recognize and repeat patterns very well. We are listening to the words formed, but once we are familiar enough with somebody's speech patterns, the rest of the information gets filled in such as the lines of a Matisse drawing, and we focus far more on our audible processing power for the purpose of the intonation and audible clues that will tell us about your emotional state. The factual information you are conveying to us is not nearly as important to us on a lower, evolutionary level as your emotional state in delivering the words to us is. Do you really care if I ask how you are feeling? Do *I* really care how you are this morning? I may or may not actually care, but the important thing to understand here is that the question is loaded with far more innuendo and verbal information than just the words alone. The tone of your voice and the *way* you answer this question, whatever the answer may be, is going to tell me a lot more than the words you speak. This is the reason for all of those polite forms of communication, such as "how are you?" or "good morning." We aren't really saying "have a nice day" or asking how you feel in order to get the verbal factual information. We want to impart emotional information and receive it from the tones and emphasis in your voice! This is also the reason emoticons and emojis, which of course are tiny little symbols of faces, are so necessary with text messaging and e-mail. They compensate for the inability to hear the tones and emphasis of the voice. It's also why we have grammar for writing, which encode these audible devices into text writing. Look at the following conversation:

> HELLO. MY NAME IS SAM.
> WHY ARE YOU SHOUTING?
> WHAT? HOW CAN I SHOUT? I'M NOT EVEN SPEAKING. I'M JUST WRITING WITH THE CAPS LOCK ON.
> What do you *mean*?
> What do *you* mean?
> I *mean*...that you were *shouting!*

The elements of grammar allow us to put verbal cues into text because we need to embellish and enhance simple text by creating visual shifts and symbols to text. For instance, the ellipsis "..." is a text grammar device to indicate a pause in speech, while using all capital letters indicates a person shouting, even though of course no speech is occurring.

We can convey these subtleties of emotion and meaning into words by using a shift in pitch, a change in emphasis, or even the rapidity with which we speak the words. Actors and actresses often get lessons in learning speech patterns by repeating phrases that are essentially the same in words, but exercising the ability to convey certain emotional states assigned to the phrases. The point of the exercises is to understand how rich with meaning human speech can be, even if the actual words are saying the same thing. My intonation and subtle shifts in pitch can completely change the meaning of a single sentence. When performing these exercises, we can rapidly understand that we communicate verbally with *much* more than just words. We communicate with a slew of audible cues encoded *into* our words. And we can do this without using the sense of sight at all. This is why dialogue is the first bastion of media that you will need in order to exercise dramatic license. You obviously need spoken words in order to create a dramatic element, but you also need to encode the emphasis, tone, and quality of those words properly.

As a multimedia storyteller, you will need to learn how to pick the right dialogue audio resources to tell your story! This means good voice acting, quality audio capture and equipment, and proper editing and output. Poor quality audio can absolutely sink any multimedia project. If you think you and your buddy can record the entire dialogue for your game with an iPhone and some funny voices, you are going to be extremely delusional. Pick quality voice actors, record them in a decent studio with solid audio equipment, and make sure to get a good editor to go over the material.

11.3.2 Sound Effects

What are sound effects? How do they differ from other types of audio? Sound effects are generally associated with action elements or main players in a scene. Sound effects are sounds that represent or re-create actual physical phenomena. Good examples are footsteps of a player in a game or the roar of a *T. rex* or a tiger from behind you. Gunshot sounds are effects. They represent a sound in the real world, in your immediate vicinity, posing some potential gain, loss, or threat, and they occur as specific indicators of events occurring in the scene or the narrative.

In the old serial radio shows, they used to devise unique sound effect devices to portray the sounds of things occurring in the physical world of the radio broadcast but must be heard instead of described. One such device was the slapping and punching effect from the hero of the show beating up the bad people. You can't just say, "pow, I hit you." You have to make it sound like somebody got the beejeezus beat out of them! Why is this the case? It's the core of the need for sound effects. Saying "now I will describe the beating Johnny Black got from the Lone Ranger" is not a visceral experience. When you have the use of audible information that you can create a knee-jerk reaction from in the audience, you must use it to its greatest advantage. Remember that being a good media storyteller is all about creating emotional reactions from the audience, often times in a way that works on their subconscious. So when the need to create a fight scene occurred in the original radio broadcast series, they would take several steaks and slap them together to re-create the sound of a human fist or foot connecting with a face, stomach, or ribcage. The sound of skin slapping skin is a very distinct one and one that generally indicates either sexual or violent contact between two human beings. This sound is ingrained into our minds and operates on us in an entirely subconscious manner, which is what the intention of the sound effect generally is. These are sounds that are associated with action in the real world, and our brain expects them to exist as action occurs in a visual experience (such as a game), or it enhances the method of storytelling when it occurs devoid of visual cues (and can sometimes substitute for them when necessary).

In a game, if you are firing a gun, it will sound like a real gun firing (albeit a lot less volume), and the realism of the game is drastically enhanced, the more the sound is realistic. In a podcast or radio show, however, there is no audible information that a gun has been fired or is firing until the sound is actually *heard.*

Sound effects can also provide clues to action in the local area of which the scene, gameplay, or action is occurring. Footsteps or rustling bushes are often audible indicators that something important is occurring near or around the center of action, which represents the perspective of the audience or player. The spatial representation of sound has been shown to be very important in judging distance, level of threat, and the size or scope of our surroundings. The human ear can differentiate from left/right ear sounds to produce a 3D acoustic representation of the surroundings, which allows us to judge spatial distance even without the use of sight. A study done by Parham Mokhtari, Hironori Takemoto, Ryouichi Nishimura, and Hiroaki Kato revealed that the human ear and inner ear structure is an incredibly sophisticated acoustic machine, able to convert audible information into these 3D acoustic representation models almost akin to sonar in marine creatures. Why is this important? Because the more sophisticated you make your acoustic delivery of media in a game, film, podcast, or otherwise, the more immersive and lifelike you can make your experience. This is why surround-sound theaters really do make a difference in the nature of the experience and why sophisticated and well-produced audio can make or break a production.

11.3.2.1 Ambient Sound

If you walk outside and shut your eyes, chances are that you won't hear silence. No matter where you are in the world, you're going to hear a multi-dimensional cacophony of action, movement, and sound. If you're in a city, you'll hear people and vehicles, the chatter of individuals on their cell phones, the squeal of a bus brake, the shuffle of feet on pavement, and perhaps even the rumble of a subway beneath your feet. If you're in the country, you might hear birds chirping, squirrels rustling the leaves of trees, and even the wind blowing around rocks, hills, and plants. In the jungle, you'd hear all kinds of wildlife, even maybe insects crawling through the brush. On the coast, you'll definitely hear the waves crashing against the sand or rocks and the gulls or other aviary life. The interesting thing is that you'll barely notice these things until you focus on them. I can definitely bet that as you sit there right now, the only thing you'd make particular notice of is if it all suddenly *stopped* and you were surrounded by utter silence! That's because you are so used to hearing ambient sound that you definitely have a filter in your brain, combing it out while you concentrate on the prominent sounds that you're interested in, such as the television, your stereo speakers, or that podcast you're listening to.

Ambient sound often clues us into what kind of environment we are *in* and, even more so, offers us clues to subtle shifts in that environment. Frantic scurrying of wildlife suddenly clues you in to a potential predator. A crack of thunder or sudden dripping sounds means rain or a nearby storm. The ambient sound that we normally process *out* of our conscious mind is always being sifted, like plankton by a whale, by our subconscious mind to warn us of sudden changes in our surroundings.

So why do we need ambient sound in a film, television show, podcast, or game? As I stated previously, the *lack* of sound is a presence unto itself. Complete silence as an immersive interactive experience might seem odd, out of place, or even in some cases spooky. And eerie silence is often used in fear-based media genres such as horror or suspense in order to ramp up tension. Why would silence make you tense? It would seem to be counterintuitive, but in reality, ceasing all ambient noise for a brief period will actually ramp up tension because that part of your brain that is so used to filtering out all the random ambient noise will suddenly become aware of the lack of things to do and notify the fear triggers in your brain that something might be amiss. When this happens, a natural ready state for fight or flight begins to engage and the suspense begins. If you can wallop the listener with a sudden, startling sound or sight (or, ideally, a combination of both) after the tension has built, it will hit them like a hammer. It's pretty much the old tried-and-true scare tactic of jumping out from behind a corner and yelling "boo" but just a little more sophisticated. The ambient sound, or manipulation of that sound, will clue the listeners in to when to begin feeling tension or when to be relaxed.

11.3.3 Music

Music is such a broad category that it deserves its own book. Unfortunately, there's not nearly enough space in this book to go over the intricacies and full breadth of musical theory and the history of music. What we want to focus on, however, is the *use* of music and the development of music for interactive entertainment and storytelling. Music is such a pervasive part of the human experience that it would be almost impossible to find a time before we, as a species, were using instruments to make sounds in patterns for rituals or merely cathartic release. Music is as old as we are, and the beginnings of it are so far back in time that there is no definitive origin we can point to.

Music, as a vessel of communication, is incredibly complex. I would challenge you to find a television show, film, podcast, or game in existence today (or ever for that matter) that doesn't use music in some capacity. It is often overlooked when planning a game or a multimedia project, but much to the detriment of the finished result. Almost every project intended as audiovisual at some point starts to require a form of music, either in the interlude, beginning, ending or otherwise. Music is the backdrop of emotional content in our stories, providing a sense of movement, flow, passion, triumph, tragedy, and energy.

But what, exactly constitutes as *music*? What defines it? It is certainly sound or audible information, but it requires certain components or attributes that we must understand in order to choose, create, or edit for our purposes in storytelling. Music is incredibly hard to define in a global or cultural sense. For instance, what is the difference between *noise* and *music*? Musicologist Jean-Jacques Nattiez (1990, 48, 55) stated that the difference between noise and music is nebulous, explaining that "the border between music and noise is always culturally defined—which implies that, even within a single society, this border does not always pass through the same place; in short, there is rarely a consensus ... By all accounts there is no single and intercultural universal concept defining what music might be."

But if we want to characterize music and separate it from things such as a sound effect and background noise, we have to give it certain attributes that we can use, choose, and manipulate in order to enhance and supplement our storytelling toolset. So we must define that which is indefinable by choosing to do so in the context of usage. So asking the question "what constitutes as music?" is a lot like the question "is *that* art?" There's no real true answer, *but* we can ask "what characteristics does most art/music consist of?"

The concept of music as organized sound is a good way to see this. Take the sound of a guitar string plucked in the note of G. That single note, in and of itself, does not constitute music as such, but several of those notes plucked in succession with a measured (or structured) temporal period interlude between the plucking of those notes could be considered music. And if I pluck those G notes in a relational tempo, and then combine other notes in a sequence, I am suddenly playing music, and not just random notes. The inference that something is music means that there is a structured pattern to the notes in the sense of time, frequency, and pitch (which is what a note consists of). Now there are all sorts of mathematical music rules and harmonies and such, but the fundamentals of music are sound and time. It kind of sounds like animation, right? And that's exactly the idea. Sound, structured over time, is equal to music.

11.3.3.1 Rhythm/Tempo

Rhythm is the time periods and frequency over which the sound is played. Rhythm really consists of the interval between the sounds. If we want a pattern to occur, then we must have a commonality of frequency or a specific interlude between the sounds. The pattern of intervals between sounds is known as the rhythm. Tempo is the speed at which the rhythm occurs.

Tempo can provide emotional information in and of itself. A fast tempo can infer feelings of tension and energy, while a very slow tempo can drag out the movement of the music, which tends to be more prevalent in sad or maudlin feelings. The movement and speed of movement of the notes is what changes with the tempo, and of course, the tempo absolutely does not have to be uniform. Just as with animation, the ramping up of tempo over time can generate feelings of tension, and the release of the tempo at particular moments in the musical piece can cause emotional cathartic release just as the snapping of the action in an animation. The manipulation of the tempo is a particular device of many musical styles, from classic rock to Wagner's operatic scores. Rhythm and tempo are ways to manipulate the movement of the notes through time, which can encode feelings into it. If you are playing a fast-tempo game with violent actions (such as a war game or action combat), you're definitely not going to want to play slow music! Your intent is to encode feelings of tension, anger, and energetic action into the gameplay. A faster tempo, or an increasing tempo, can effectively convey that sensation much better than a slow or tepid one. This would seem to be intuitive, and of course, it *is*; however, audio, music, tempo and rhythm are things you should really pay attention to when developing an immersive experience.

11.3.3.2 Melody

A melody is the placement of notes in a sequential order (usually to a tempo) or the equivalent of sequence in storytelling fundamentals. The sequence of the notes, as they relate to one another, will create a pattern that is defined as melody. The melody can convey information about movement and a feeling of spiraling up or down, with an equivalent mood (or tone) associated. Because there are 12 notes on the Western musical scale, and those notes can exist on multiple octaves (each ascending octave being higher pitched than the other), there are nearly infinite combinations of notes to put inside a melody. But the sound, in an emotional sense, can be much like color from a palette—certain combinations can produce feelings in people. These combinations and feelings are semi-subjective. There appears to be a universal element, which can be interpreted liberally in one direction or another, but still holds to a core sensation. The ability to put these notes in the right order to the right tempo is the job of the composer—they're responsible for the conveyance of emotion through music alone. Melody is one of the tools at the musician's disposal.

If somebody notices a song or finds himself or herself singing along to it somewhere, it's often described as having a good melody. This catchy phenomenon is an artifact of our pattern-loving brain. The pattern, produced in short pieces, is remembered and repeated by your mind as you find yourself singing along to it in the car on your way to work, even if you're actually listening to the news and not music at all. One of the most important parts of television and radio advertising is the jingle or a simple melody featuring the product that will stick in your mind at a later date. The melody, combined with the simplified note structure, will often linger in your mind literally forever, like a phone number memorized in childhood. If anyone remembers the "Hot Pockets" jingle or "By Mennen" from the television advertisements, you will know exactly what I'm referring to. In fact, the chance that upon remembering the jingle you're singing it in your head right now (and probably cursing me for triggering the memory) is extremely high. What's the cause of this melodic permanence? It's simply a function of your brain's high capacity and love of associated patterns. The shorter the jingle melody, the more likely you are to remember it. This is extremely important in creating interactive entertainment, or simply just in branding a product. If you can create a life-long memory in association with a single product, it's an incredibly powerful marketing tool.

11.3.3.3 Voicing

Voicing is a lot harder to pin down than rhythm and tempo. It's not so much about the note itself as it is about the noise surrounding the audio tone that goes *with* the note. Since every sound coming from an organic source (and not a digitally generated signal) will have some sort of irregularity, those irregularities in frequency and amplitude will produce a very unique sound that your ears and brain can easily distinguish once it has heard it enough times. This is actually due to the fact that different surfaces, instruments, and sound-generating devices will produce those irregularities in a patterned manner that we can recognize. This is *exactly* the reason you can distinguish the individual voice of your friend, child, lover, or parent in a crowd fairly easily.

The unique patterned irregularities even occur in the playing of instruments, which we usually want to associate with some level of regularity in frequency in order to play musical notes tuned to a particular scale. But every instrument has its own set of deviations from the frequency as well as fluctuations in the amplitude and change in amplitude, which, we say, give it a particular *voicing*. And it's no accident that we use the term *voicing*; since we are so tuned into the sound of the human voice and can easily distinguish one from another, it's very easy to associate the idea of *voice* with a particular instrument.

What does voicing impart to the quality of a piece of music? It's hard to pin this down specifically, because it is always subject to interpretation, but certain instruments, like certain people's voices, can have a dramatically different effect on a person. For instance, a note played on a violin can have a calming effect while the same note blasted on a tuba will be anything but! A trombone, like most brass instruments, has a metallic and harsh sound that is very distinctive. A flute, oboe, or other woodwind, on the other hand, is often considered to have a softer voicing. So voicing is a lot like tone in terms of storytelling—it allows you to set a general emotional reaction to a note or series of notes. Just like ramping up or down the tempo of a song, changing or composing the voicing (using various instruments) can have a radical effect on how a song is perceived or how it feels to the listener. For instance, taking a Megadeth song and having a folk singer perform it with an acoustic guitar is going to drastically change how the song feels, even if it's the same notes played in the same progression. So voicing can affect the general emotional response of the audience just as much as the tempo and rhythm.

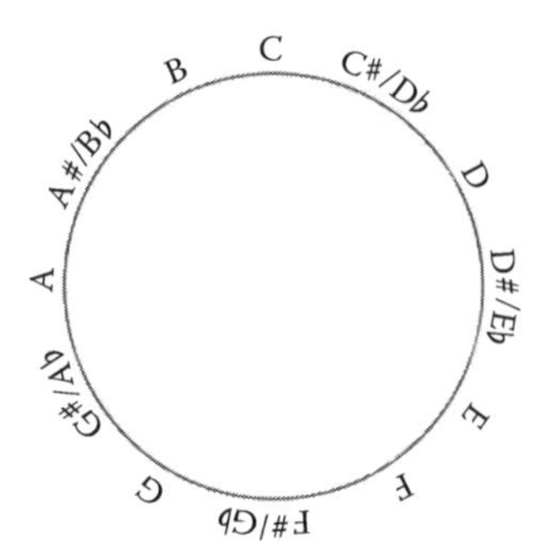

FIGURE 11.2 The Western musical scale with all notes.

11.3.3.4 Key

The key of a song and its effect on the listener is often just as mysterious as the use of color in imagery. A key is essentially a musical structure that says certain notes mathematically go together or form harmonious sounds when we hear them played together. The combinations of the notes in a certain order are called *scales*, which are sets of harmonious notes. There are major and minor scales, which have certain root notes associated (see Figure 11.2).

Certain scales or keys can be said to have certain properties as they pertain to emotional responses. Minor keys are often seen as sad keys or more melancholy than other keys. But honestly, there's no real rhyme or reason. Certain keys among musicians can be thought of as possessing certain characteristics that emote in certain ways, but once again, it's also the voicing and rhythm structure that change how you feel about a particular piece of music.

REFERENCES

Geil-Neufeld, J. (2015). Who's listening to your podcast. Maximize Social Business. Available at http://maximizesocialbusiness.com/whos-listening-podcasts-2015-18213/.

Nattiez, J.-J. (1990). *Music and Discourse: Toward a Semiology of Music*. Princeton, NJ: Prince University Press.

CHAPTER 12

Exercises

THESE EXERCISES ARE CREATIVITY-STIMULATING items designed to begin to comprehend and develop skills in using images, video, animation, sound effects, and music to tell effective stories. One of the greatest skills of the digital storyteller is understanding what media to use in what place to get the most out of the format. One of the great strengths of a good multimedia storyteller is understanding what elements will complement and enhance the basic content of the story.

12.1 EXERCISE 1: TELLING STORIES THROUGH DRAWINGS

As we have seen, symbols and drawings can be used to substitute for complex ideas and thoughts without ever using words. If you've ever read the funny pages or owned a Calvin and Hobbes book, you've seen entire concepts, ideas, and narrative elements of a story be told through simplistic drawings. In this exercise, you will use a series of drawings to tell a story *without* the use of words. Figure 12.1 shows a simple cartoon which tells a miniature story without use of words.

Create your own comic, with stick figures (if you can't draw at all, you can at least manage a few sticks and circles). The important elements of your story, especially the narrative action, should be easily understood. In this exercise, the intent is to show you how well you can tell a story, even without the use of human speech, word-based narration, or preconceived context. This is actually a vital skill for storyboard artists in films and games, in which the artist is called upon to create sequences of action for laying out camera shots. These storyboards are used to give people working on the film a visual reference model when setting up the action.

FIGURE 12.1 A cartoon telling a story through simple action.

12.2 EXERCISE 2: TELLING STORIES WITH AUDIO

Your second exercise in media storytelling is to tell a story *without* the use of words! In the 1981 animated short film *Crac!*, by Frederick Back, an entire story with a fairly complex cast of characters and concepts was told entirely without the use of spoken words. Back created a painterly look with his stylized hand-drawn animation and used folk music and background noises to create a story about the modernization of society, as told through the perspective of a rocking chair. This short film was unique in its ability to convey complexity through art and sound alone. Your task in this exercise is to similarly perform the same task, on a slightly different level.

1. Choose a specific theme for your project. Some themes in the following have been successfully used in some of my college classes by students:
   - World War II
   - Vietnam
   - The Civil War
   - The Great Depression
   - The Chinese Communist Revolution
   - Dogs/cats/pets
   - Ancient civilizations
   - Medieval Europe
   - Sports/football/basketball
   - Searching for a job
   - Marriage
   - Parenthood/babies
   - Nostalgia (1950s, 1980s, etc.)
2. Using simple video-editing software, put together a three-part video series that tells a story about the theme you chose, but uses these specific tones or predetermined emotional states to impart on your audience. You can use any audio, animation, music, still images, or video that you like, but you absolutely must not directly use dialogue or words (signs and background words are OK, but no subtitles or text directly on the screen).
   - Funny
   - Exciting
   - Sad
   - Triumphant

3. Publish the video and see if your audience gets the feeling of the intended emotional state.

When working on this exercise, it's important to try and manipulate the audience as best you can with creative use of audio, video, and sound. The principle of *imprinting* will become very important here as a thing to both make use of and avoid overuse. Imprinting is the process by which we assess similar patterns of storytelling and repeat them in our own creative work. It's not necessarily a bad thing, but over-imprinting can often lead to viewer fatigue and a regurgitated or simply ripped-off feel. It's up to you to create a great presentation without making things look too derived from every commercial or advertisement that everyone has already seen, but yet make it effective.

CHAPTER 13

Conclusion

CONCLUDING THIS SECTION, WE have to understand that *multimedia* is simply the term used for transmitting information through multiple forms of recorded sights and sound. These recorded elements of visual and auditory information are supplements to our word-based verbal communication. As you have seen, the use of recorded images is almost as old as the human species itself, as is the desire to communicate information through them. Technology has rapidly increased over the past century, enabling us in a relatively short period to have instant, ubiquitous access to images, films, animation, and audio-based entertainment.

Digital storytelling has the advantage of being able to benefit from these multiple forms of media to supplement and integrate into the storytelling process. As these things have become instantly available and more easily manipulated, the need and desire for multiple forms of content is continually growing. Streaming video, real-time 3D graphics, and integrated surround-sound are now far beyond novelty items in the toolkit of a storyteller but rapidly becoming standardized tools. Storytelling is an expansive art that seeks to develop quality content from wherever it can, whether it's banging two sticks together in front of a campfire to simulate the sound of a horse's hooves to creating stereoscopic renderings to make a film 3D, the function of this media is to enhance the impact of the story by connecting to the audience in a fundamental emotional manner. Media not only supplements the emotional content of the words used to construct a story, but it can also often encode information and subtleties that the dialogue and narration alone cannot.

And what's on the horizon? As of the writing of this book, serious efforts are being made to retool the paradigm of entertainment through the use of virtual reality kits like Oculus Rift and Google Cardboard. Augmented reality devices and methodologies are rapidly reaching the point of viability with the first Google Glass and now Microsoft's Hololens set. On the horizon and in the very near future, we may just find ourselves as extras or even primary actors in a universe of our own or at home watching films in a virtual theater. We could be participating in a fully spatially realistic film as the main character, seeing the world from their eyes, or possibly controlling worlds constructed of our own imagination as we act like individual deities. The shifts in technology are once again opening doors to expanding our ability to manipulate perspective and enhance the story through innovative use of media.

III

Interactivity

CHAPTER 14

Interaction Basics

14.1 INTRODUCTION

What is *interactivity*? *Inter*, the root of the word, means "between two things," and, of course, *activity* means "to *do* something or make an action of some kind." So by our very definition of the term, we must be *doing* something in order for it to be interactive. We must find ourselves making conscious decisions that control some aspect of our immediate surroundings. "Wait though," one might ask, "Isn't *life* always interactive? Aren't we *always* choosing or affecting some aspect of our environment just to even be alive? Isn't 'interactive' just 'not being in a coma?'"

Of course, it is correct to say that we are always interactive to some degree or another. Even sitting on your couch watching Netflix mandates that you made some choices that affected an outcome. You chose to sit on the couch instead of going to a Yoga class. You chose Netflix over Hulu or regular cable television. You chose the program you're watching. You may even have chosen to half-watch the show while you fiddle around on your phone or check Facebook on your iPad or browse the Internet on your laptop at the same time. Chances are that you're in the middle of some interactive choice right now, no matter *what* you happen to be doing unless it's sleeping or in a drug-induced stupor. But the level of interactivity and synchronicity of that interactivity varies vastly from one thing to another, especially when it concerns the delivery of story or news-based content to your laptop, phone, television, or radio. How *much* control you have over the content and how *soon* after a choice is made do you get the results are vastly different from medium to medium.

In this section, we will explore these elements and different levels therein, trying to understand how we can better comprehend, explore, designate, develop, and design for the concept of interactive media. Not only will we learn how the design and development of interactive media developed in the past, but we will also see where it is going in the future and learn how to better prepare for newer, faster, and completely different methods of interaction. Interactivity and media technology are intimately intertwined, as are forms and distribution of media, and we will see that we are living in a truly transformative time when the paradigm of how we relate to content, stories, and all other forms of interactive entertainment is rapidly going through a massive shift.

14.2 ATTRIBUTES OF INTERACTIVITY

Let's first look at the fundamental attributes of interactivity and how we can further characterize the differences between types of interactions. Interaction, as stated earlier, is not a one-size-fits-all category. When someone uses the word *interactive media* or *interactive entertainment*, they can mean one of a dozen different models that fit that description. Interactivity must be further defined if we are going to develop a common set of models that people can relate to. Interactivity is about making choices, which are then imposed as deliberate actions of some kind, which, in turn, affect the world around you or the media you are currently engaged in. By definition, you are no longer a passive entity in the form of media entertainment or storytelling you are the recipient of—you become both *actor* and *audience* simultaneously.

14.2.1 Level of Control

The level of control is how much your choice actually affects the media. This is a sliding scale from 0 to 10. Certainly, we can say that choosing to play a game or watch a movie is an active choice unto itself, and it's the *lowest* level of interactivity that can be assigned to any form of media entertainment or presentation. This is because the only level of control you have is *on* or *off*. So any television show, radio broadcast, theater play, or podcast is going to score a 0 on the level of interactive, provided that that's the only level of control you have. Most of our entertainment and story-based content in the twentieth century was based on this type of model, which is why, in previous chapters, I have rated them as extremely *passive* forms of entertainment and stories. There's nothing wrong with that, of course; it has maintained a high level of popularity and proliferation in our society even now, in the context of our monumental paradigm shift toward more interactive types of entertainment.

The next level of control that an audience, or participant, can possess is in the types of entertainment previously labeled *contest television*. Contest television takes your usual form of television shows, generally in some kind of talent show setting, and allows the audience to vote. *American Idol* is the longest-running and most successful model of contest television, and indeed the popularity of the program was no doubt in part due to the insertion of that minute but vital element of control. How much control do you, as an individual, have? Not much, it seems. One vote out of millions doesn't count *much*, but it still creates that bidirectional level of interaction between you and the material you are watching. Even if you only have a tiny, tiny, voice in the final decision, you still got to execute that voice. That level of control, even at its most minute, gives the viewer a small sense of empowerment. When you watch the show and vote for your favorite, you have suddenly entered into the realm of *interactive* entertainment. Technology has made it possible for millions of people to vote for their favorite easily and from anywhere in the world, as long as they have a phone that can text a number.

What's the highest level of control? What would score a 10 on the sliding scale? You will note here that I'm skipping the middle, and that's for the specific reason that so many different types of interactive media exist in between the lowest rung and the highest rung that it would be almost impossible to list them all, especially before we defined what the highest level might be! *That* role belongs to immersive, real-time interactive 3D/2D video entertainment. Now we have to define the concept of a *game* later, and many real-time applications aren't really games by the classic definition, which is why I am using this somewhat long-winded description. The important aspect of the game-like application is that the user has a very high level of control over the action. There is an input device of some sort, usually what we call a *controller*, or if you're old (like the author), you might call is a *joystick*. But all age-related humor aside, a game or application has the feature of constant input controlling the action. Whether it's a sports game, a racing game, a first-person shooter, or an interactive world like *Second Life* (in which you don't play a game so much as create a secondary life for yourself), the principal aspect of control is that the user or player has a tremendous amount of it. Indeed, in games or game-like simulations, the user must often exercise constant control in what we think of as *real time*, which just means the *action* time in which we currently exist.

We will explore time as a concept in interactivity in the next segment; however, the aspect of control is what we want to explore here.

What control *do* you have in a typical *Halo*-like first-person shooter game? Well, the perspective is set from that of a character as if that character is *you*. And the control over that character's actions and intent is almost completely autonomous. You can move, fire, jump, attack, defend, and explore anywhere you want, given the limitations of the environment and other entities in the game world. You have an incredibly high level of control over the physical movement, navigation, and combat or interaction with the environment. What don't you have control over? Usually, there's a global aspect to the game, in which you don't have any control over whatsoever. This is the domain of the game developer, and they have chosen what you can and can't interact with. You also only have limited control over other players and nonhuman entities (such as enemies or sidekicks). Those characters are also controlled by the game and the game logic. So you *do* have a lot of control, but you don't have *total* control over the game or application you are engaged in. Mostly, you have control over a single entity, and that control is almost always complete or nearly so. Figure 14.1 shows a basic schematic of our conceptual slider and level of control.

What are some of the levels in between total control (a value of 10) and almost no control (a level of 1)? Well, now that we can see how total control is defined, we can say that somewhere between 1 and 10, there are multiple layers of ability to control the environment, circumstances, and players in the game. Some interactive entertainment formats, such as graphic novels or branching fiction, allow the audience some level of control over what narrative they will receive, dependent on various choices and movements. If I can control the things the main character says or does, but among only a few predefined choices, then we can say that the level of control might be a 3 or a 4, some control over what happens next, but not total control over the story or physical movement of the characters.

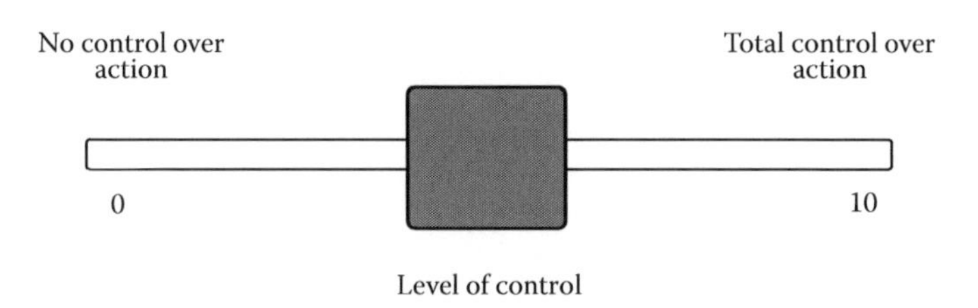

FIGURE 14.1 Levels of control diagram.

A game that lets you move your characters only in certain ways, or limits when you can move them, can be said to be an entity with a level of control somewhere around the middle, with a value of 5, 6, or 7. Think of this like chess. You can move your pieces certain ways, and in that way, you can move each piece determined by predefined rules. Also, you can only move when it's your *turn*, and any effort otherwise would be considered unfair or simply not be possible if playing on a computer. This limitation of your control over the game and the times that you can control the character are what determine the value of the slider. Many real-time strategy games are like this, and, of course, they all derive in some form or fashion from the concept of games such as chess, backgammon, go, or even good, old-fashioned checkers. Turn-based combat games such as *Final Fantasy* are also games that limit the times and the commands you can give a character or characters. In these types of games, you have limited control in a limited time window.

14.2.2 Synchronicity

Synchronicity, when speaking in terms of interactivity, is a measure of the amount of time which elapses between the user input and the game reaction. It can also be seen as a sliding scale between 0 and 10. Figure 14.2 shows the diagram of synchronicity.

In a first-person shooter game, the time between hitting the trigger button and the firing of your weapon is so fast it might as well be instantaneous—unless the weapon is a "charging weapon" which requires some amount of time to charge before firing. So this is considered fully synchronous or reaching a level of 10 on the synchronicity slider. This is important because the more synchronous the interactivity, the more engaged the player will become when playing the game. If it took 2 s to fire a gun after hitting the trigger button, you would quickly throw your controller across the room and give up. This kind of game requires real-world instant or near instant time intervals between input and action.

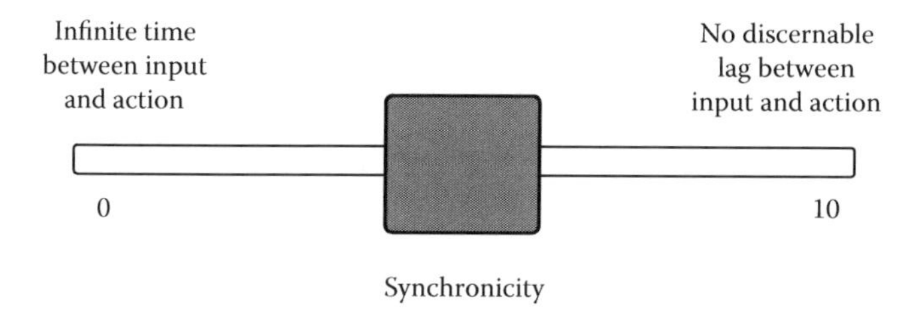

FIGURE 14.2 The synchronicity diagram.

Other games, however, do not require this level of synchronicity. Consider the aforementioned *Final Fantasy*, one of the most successful and popular role-playing games of all time. You don't click a bunch of buttons to attack an enemy in real time. Turn-based combat is about setting up a series of attacks and defenses from multiple party members, which are selected and delegated *before* the attack occurs. The players then watch the action as it unfolds, and the monster, or enemy, responds. Games such as *Pokemon* also use this tactical methodology of turn-based combat. This is a level of ~5 or 6 on the synchronicity scale. You make decisions, tell those decisions to execute, and they play out the scenario as you watch. This is a much different experience than a first-person shooter or a fighting game! Your decisions can be thought out at a slower pace, and strategy becomes as important as reflexes in this case.

In any case, a high level of synchronicity is not necessarily better than a low level. It's simply a manifestation of a much different methodology. If you are working with low levels of synchronicity, you will tailor the rules, timeframes, and resulting action to match the necessary delay.

Contest television, in the form of *American Idol*, is a great example of tailoring synchronicity to your format. It exhibits the lowest level of synchronicity in terms of interaction. If you are voting for your favorite *American Idol* candidate to win, that vote takes several hours to determine the results. In this case, synchronicity is something that the developers of the contest rules took into consideration! You can only vote for your candidate inside of a certain window, after the show is over. This means that watching the show on reruns, or skimming highlights on YouTube or your cable box digital recorder would severely diminish the experience (since you wouldn't get to vote). This is most likely a prominent reason why the Nielsen ratings were consistently so high with these programs. People had to watch in order to participate interactively. Now, the results of those votes didn't get returned to you for some time, but when they *did*, the anticipation of finding out if *your* person won would make the engagement in the activity all the more exciting, despite the fact that you were only one vote in a giant sea of viewers. But the designers of the show experience took all this into consideration before putting it on the air. They wanted the show to be watched while being aired, and they wanted you to get excited about the result! This is a great example of tailoring the synchronicity to fit your design or situation. If you need to implement a delay between audience input and resulting action, you should make it work for you.

14.2.3 Collectivity

Collectivity is an interesting feature to interactivity, and although it currently only really exists in a few models, it has a powerful effect on the human psyche. Collectivity is the concept of *crowdsourcing* some aspect of an interactive entertainment model (Figure 14.3). Crowdsourcing can be as simple as the voting process, as we see in contest television, or as complex as the volume of certain words on Twitter being plugged into random data represented as game-based events or circumstances (imagine the weather conditions in a racing game changing depending on how many people said "rain" or "snow" on Twitter). Collectivity has a powerful influence on humans because of our profound enjoyment of all things social and connective of other human beings.

Social media–based stories often have an element of collectivism, especially in the feedback, sharing, and response elements of the format. Despite the low level of control an individual may have over any social media story or entertainment, the fact that hundreds or thousands of people can up/down vote, like, or share any element from any post can add a tremendous element of social connectivity to what would otherwise just be a top–down method of entertainment and storytelling. People can make requests, have conversations, and even at times communicate with the story designer and creator themselves through the advent of social

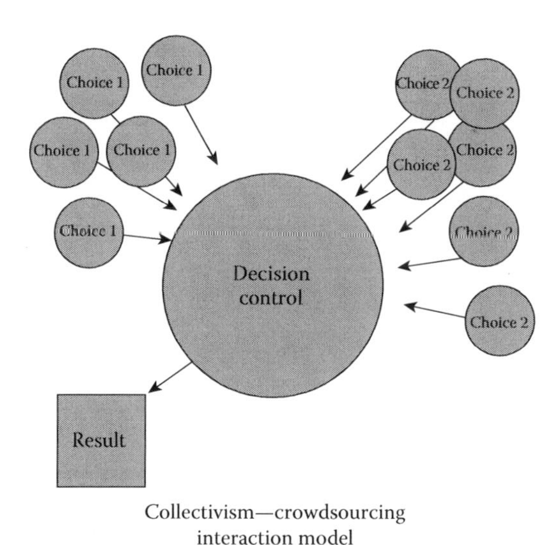

FIGURE 14.3 Social media and contests use the collective, crowdsourced interaction model.

media. Although storytelling and entertainment through social media is still in its infancy as an interactive format and tool, it contains some very powerful elements that are only now being understood as they are being developed and studied. This kind of collective social input to the development of stories and interactive entertainment will only grow as we learn how best to produce success from it. Models of social input to the development of a story are currently in the works as we speak.

CHAPTER 15

Interactive Media Types

WHAT CONSTITUTES A VENUE of interactive media? How does it differ from non-interactive media? This is an important question to explore because it's hard to pin down exactly what a thing is without a specific and publicly accepted definition.

As we learned earlier, interactive media can be considered anything that not only follows the format of media presentation (words, video, animation, or audio) but also allows you to alter the action in some way or sense (other than turning it off). But *how* that media reaches you is an experience entirely dependent on some combination of physical hardware device and software engineering. There are multiple aspects of these different venues of distribution, and their characteristics and capabilities in some way influence the time and place you interact with them. They all have some specified purpose as it pertains to storytelling, information sharing, and data gathering.

15.1 KIOSKS

A kiosk, by its formal and traditional definition, is a stationary element that contains information intended to present information or interactive experiences for specific purposes, often in an informative manner or to tell a story about a particular person or piece of information. Museums often use these kiosks to tell stories about nearby art or historical objects. The physical location of a kiosk is set to a particular place, so that it can be associated with an object nearby. Although the traditional kiosk object is usually a physical booth-like device with some type of input element, such as a touch screen or controller, newer mobile-friendly kiosks are starting to be developed for places such as zoos and museums in which your specific location can trigger information and added content to enhance the experience without having to maintain and set up multiple booths for the same purpose. This mobile kiosk is still physically present, however, and tied to a certain location, which is imperative to the nature of the tool. Kiosks can be of great use in offering a myriad of information about a place, company, or historical story. Often, companies will use these kiosks to provide interactive information about their history, products, or future plans for development. Interactive kiosks are often used to showcase or promote upcoming developments and future plans for expansion of a company, product, or public work to inspire interest.

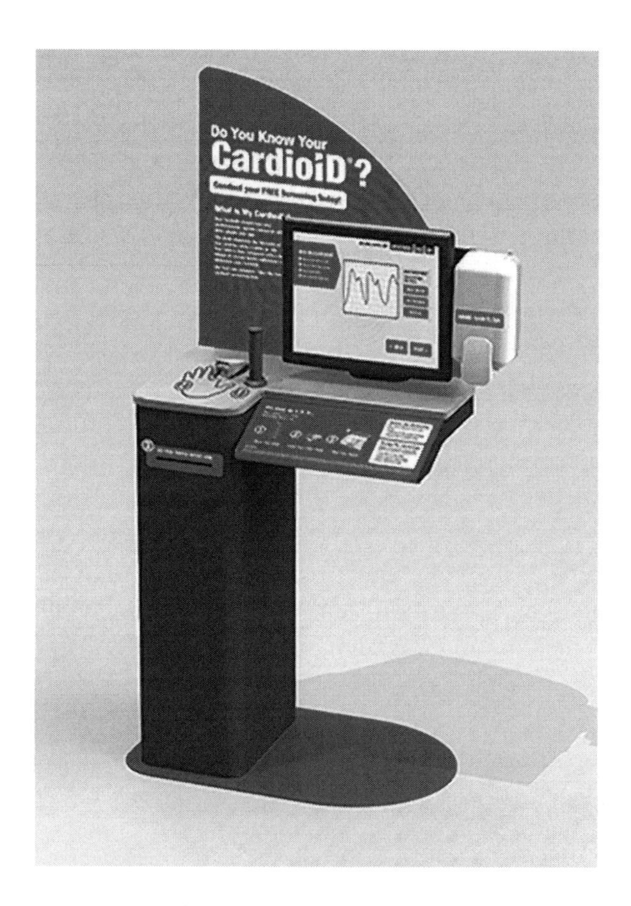

FIGURE 15.1 A traditional kiosk, which is there to create an interactive experience of some kind for the user. In this case it is a hear-rate monitoring app, which has been replaced by devices like the Fitbit and the Apple Watch.

The possibility of interaction with a kiosk is fairly open. The use of multiple input devices is frequently seen, including physical motion detectors and touch screens. Most of the time, the point of the kiosk is to present information in some novel or interactive manner, so the touch screen and menus will be the most prominent tool for providing input (Figure 15.1).

15.2 WEB

Possibly the most prevalent and prolific venue for interactive development and entertainment is the World Wide Web. The web uses several technologies for providing a processing interactive entertainment, all of which ride on top of the browser/hypertext markup language (HTML) model. This is an incredibly flexible model that allows a tremendous amount of interactive media to be developed and distributed worldwide with some level of universality in terms of distribution. This means that content developed in one place will look and act the same across multiple operating systems, computer monitors, mobile screens, and otherwise.

Web-based media is a great venue for interactive entertainment because it is able to manipulate and interact with literally every type of digital media. Audio, video, still images, motion graphics, and even real-time 3D graphics can be generated, streamed, and interacted with almost instantly across the world. In order to do this any other way would require identical dedicated hardware (like an Xbox console) on both ends.

But aside from e-commerce and Wikipedia, how exactly are we using the World Wide Web as an effective entertainment and storytelling device? Outside of games (which will be covered later on), what other story-based content is being developed for delivery through the web?

Most of the content now being created and distributed through the web can be seen as belonging to certain subcategories: supplemental content, web-based comics, episodic tube shows, adver-content, podcasts, and the emerging form of storytelling known as *social fiction*. The method of delivery and distribution is always through the web, or in conjunction with the web-browsing experience, but these methods of web delivery are always *using* the web as a delivery service, with HTML, cascading style sheets, and related technologies as the shell platform. This provides a universal delivery method for vastly different contents, which is why the Internet and web technologies are an extremely important facet of our modern ability to create and distribute story-based content to anyone, anywhere, in a format that is universal. Like the printing press in the nineteenth century, the web and web-based technologies have dramatically shifted the paradigm and allowed us to stream multimedia story-based content across the world simultaneously and instantaneously. This means that the same story, with the same images and sounds, can be instantly downloaded and viewed by anyone, anywhere. The real question to ask is how this new technology is changing our storytelling skills, options, and abilities through this new interactive and near ubiquitous venue.

15.2.1 Second-Screen Content

The phenomenon of *second-screen* content or supplemental content for what is otherwise a standard unidirectional passive form of entertainment (such as a streaming series or television show) is now becoming not just a novelty but also a serious necessity for any high-quality level of programming. The ability and need to process multiple streams of data simultaneously has made second-screen content a must-have for any series online or otherwise. The second-screen is generally a mobile device or tablet in which the viewer looks up information and background stories from the characters, plots, and subplots in the show. Thus, while they are watching the action of the narrative content, they can access supplemental information, catch up on previous events, or just query specific details of what would be an otherwise glossed over part of the series. This second-screen usage is rapidly increasing, and the need for good layout, accessibility, and breakdown of story elements is a really interesting area of study.

Here, as in Section I of this book, you need to compartmentalize the pieces of your story in order to break them off and offer them as separate entities in your supplemental content. A character is an object, a module, and you can display them inside web-based content as such, giving extra details about their place, role, and attributes inside the greater story. *The Walking Dead*, a popular zombie survival horror fiction, popularized the supplemental content for second-screen viewing, and due to the phenomenal success, it was mimicked by dozens of other shows. This object-oriented model of storytelling goes well with the advent of technology and pushes the frontiers of what is possible with storytelling into the twenty-first century. A story is not a one-off concept, like a novel, but an engaging universe in which relationships, connections, and an unfolding narrative are ways to involve people inside a world. The single-concept film is falling by the wayside in favor of universes because the potential for expansion is far more lucrative and congruent with the evolution of content viewing. The web offers a great vessel for that content to supplement the more traditional "TV-like" episodic format.

15.2.2 Comics

What is a *web comic*? How does it differ from a regular comic? The comic book format is incredibly well adapted to the web, in the sense that vivid imagery and limited dialogue are easily distributed and engaged with through an interactive venue such as HTML and a browser. What was once only able to be purchased at a comic shop can now be published and distributed worldwide in a matter of seconds. Web comics range from fully interactive to completely static.

Web comics, in the completely static form, are just like comics on paper or in a book. There is no interactivity besides navigation, forward and back as if you were flipping pages in a comic book. The only real difference is the distribution method and availability. Web comics in the fully interactive model, however, can have animations, buttons, tasks, and sound controls that are obviously lacking in a printed publication. The addition of vocal narration and animation alone can enrich what would otherwise be a fairly one-directional and static format. Adding small amounts of interspersed animation and effects can turn a boring idea or story into a fully lively experience.

15.2.3 Tube Episodes

YouTube, and its clone sites, is a great venue for the "public-access TV" of the Internet. If anyone out there is as old as the author, they might remember cable public access channels, which would feature dizzying arrays of bad talent, bad production, and silliness of all kinds from anyone with a will to stand in front of a low-resolution camera. Cable public access shows were a hodgepodge of anything that local celebrities or aspiring actors felt like doing, when they were sure nobody was watching (and indeed, they had no way of knowing *who* was watching).

YouTube replaced that with a service that not only reached worldwide distribution instantly, but was also accessible by anyone with a computer and a webcam. On top of that, there was a level of accountability for popularity in the number of total views that content would receive—instead of a statistical Nielsen-based rating that could only extrapolate how popular a show was based on statistical analysis and projection, YouTube viewers and content creators actually *knew* exactly how many people watched their content. In short order, it became home to multiple content creators looking for an audience. The content was incredibly dense, but the count of viewers and the algorithms of content that you might be interested in pushed the site to be one of the most popular in the world. YouTube presents a semi-interactive, democratized source for content and distribution hub for content providers.

YouTube fiction was soon to follow the tutorials and other various contents that first dotted the landscape (Figure 15.2). In this sense, YouTube fiction is similar to social fiction, but slightly different in that the only social aspect of a YouTube element is the option to comment per video, so I am treating it as a separate entity. YouTube fiction often masqueraded as nonfiction, in the murky teenager daily diatribes of LonelyGirl15, which told a fairly captivating story about a teenage girl and her group of friends through a series of personal diary episodes where the main character was supposedly recording her video diary. The series became incredibly popular, and shortly afterwards in the subsequent seasons, things surrounding what originally appeared to be innocent teenage angst became a gateway to an unfolding narrative that involved secret organizations, teen disappearances, and dark forces at work. The show was an unbridled success, spinning off multiple fan-fiction derivatives and theories about what happened in the final episode. Like the 1938 *War of the Worlds* radio broadcast by Orson Welles (Figure 15.3), many people originally thought that the story of LonelyGirl15 was true, until the seasons progressed and it was discovered to be a scripted "tube-reality" show. Many of these supposed reality-based shows are common through the venue of YouTube and, subsequently, podcasts, because the format lends itself so well to a gritty "reality feel" through the use of webcams and low-budget production.

FIGURE 15.2 A still-frame from the LonelyGirl15 YouTube series. Characters and plots were all told through web cam footage.

FIGURE 15.3 Long before LonelyGirl15, Orson Welles pioneered the false reality show in his 1938 radio broadcast of *War of the Worlds*, by H.G. Wells.

15.2.4 Social Fiction

Certainly, we can consider all social media as some primitive form of story-based content, and the story that is being carefully crafted and honed is generally locked to an actual person's life and times. The narrative is almost always crafted deliberately and for various psychological reasons which are far beyond the scope of this book! But what about fictional stories? Pioneering efforts in the world of fictional social media are happening right now, and the potential of the format is only now becoming clear. Social fiction is a new format that is just emerging, as of the writing of this book. The concept is to take a slew of fictional characters and create social media accounts on Facebook, Twitter, Instagram, Vine, or Snapchat for these characters (or a combination of them). These social media accounts provide the social media window into the lives of these fictional characters, with story-driven content being delivered on an hourly, daily, or weekly basis. The content is still based on a tradition notion of storytelling, however! Just because these are told *through* the venue of social media doesn't mean that they are absent real stories. It just means that the method of presenting the elements of narrative, sequence, characters, perspective, setting, and tone are completely different from something such as a book, television show, or film. The format drives the compression of the content, which means that the story and interaction between the characters and narrative are often broken into tiny pieces and fed as status updates, shared photos, videos, surveys, and discussions through a publicly accessible site. Not only is the format able to break apart these story pieces into smaller chunks, but it also allows the audience to interact with those pieces, in the form of comments, requests and surveys. This way the viewer can interact with the content and even drive the content to some degree as the storyteller tries to keep up with requests by the audience. This is a midlevel of control over the narrative and a low level of synchronicity, but it seems to still provide the audience with a sense of interactive participation.

As previously mentioned, the most successful version of this emerging genre of entertainment to date is *DadBoner*, a fictional Twitter account by Karl Weitzin, a fictional buffoon-like character who is striving against middle age, divorce, and a generally negative outlook on his personal fitness and health. Created by comedian Mike Burns, the Twitter account belted out a complete story in little bits, one at a time, with time for fan involvement and commentary.

There have been multiple attempts into the genre of social fiction, with some mixed results. This format is emerging, and it has to mature before the tenets of successful methods can really be assessed. The major hurdles in terms of content development for storytellers are that the story is constantly moving forward, and social media is an element of storytelling where the fans and viewers will expect and demand a tremendous amount of content with a level of frequency that may be hard to keep up over a long period. As a functional story through social media, there must be a consistent amount of material being written and distributed with heavy frequency that may take a serious toll on any creative team behind it. The problem of sustainability is also an issue with stories that are told through social media—they can only last so long before people get bored with them or move on to other things. Since there is really no benchmark for this kind of entertainment yet, it's still an area where more study is necessary.

Interaction between the important elements of the story and the audience is a place where much experimentation should take place. A social fiction story can have the same narrative told through multiple or single perspectives, since the format of the venue can be done through more than one social media account. Perhaps the revolving multiple perspectives could be used to show the same narrative from completely different eyes, in another character's Facebook or Twitter feed. The audience could then choose the perspective they prefer, or even watch all of them in order to become more immersed in the content. The possibilities will be explored as more and more of these social fiction formats are explored.

15.2.4.1 Adver-Content

Adver-content is the most nebulous but, perhaps, the most prolific and pervasive aspect of story content for web. Advertisers are one of the majority financiers of the Internet. Much like television, the Internet and the World Wide Web would simply not exist without money from product and service advertisement. So if it is such a big part of the financial backing of the medium, it must have been proven effective, and indeed, this is the case. Internet advertising provides a huge proportion of advertising budgets *because* it is so effective.

A problem that advertisers and marketing specialists have, however, is *how* to market and brand online. In the ever-evolving world of the web, multiple formats of marketing have been tried and abandoned in hopes of finding a new way to reach out to consumers. The first ads were the banner and pop-up advertisements, a tactic that was not only annoying, but also intrusive and unlikely to provide results for the product.

What are the other options? Social media is the most obvious new venue for advertisers, and indeed, they have pounced on it vociferously in the recent past. Due to the rapid proliferation of social media outlets such as Facebook, Pinterest, or Instagram, and the speed at which they quickly began to take up a large amount of their users' screen time, media marketing saw the incredible potential as an advertising tool. The first advertisements were on the fringes of the screen space, but mobile devices and cramped pixel real estate soon made it necessary to start streaming ads into the regular content of the user, such as in your Facebook timeline or Instagram hashtag search. Even Tinder, the popular dating app, now has between-swipe ads. But the problem with these ads, despite the clever positioning, is that they're still pushing content to you despite your desire not to see it! Advertising is still an intrusive and unwanted part of your web browsing experience.

The next step in media marketing, and one heartily in development by marketing divisions, is the ability to create a two-way street with the consumer. Instead of popping an ad into your timeline or Tinder swipes, the marketers want to create a world of stories from their content that you can actively engage in. This bi-directional marketing, still in its infancy, is drawing interest from multiple parties as a way to push advertisement into the twenty-first century. Creating a story through social media and allowing the consumer to engage in that story is an exciting new way to generate clicks, likes, and buzz about an ad campaign. Earlier we discussed social fiction and how it is in development as a method of content delivery for entertainment, but it could also be used as a powerful delivery tool for any marketing material. Imagine the mascot of a big chain having their own Facebook page with mini-adventures and posts with comically based material or an Instagram account of the image-based adventures of a certain character, such as the recent Fashion Santa Instagram sensation, where Toronto's Yorkdale Shopping Centre hired model Paul Mason to wear designer clothing and take selfies as a slimmed-down, fashionable version of the classic Santa Claus. This was a masterful use of the social media venue to create a new character and use his or her story to garner huge amounts of interest from the worldwide population that regularly posts and looks at Instagram accounts! Due to the success of these social media campaigns, my prediction is that you will see the concept of social fiction become used in this manner in an increasing percentage. It's far more engaging to follow someone on Instagram than to have a pop-up image happen in your timeline or on the sidebar. Creating compelling story content like characters and narratives for the purpose of advertising is a great way to engage consumers in your product.

Advergaming is another tool of the marketer to get their story and content across to individuals who are accustomed to gameplay online. Advergames are brief, free games found on multiple websites, usually for the purpose of engaging younger demographics in a product or familiarizing them with a new brand. Although advergaming has been far eclipsed by social media as the web-based favorite, it was taken very seriously by the advertising world and still remains a viable option. Multiple studies were done with children and sugary cereal-based games, with the results of those studies driving the game design for advergames produced by companies such as General Mills and Kellogg.

Although advergames are less prevalent now than before social media eclipsed them, there is still a huge venue for the concept. Many popular multiplayer, online games such as *Minecraft* and *Warcraft* have huge potential for marketers to create their own content, levels, mods, and characters to seamlessly insert into the game. Open-world games such as *Minecraft* are incredibly popular and an extremely ripe area for some kind of creative marketing. Offering free content and gameplay inside an already open architecture game is a marketing space that I predict we will see proliferated in the very near future. It saves the time and effort of creating custom game engines and completed content for short periods while enhancing the reception of the player because it is in an environment which is already comfortable. I believe that if you combine this with contest and incentives you can have an incredibly effective media advertisement campaign for products that appeal to the game-playing demographic. In fact, there are several companies, such as Adbolt, currently offering services for *Minecraft* in-game ads! As of the writing of this book, there are multiple advertising services beginning to offer in-game ads for popular mobile and desktop games. Often free versions or content is enabled for public consumption, with the cost offset by the revenue from advertising.

15.2.4.2 Podcasts

Podcasts are the novelized and on-demand form of what is essentially an extremely old format. Radio shows in the pretelevision era were incredibly prolific and popular as 15- to 60-minute formats of story-based narrative content, news, and variety shows started their long road to the podcast webisode/episode of today. Most podcasts are limited to an audio-only format, and indeed, the most popular breakout example of the format, known as *Serial*, used an investigative journalistic approach to a real-life cold case murder investigation from the mid-1990s.

Being constrained by the audio format, podcasts have the disadvantage of not having visual information but the added advantage of being convenient for people who drive long distances, commute to work, or just want a distraction on the stairmaster. Podcasts have quickly gone from a radio talk show environment to a completely fictional docudrama style based on the *Serial* style of investigative journalism, but usually dealing with topics such as the paranormal or science fiction. Popular knock-off episodic content includes *The Black Tapes*, *Tanis*, *Limetown*, and *The Message*, which are all science fiction or paranormal versions of the original *Serial* podcast.

Are podcasts interactive? They certainly have some potential interactive features, much in the same way that a YouTube web series could be interactive. Fans can comment, e-mail, and visit the website where there are often multiple forums and fan-based content posted. Creating this alternate or supplemental web companion material is an important part of content development, as discussed earlier, and podcasts are small and agile enough to respond to fan queries, e-mails, and requests in a timely fashion (increasing the level of synchronicity and control). So you may not, as the audience, have *much* control over the material or path a podcast takes, but you could envision a version of this format that allows for the audience to make choices in close to real-time that affect the outcome. The potential is actually there, even if the format hasn't quite grasped it yet.

15.2.4.3 Wearable Tech

Wearable tech and augmented reality are just breaking the horizon of our consciousness, and the hardware is in its infancy (as were mobile devices in 2004). We can't quite imagine creating story-based content for the advent of the slew of augmented reality systems such as Microsoft Hololens, or the recently released Apple Watch, but the need and possibility for these is definitely on the horizon.

For instruments such as the Apple Watch or wearable technology that moves, breathes, and lives with you, developing an interactive media experience is a challenge. While it has a constant stream of information about where you are, what your vitals are, and the accelerometer input, the interplay between constant contact and a game or interactive story-based experience is still in the very beginning stages of development. Developing a creative interactive experience from wearable tech is a completely open venue!

One of the most important changes in the paradigm shift from traditional web-based content to mobile-content is the ability of your mobile device to know exactly where you are at all times. Using location as a device or element in your interactive entertainment experience can be a great addition to the immersion level, but at the same time, the mechanics of location and GPS have to be designed into the game or interactive content in a very specific manner. Location-based information could easily conflict with or tank your interactive experience, especially if you depend on your audience to physically change their location while engaging in the activity. Most research and current trends in the world of location-based gaming are centered on the idea of *locality* against *location*, which is a way of using your location in a nonsynchronous manner!

Using locality vs location in a game is best exemplified by the (now discontinued) mobile game *Shadow Cities*, by Grey Area. The game superimposed a magical world over the real world, using the local map of your area. You could fight demons, capture spirits, and build energy towers to foment your progress as a mage in one of several factions and gather power and experience. The caveats, however, were that you were only able to exude certain powers in certain areas, usually several square miles, when you were actually in that area. You could build, attack, and engage spirits inside of your local realm, but you had extremely limited abilities outside of the area in which you were physically. The nice thing about this locality model is that you didn't have to literally move in order to play the game—the game was dependent not on you moving to interact with it, but it did contain some level of connection between your physical location and the input or conditions of the game. This connects the game to your local surroundings without forcing you to get up and move around while playing.

New venues of entertainment based on augmented reality are just now on the cusp of viability, such as the Microsoft Hololens and (now defunct) Google Glass. Experimental systems such as this are beginning to push the way we imagine the gameplay of the future will take shape, with a mix of physical reality and a superimposed layer of digital information on top of it that is unique to an individual or even possibly able to be shared between one or more individuals. There's really no schematic or model for success in this field yet, which is a reason it is both extremely promising and unpredictable. Augmented reality is an interactive frontier that deserves a serious range of study and experimentation.

CHAPTER 16

Games

WHAT EXACTLY *IS* A *game*? Defining this model of interactive experience is absolutely essential if we are going to explore it in any meaningful way. Creating a theoretical model of what we can even consider a "game" will help us understand all the elements of a game and how they can be conceived and created successfully. We can consider a game to exist on the highest level of the interactive experience, with high levels of control and synchronicity. This is one of the reasons that games are harder to make in many cases than noninteractive entertainment. There is a huge amount of intricate, connected pieces to create in order to make a top-level game experience successful. Digital game development has only been around since the early 1980s, and although the concepts and understanding of digital interactive entertainment as an art form and a science have been explored in those past 35 years, the rapid movement of technology and speed at which we have adapted to that movement has made it nearly impossible to create any cohesive set of rules or design principles that fit everything.

Just as we broke down the concept of the story as a theoretical structure in Section I, we must do the same for the game. A game is unlike any of the previous interactive forms of entertainment mentioned because it contains within it very specific structures that must be present in order to qualify as such. Kiosks, podcasts, contest television, and social fiction forms of entertainment use interactivity to *enhance* the story for the audience. In a game, a certain level of interactivity is absolutely essential for it to qualify as a game.

So what *are* the essential elements of a game that must be present in order for us to consider it a true *game*? I will list these in the following and describe them in order of importance.

16.1 OBJECTIVE

The very first thing you need in order to consider something a game, whether it is a board game, a mind game, or a console game, is an objective. A player walks into a game, whether it is *Halo 4* or chess, with a clearly defined set of objectives. In a game of chess, it is to capture the other player's king by trapping it. That's it! That's your objective in every game of chess. There are infinite methods, combinations, and means to achieve that particular goal. But regardless of the strategy or method, the objective is always the direction in which you and the opposing player are moving. At no time during a game of chess will you decide that capturing the opposing player's rook piece satisfies the objective. So a game must have that defining objective as the engine of gameplay—without it, you really aren't playing a game in the true sense of the definition. This means that very many open-world simulations and online worlds such as *Second Life* aren't really games in the true sense. They are more like simulations, which mimic aspects of the real world in online virtual communities but have no definable objective. *Minecraft* is debatable—certainly, there is some kind of objective goal, but often, people use the open-world architecture in many different ways other than as a game.

In many complex console-level digital games, objectives can be *global* or *local*. Global objectives are generally fairly simple: save the princess (*Mario*), kill the dragon, save the universe, survive a zombie apocalypse. The local objectives can be simpler—escape a castle, kill a troll, find a gem, etc. The local objectives are there to get you one step closer to the global objective of the game.

In a game of *Halo 4*, or similar first-person shooters in single-player mode, the objective is to get to the end of each level. There might be constraints, dependencies, and specific obstacles in achieving that goal, but your ultimate objective is spelled out to you when beginning the game. Objectives can vary, and tasks can be set inside of a complex console-style game, but the one single important aspect of a game is that there is an objective goal that must be achieved. But always keep in mind in every game that there will always be a planned and specified objective goal for the player to accomplish.

16.2 RULES

Rules are the second most important element of a game. Rules are constraints under which you are challenged to accomplish your objective. Rules are the structure inside of which the game exists. Without them, it's really difficult to imagine an experience that would have any significance! Rules are there to provide a framework for what you can and can't do while pursuing the objective goal of the player.

Rules can be simple or complex, but they are always based on two things: dependencies and physics. Dependencies are elements that require an action or a previously acquired item. Dependencies are there to guide the player into certain actions and threads before they can move to other ones. The dependency in a game of chess is that you cannot make a move when it is not your turn. To do so violates the rules of the game. In a first-person shooter on a console, one of the dependencies for firing a weapon would be that it must be charged or have ammunition, which is a separate item that you acquire at some other point in the game. The idea behind the dependency is to have an added structure and challenge to the game or (in the case of chess) to allow your opponent to react to your action. Dependencies are also found in the area of currency, which is some kind of coin or amount of goods that it would take in order to acquire armor, weapons, objects, or other items one might need in order to facilitate the achievement of one's objective.

Physics are rules that are affected by the physical universe. They naturally govern movement and navigation throughout the game world. This is a very intuitive part of gameplay because it mimics, in some way, the natural physical forces of the real world, but often in an exaggerated or enhanced way. Movement through our natural physical world is governed by things such as mass, gravity, kinetic energy, friction, and centrifugal force. These are all things that can be manipulated to give the game a realistic feel or completely redesigned to become almost abstract in nature. But the forces will govern your movement. For instance, in a game you may have gravity and mass affecting your character, but perhaps on another planet where the forces are different, the character might be able to jump very high, but not actually fly. How high they can jump and how long the "hang time" could all be subject to the direction of the game and could even change with different environments to provide more challenge. But the basic elements of the forces would mimic our actual world. Manipulating the aspects of physics can lend an otherworldy feel to an otherwise standard first-person shooter or third-person action model.

16.3 REWARD SYSTEMS

As previously mentioned in Section I, reward systems are the heart of what makes a game successful and hold the player's attention. A reward system is a way to generate incentive, which in turn drives the player to want to return to the game and play again. If there is no incentive to play a game, there is in turn no reason that the player will return. Reward systems are deeply embedded in the concept of gameplay because they mimic the body and brain's natural response to certain stimuli and real-world situations. The brain and body have developed very specific neurological chemical reward systems for use in the survival of the species, in the forms of adrenaline, hormones, serotonin, endorphins, endomorphins, oxytocin, pheromones, dopamine, gamma-aminobutyric acid receptors, and many other chemicals that we are just beginning to understand as we unravel the intricate machine that is the neurochemistry of the human body and brain. These reward chemicals provide extremely powerful incentives to the human mind in order to get them to repeat certain processes. When this system is used in a complete natural setting, the rewards are powerful enhancers of positive action, such as eating, mating, and survival. When fermented or extracted from plants as chemicals or purified by synthesis in a laboratory, the same chemicals that exist inside of our body naturally can wreak havoc upon us in the form of intense craving and addiction, as we can clearly see in the pharmaceutically enhanced landscape of modern life where opiates, cocaine, methamphetamine, antidepressants, and benzodiazepines can cause extremely destructive and addictive behavior patterns.

Reward systems in regular life can also be triggered by neuroses and mental illness. Hoarding, compulsive behaviors, and other personality disorders can be triggered and chronically enabled by a malfunctioning or overactive natural chemical reward system. Anything that can influence human behavior to chronically self-destructive levels *has* to be an incredibly potent element of our psyche that can be manipulated and utilized in order to create more powerful and compelling experiences. Using the natural reward system to make gameplay compelling is an essential element of game design. Using these naturally occurring reward systems in games is a common tool used to make gameplay more enjoyable and stimulate the player to repeat the experience. Anything in a game that compels the user to play again can be considered a reward system, but there are seven specific systems that I have identified in gameplay: collection, achievement, catharsis, competition, role-playing, discovery, and social interaction.

Games often have a combination of these reward systems inherent to their structure, which compel the player to return to the game and repeat the experience. Creating compelling content as a game developer means that you want to have the maximum amount of hours possible to hold the player's attention! If you don't offer them some reason to come back and repeat the experience, your accumulative play time on a per-player basis will be pretty low. Reward systems are there to inspire and encourage repeat play, in order to make the game more successful and memorable (and to sell more copies, of course).

16.3.1 Extrinsic vs Intrinsic

A reward can said to be *intrinsic* when it occurs only while playing the game. As soon as the game is turned off or the player ceases to engage in play, the reward ceases to occur. Many reward systems occur during engagement of the activity and do not carry over outside of the concurrent gameplay time. These are things such as a cathartic act, such as playing a game where you are a huge robot blowing up buildings (my personal favorite). During the gameplay, you may feel elation from your adrenaline and testosterone from shooting rockets at buildings and unleashing incendiary destructive mayhem on the city below like Godzilla. But the minute you turn the game off, the elation quickly fades away.

Extrinsic rewards, conversely, continue *after* the gameplay is over. This is a more complex level of reward, because you are no longer engaged in the game. One example of this would be a level system in a game, where you have a character that can move up a level in some fashion, achieving rewards, powers, and abilities based on that level. If you turn off the game, there is a persistence of reward in the sense that your character is *still* one level higher. Even when you aren't playing the game, your character, which represents *you* (remember the Voodoo Principle) is on a higher level than before. This means that in some small way, you can vicariously accept the accomplishment as one of your own. After all, it was *you* who did all the work to get him there!

Some reward systems have both intrinsic and extrinsic characteristics, and some are distinctly one or the other. You can think of reward systems that have both characteristics as similar to going out for a run—some people actually enjoy the run itself, while some people only enjoy it *after* the run is over. Usually, this is what separates runners from nonrunners! Nonrunners may run, and they may feel good afterwards, but they never feel good *during* the run, while runners tend to enjoy the act itself.

16.3.2 Collection

Collection is the act of gathering things and holding on to them, either in the form of currency, food, or other aspects of the game which are essentially just there to be collected. Collection reward derives from the evolutionary system in which the act of putting away valuable items (such as food, money, or precious objects) to use at a later date when the need arises is of positive value. Hoarding is the out-of-control version of this act.

Collecting is an intrinsic *and* extrinsic reward system. The act of seeking and obtaining items itself can be rewarding and enjoyable, while the sensation of ownership of those intangible goods can persist after the game has been disengaged. If your character has accumulated a huge amount of wealth in the game, you are still connected to that wealth when not engaged in gameplay. Even if this wealth is purely fictional and has no real-world value, the player will still carry the sensation of ownership of that wealth outside the game with them. Thus is *persists* even when not playing the game.

16.3.3 Achievement

Achievement is perhaps the commonly used tool in games. Achievement is the process of moving up in a natural hierarchy or becoming better in some way. Achievement is a public acknowledgement of some kind of accomplishment on the part of the player, such as a level up or a better ranking. This allows the player to compare himself or herself to other players and self-determine his or her status by feeling good or bad about it.

The quest to the point of achievement, or striving for that achievement, is an intrinsic reward system. The act of moving toward achievement will stimulate the reward system. Achievement is also an extrinsic reward system in the sense that it carries with the player after the game is complete or no longer being played.

16.3.4 Catharsis

Catharsis is the mechanism, as previously discussed, in which stifled emotions and pent-up frustrations can be experienced through actions of another person. In this reward system, the player feels good because they can experience something that they aren't able to experience in the real world, such as blowing up a building as a giant robot, or they experience something emotional that they can relate to, which is happening to somebody else. In modern games, the catharsis is usually being able to do something which, in the real world, would have dire consequences, relatively cost and guilt free. Games such as *Grand Theft Auto* are rife with cathartic elements, in that they allow the player to make decisions and do things which are considered morally corrupt or unacceptable in the course of daily life, but can be done with impunity and a basic removal from consequence in the game.

Catharsis is one of the primary motivators of all entertainment-based content and plays a large part in the communication of emotions to the viewer. Allowing the player or the audience to experience something they haven't ever experienced or relate to a similar emotional experience that they have had will strengthen the connection between them and the story or game that they are watching or playing. Catharsis is the fundamental vessel through which overwhelming emotions are communicated and shared between human beings. Catharsis in modern game-based entertainment is often characterized by extreme violence or destructive tendencies, but only because they are *able* to create an immersive environment in which the ability to engage in violent or destructive behavior is free of consequence.

Many people criticize the interactive entertainment industry for the proliferation of violence in gaming, and, indeed, if you look at the top-selling games every year, a good proportion of them will be based on violence of some kind. Swords, guns, knives, fists, and explosions seem to be the main staples of the game industry. There are many schools of thought on the nature of this violent focus, but it's important to understand that human beings by default have incredibly latent violent tendencies. Human history is rife with examples of incredibly brutish and appalling acts of violence, often endorsed and encouraged by the public. The Aztecs brutally sacrificed young men and women by laying them naked across a stone altar and ripping their still beating heart out of their chest with an obsidian dagger while crowds of people watched below. The Spanish conquistadores were appalled at this act of brutality, but just that same year in London, people were still being publicly drawn and quartered, which is a pleasant way of saying "hung by the neck until half-dead and then emasculating them, ripping their intestines out with a knife and followed by a beheading" all in front of a jeering crowd. So the Europeans had little room to speak in regard to public brutality.

Even though we now live in a "civilized" society that frowns upon such violent behavior in real life, we tend to idealize it and romanticize it. People who criticize the game industry for stimulating overviolent behavior should take a look at television or film instead, where the incidence of violence is just as heavy, if not heavier. It is the element of catharsis, which we are discussing, that is the primary catalyst for the volume of violent content in games and entertainment media. Catharsis in the form of entertainment violence provides that pressure valve release for the latent violent tendencies of human beings in a world where actual physical violence is far less common.

There are many ranges of emotions *other* than violence possible in a game, despite the heavy influence of violence. Fear and horror games are great examples of cathartic environments in which players get to experience fright or suspense on multiple levels, which can release the pent-up emotions in that regard. Humor is another cathartic vessel through which a player can enjoy an experience in an interactive manner and feel some personal emotional reward as they laugh at silly characters or circumstances.

The cathartic release effect is near ubiquitous in game-based content, whether by design or by the nature of the format. It would be difficult to imagine a modern game without some level of catharsis that is inherently present. The effect of this reward is very powerful and, indeed on its own, will create an urgent desire to repeat the experience by continuing to play the game.

16.3.5 Competition

Competition is an incredibly potent motivator for human behavior. True competition requires other human beings in order to qualify. You can only get this benefit from directly playing or engaging another human being. If we use the classic chess example, you can see that you are engaged in a game of skill against another thinking breathing human. The reward from playing this other person comes from actively desiring to defeat this person. The act of total concentration and immersion in the act of desiring victory is the intrinsic aspect of this reward system, while the sensation of achieving that victory over the other person or group of people is the extrinsic aspect of that reward system, in the sense that until you play that person again, you will retain the sensation of being the winner. The idea of the *winner* and the *loser* is a deep-seated concept in the human psyche, connected to our feelings of self-worth and self-esteem, and is in some ways very necessary for us to place ourselves on a pecking order or a hierarchy of significance and value. Social hierarchies are incredibly important to society, and the fact that we can move up a notch (if only in our head) by defeating somebody else at something is a powerful motivating force.

Competition is often used in sports games or fighting games as the primary reward system and motivating factor. The upside to this is that it's a very powerful motivator, but the downside to this is that it requires more than one person at a time to play simultaneously. That might be hard to coordinate at times, but many tournament-style games are popular, where you can join a team and play against other users online, which allows you to find competition anywhere, anytime. Internet technology has moved along enough to allow this to happen globally, which exponentially expands the possibilities of competitive play. You now have competitors from hundreds of countries to choose from.

16.3.6 Role-Playing

Who hasn't, at one point or another, wanted to be somebody else? Especially somebody with super powers, magic skills, or extraordinary abilities of some kind? In 1977, Gary Gygax completed work on his iconic *Dungeons and Dragons*, which was considered one of the seminal role-playing games of the century. In this pre-video game world, the *Dungeons and Dragons* model was based on the creation of a character, with various skills and abilities, that could interact with adventures and creatures and other characters through modular dungeons and adventures. It was incredibly popular and spawned multiple knock-off role-playing enterprises, which eventually morphed into computer games as the technology grew and expanded. But the heart of the concept is still the same: the individual builds a character, which is a representation of himself or herself as an avatar, and that character enters into a world in which he or she interacts with other characters.

The Voodoo Principle is hard at work here, in the concept of embodiment, which is the transference of a small piece of the player's psyche into the virtual character or avatar. Your avatar is your representation in the virtual world, and when you build your character, you begin to breathe a small piece of yourself into that character, which connects you emotionally to it. Role-playing is incredibly extrinsic, in the sense that you carry the emotional connection to that character with you, even when you are not playing the game. You may only actively engage with the world or other characters during gameplay, but after the gameplay is over, you still carry the ideation of that character in your mind.

16.3.7 Discovery

Discovery is the act of figuring things out or uncovering a mystery. Curiosity is a natural human trait and one that pervades our everyday existence. From Rubik's Cube to crossword puzzles to Sudoku, we have an incredibly quizzical mind which has served us well in the evolutionary sense as a species. There is a special feeling that we all get when we figure out something or solve a puzzle. It is an intrinsic reward system that releases dopamine into our system after the successful act of discovery and, therefore, a very powerful motivator in all forms of entertainment. In books, television, and film, we have a pervasive element of discovery in the form of murder mysteries, which have been a popular staple of entertainment for over a century. What do Agatha Christie, Scooby Doo, Matlock, the Hardy Boys, and Humphrey Bogart all have in common? They are all detectives who lead the audience on a path of discovery as they turn over clue after clue in the pursuit of the final truth! The act of discovery is a very powerful reward system, but it is also very fleeting. The minute the elation of discovery disappears, it is gone forever, and the quest must begin anew. For this reason, most mystery-based entertainment elements must contain some sort of episodic nature, in which there is a fresh mystery every week to continue interest and keep things novel. Mystery-based gameplay is subject to similar constraints, in the sense that once the game is over and the mystery has been solved, repeat gameplay is a lot less likely. But the sequel will always provide fresh material, of course!

Interactive games often use the element of discovery to enhance narrative content. Mysteries are a great way to engage the player in the story behind the game. There are specific genres of gameplay that revolve around the uncovering of the narrative, plot, characters, and other important aspects of the story by making the player responsible for the act of discovery. This device is instrumental in creating the reward of finding out elements of the story that are obscured or unknown. Pivotal games such as *Myst*, which was produced for the Macintosh in 1993 by Broderbund and designed by Robyn and Rand Miller, were instrumental in bringing the element of mystery and discovery to interactive entertainment. *Myst* was a puzzle-based mystery first-person game which featured rich narrative content that had to be uncovered as the gameplay progressed. This became the model for multitudes of similar games over the next 20 years and still provides a structure for mystery-based gameplay today. *Myst* was hugely successful and held the record as the best-selling PC game until *The Sims* overtook it in 2002.

16.3.8 Social Interaction

The human being is a social creature. It is not only an inherent part of our nature, but indeed an actual *need* that must be met in order to keep emotionally and mentally healthy. Solitary confinement in prisons is just as effective of a punishment as physical abuse because it deprives the individual of human contact. And it is demonstrable in multiple psychological experiments that total isolation from other human beings causes emotional and mental breakdowns after a certain amount of time. We are social creatures, and we crave that social interaction on a daily basis.

For this reason, social interaction is a hugely important reward system for multiplayer games. In a world where you can interact and communicate through the gameplay with other human beings, all the same chemicals and sensations of well-being can be released just as if you were at a party. *World of Warcraft*, arguably one of the most-played and successful games over the past decade, is a perfect example of a game that uses social interaction as a primary reward system. The ability of players to communicate and bond with other humans in the game world is often cited as the most alluring or important thing to chronic players.

Warcraft was such a successful user of reward systems such as role-playing and social interaction that it quickly became the subject of multiple addiction stories, rife with examples of people who had lost their job or somehow ruined their life because they were unable to stop playing. Any game that can completely take over somebody's life as if it were a narcotic drug can be examined and lauded as having an incredibly successful reward system design. There are even several groups in existence now acting as advocates for people who are "addicted to *World of Warcraft*" and have form collectives such as Alcoholics Anonymous to combat the problem.

The important thing about this "*Warcraft* addiction" is the evidence that the reward systems in the brain stimulated by playing a game can be just as potent and compelling as a narcotic drug such as cocaine or heroin. While the moral implications of such a thing are far beyond the scope of this book, the psychological implications are fairly crystalline. Game reward systems are powerful motivators and can have serious control over whether somebody will repeat the game experience.

16.4 CHARACTERS

Game characters are special kinds of characters. Those critiquing the gaming world for having one-dimensional characters are not entirely incorrect in their supposition, although that trend is beginning to shift as the game-based stories become more and more sophisticated. But the character in an interactive experience is a very important element—they must have certain characteristics in order to become compelling to the player at all. Characters in games are not the same as characters in movies, for the reason that the player gets to either *be* them (by direct control) or interact *with* them, in conversation, battle, or otherwise.

16.4.1 Archetypes

In his interview series with Bill Moyers and in his subsequent book *The Power of Myth*, Joseph Campbell outlines fundamental aspects of the human experience as told through mythology. He speaks of various aspects of human psychology and how these elements are channeled through myths and the characters in those myths. The archetypes of characters in comic books and video games are often similar to his concepts in this book, which tends to lend itself to the framing of the characters and persons in these myths. Mythology, comic books, and games have very similar roles in society, with many seeing comics and superheroes as the modern versions of the old mythological heroes such as Hercules, Odysseus, and multiple others. One of the defining characteristics of these heroes is their heroic attributes, which are exaggerated versions of our natural human tendencies.

In the mythological universe, there is often a lack of moral ambiguity. Bad people are bad people, good people are good people, and very rarely do we see any conflict in between. Archetypes are ways to play out moral lessons and categorize heroes and villains. In games which are often an extension of a comic book-type universe, we can see the same pattern. One character is the hero; another character is a villain. This decidedly 2D depiction of heroic and villainous characters lends itself well to games because the stories, which have far less opening for specific copy, can be told in a much simpler way. You know the good people from the bad people, and you generally have a specific mission to carry out in that regard.

Characters in the heroic universe have powers and abilities that generally far outstrip the ordinary human being. This, combined with motivations and objective goals, can make them very idealistic and seemingly simple.

16.4.2 Hero

The hero is the good person, pure and simple. His or her motivations are always pure, and his or her moral core is solid. He is always tested, again and again, usually in a series of adventures, on a quest, or in pursuit of rescuing a distressed human (usually his or her spouse, daughter, or other victim archetype). The hero has abilities and powers that rise above normal people, while not being invulnerable or possessing weakness. The hero is represented ubiquitously in modern comic books and games. From the master chief of *Halo* to Mario from Nintendo, the hero is well represented in all forms of interactive media entertainment! He or she is the idealistic representation of the purity of good and all that it stands for and incorruptible morality.

16.4.3 Villain

The villain, in sharp contrast to the hero, stands for chaos, pain, and personal gain. He or she has no moral core and often does things strictly to harm or impede the hero. His or her goals are also pure, in the sense that he or she wants only one thing, be that to destroy the hero, gain some form of ultimate power, or create complete and total chaos. The villain is necessary often as an obstacle and a narrative shill for the hero's quest or objective. The objective for the hero will often be to prevent the villain from obtaining power, rescue the victim from the villain's grasp, or prevent the villain from destroying the world in some way. Sometimes the narrative construct will feature the hero escaping the villain in some form or another. The villain often possesses similar but warped versions of the hero's powers or complete opposites. The dichotomy of the villain and the hero is often a narrative device in and of itself; think of Batman (Figure 16.1) and the Joker (Figure 16.2), Superman and Lex Luthor, Professor X and Magneto, and various other combinations which are examples of a dual morality and good/evil in opposition. The concept of this duality is almost as old as humanity itself. Zoroastrianism is a religion from ancient Indo-Persian roots that proposes a ditheistic concept of the ultimate creator and good deity Ahura-Mazda and his opposing force representing chaos and evil Ahriman, who is the destructive force. From this concept of dualism, we also derive the Christian elements of God and Lucifer, locked into an eternal struggle of good and evil forever. This legacy of conceptual duality is so strong in the psyche that it bleeds over into our modern mythology of superheroes and game characters, creating the hero/villain

FIGURE 16.1 Batman, a classic archetypal hero.

format. *Star Wars*' Jedi/Sith duality is just another in a long chain of examples of this basic human concept.

16.4.4 Victim

The victim is the helpless force and is usually a narrative shill used to create the rescue format. The victim is weak and powerless, represented by a child, a female, or at times a man-child in some capacity. The victim is in constant need of rescuing from harrowing situations and impending

FIGURE 16.2 The Joker, the archetypal villain and nemesis of Batman. This reinforces the Zoroastrian concept of order versus chaos locked into an eternal struggle.

doom, often at the hands of the villain, whose intentions is to draw out or cause harm to the hero in some capacity.

The most classic of all rescue games is the original *Donkey Kong* (Figure 16.3), in which a giant ape kidnaps Mario's girlfriend and absconds with her to the top of scaffolding, raining barrels and fireballs down below to create obstacles to Mario's upward progress. This was extremely reminiscent of the film *King Kong* (and indeed, borrowed from the film name), in which a similar rescue story was told.

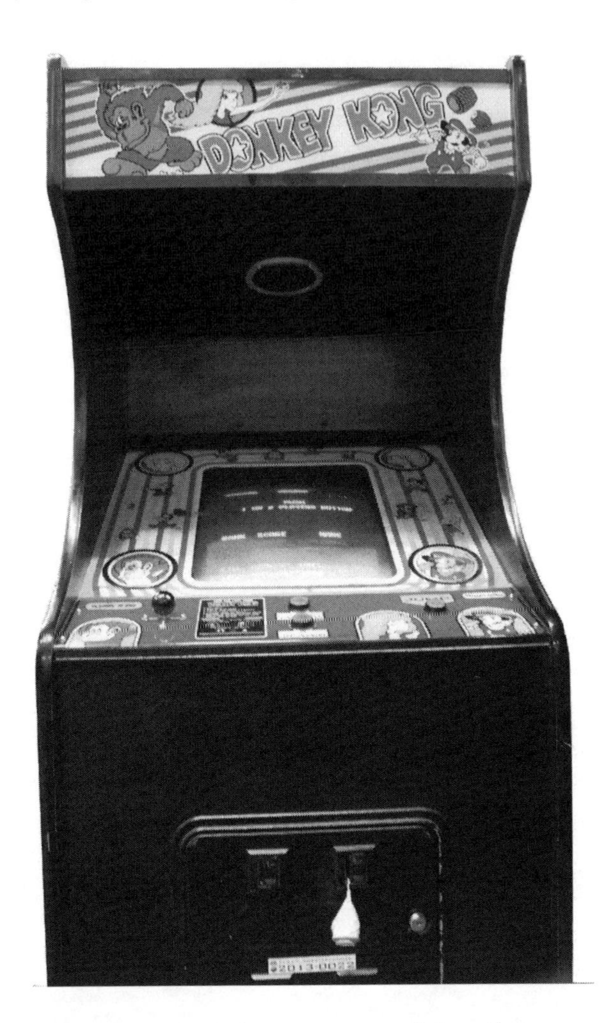

FIGURE 16.3 The original *Donkey Kong*, one of the all-time most successful arcade games and the gaming world's introduction to Mario, possibly the most prolific game character of all time.

16.4.5 Mercenary

The mercenary is a character that is almost completely neutral in all forms. They are neither good nor evil, but they work completely inside of their own personal gain. Often in the narratives, the player will be given the mercenary to play as a character, but over the course of the game, they will be given the choice of moral goodness over personal gain, with the narrative pushing in one direction over another. The conversion of the mercenary from neutral to good (or at times, evil) is a primary narrative device in modern mythology. Han Solo in *Star Wars* is a great example of a self-interested person who is converted through a series of events to work for the light side of the "Force" in favor of his own self-preservation. This mercenary character is a common theme in games for various plot devices, even in many forms staying a mercenary or bounty hunter the entire game. The mercenary provides a good dose of moral ambiguity into the otherwise one-dimensional structure of character archetypes.

16.4.6 Reluctant Hero

The reluctant/unlikely hero is a subset of the standard hero archetype, but with the slight twist of not really wanting to *be* the hero. Generally, he or she is somehow coerced, tricked, forced, or convinced to become the hero due to some kind of circumstance. This is a twisting of the usually one-dimensional hero narrative, by adding some extra humanness to the standard model. The unlikely hero is the person without any extraordinary abilities who somehow, despite all odds and forces compiled against him or her, manages to save the day. Frodo Baggins and Samwise Gamgee of *Lord of the Rings* fame are excellent examples of unlikely heroes. They seem completely helpless and unlikely to succeed in the mission that they are given, but despite armies and powers of great might, they manage to make it in the end.

16.4.7 Tortured Villain

The tortured villain, as the unlikely hero, is a twist on the standard villain model. This archetype fills the role of the villain in some capacity, but only due to some traumatic event or desperate desire to alleviate some personal chronic pain. The tortured villain can be used as a comedic element, as a destructive element that is somehow fixed by the alleviation of pain (the mouse removing the thorn from the elephant's foot, for instance) and afterwards reverts to good person status. Or the tortured villain can be the dramatic element and wildcard in any narrative, as Tolkien made Gollum in *Lord of the Rings* and *The Hobbit*. These wildcard characters can be used as incredibly unpredictable and destructive forces in any narrative.

16.5 OBSTACLES

How much fun would it be if the player, in pursuit of his objective, could just get there immediately? A game cannot let the player just achieve said objective, or the game would be too easy! There must be some struggle or difficulty in the form of obstacles, in order for the challenge to be present.

There are several kinds of obstacles that can be created as a part of the game and narrative experience.

16.5.1 Puzzle Obstacles

Puzzles and minigames are often used as added content for obstacles inside of a game. There are often miniobjectives inside of the larger game structure that make the player work to find solutions in order to move ahead in the game. Puzzles can be games of skill, chance, or logic that require certain things to be done in order to find a door, move through a maze, or open a lock. These puzzle obstacles allow the gameplay to be extended in some sense, stretching out the time it takes to move through environments and providing a break in the action and flow.

16.5.2 Nonplayer Character Obstacles

NPCs, or nonplayer characters, are artificial intelligence (AI)–driven elements that are represented by characters that create impediments or literally attack the player. NPCs are driven by either specific patterns or movement or by a hierarchy of objectives, which can vary by type. You can think of NPCs as the zombies, devils, vampires, Nazis, aliens, robots, monsters, and any other life-forms that actively impede, slow down, or otherwise create obstacles for the main player.

In a narrative sense, these NPC elements are *rarely* other human beings, in the sense that they rarely represent living breathing humans. The Voodoo Principle, as discussed previously, can work in both directions. In order to make a superrealistic game rife with violence, the moral nonambiguity of the hero means that they aren't really allowed to kill other humans. So humanoid characters can be bereft of souls by turning them into nonhuman (robots), alien, inhuman (Nazis), or mindless undead (zombies). This is not universal, of course, and certainly you could make a game where the main character kills other human beings, and indeed many games such as *Grand Theft Auto* or *Call of Duty* have such parameters with other combatants and innocent bystanders, but the narrative device of creating a game with humanoid, nonhuman NPCs that the player can easily slaughter without moral dilemma is quite common (and probably a good way to avoid an M rating). Of course, the inverse can lead to comical content, such as the hero dog character gunning down cute kitten soldiers in a species-to-species war game, but this is a deliberate twisting of the device for comedic effect.

Procedural and sophisticated AI-driven enemies and NPCs are beginning to replace the old pattern-based AIs, with less predictable and more realistic and random results. The recent game *Alien: Isolation*, by Creative Assembly released in 2014, was a great example of an entirely procedurally driven enemy AI. The main creature was driven by its own personal set of objective goals, which were mysterious to the player but provided a structure that was both unpredictable and challenging.

16.5.3 Human Player Obstacles

Tournament, fighting, and massively multiplayer online role-playing games are rife with examples of human players creating obstacles for other human players. One engaging thing about playing other human beings is their complete unpredictability and simultaneous predictability. Humans can illustrate predictable behavior inside of a game structure but, at the same time, be completely aware that other characters are looking for that exact pattern and suddenly behave in an unpredictable manner in order to prevent this from becoming a weakness. The human ability to predict, prognosticate, and analyze other human beings, *especially* the ability to trick or pretend to do things is an immensely complex set of possible outcomes. This is why the games which involve other human beings as obstacles to your goals have the largest amount of possible outcomes and gameplay experiences. Human beings are far better than an AI at providing a rich, unpredictable, and strategic experience. The human players dramatically increase the instance of the competition reward system, since the player will be in direct opposition to other human players.

16.5.4 Environmental Obstacles

Sometimes the environment itself creates barriers and obstacles to prevent the player from achieving their objective. Things such as snakes, pits, lava beds, fireballs, projectiles, crocodiles, water traps, and pretty much anything else that you can imagine will form impediments to the player's progress. Using the environment to create difficulties in progression through both gameplay and narrative are incredibly common and a good way to break up the action and add layers to game difficulty.

Using the environment obstacles to enhance and combine with the setting of your story is good story/game design and can strengthen the connection between the setting of the game and the setting of the story. So, for instance, if your story/game occurs in a jungle setting, you can use water traps, crocodiles, and snakes to enhance the natural perils of the environment and create a more lifelike structure to your game.

16.5.5 Dependency Obstacles

Dependency obstacles are blockades or impediments to the progress of the player, which involve obtaining hidden items, completing a certain collection of items, or accumulating a certain amount of currency before being able to progress. This uses the collection reward system, triggering the human reward response from obtaining these items even before being given permission or access to other levels, weapons, or objects.

Achievement reward systems are also just as likely to be engaged in this instance, because the collection of things such as experience points can be used to increase the level, abilities, and status of the player.

16.6 ENVIRONMENTS

Environments are the setting of the game. Often, games will have either a single, comprehensive environment that is maintained the entire length of the gameplay (such as *Bioshock*) with separate levels, compartments, or segments, or a host of multiple worlds, levels, or designs that have vastly different characteristics.

The single, comprehensive form of game setting is useful for creating a consistent and static time and place for the game to occur. This will provide a grounding effect, where the consistent and pervasive atmosphere of the single level acts as a tool to keep the player in the moment and immersed in the story at all times. Imagine a game that was set in the Vietnam War era. What would you do to keep the player immersed in the environment and setting of the story? You might want to make the entire game inside a certain type of jungle setting that was as authentic as possible.

Environments in a game are vital to create the illusion of a specific time, place, and level of technology. These settings are a vital component of making the player feel as if they are engaged with the story and narrative as it takes place.

Multiple segments and levels are good for providing a larger or expansive sense to the gameplay and universe as it pertains to the particular episode of the game. Expansive universe games are important for bigger worlds that have multiple components, factions, and episodes in the series. *Halo* is a great example of a game franchise that consistently updates and expands the environments for each new subsequent title.

16.7 OBJECTS/VEHICLES/WEAPONS

Vehicles, objects, and weapons are a category slightly separate from environment or character because they operate in both realms. They are used by the character, but they must mirror the time, place, design, and technology level of the environment. Objects, weapons, and vehicles create methods of interacting with all the elements mentioned earlier and create a richness to the game that prevents staleness and repetition.

Weapons are often set with varying properties and attributes that make them effective in certain places, but ineffective in certain other places. Ammo capacity, damage levels, rapidity of fire, and accuracy are all varying attributes that can be manipulated by the designer to make the gameplay more interesting. Weapons can be used as a reward for achieving a goal or objective, or used as a dependency for moving to another level or progression.

Objects are defined as anything in a game that has value or purpose to the player, such as potions, healing syringes, spells, explosives, enhancers, or psychic abilities. They are usually obtained through scavenging, rummaging, or searching or can be used as rewards in various circumstances.

Vehicles are an enhancer for locomotion and movement, offering the player a faster way to navigate the environment. Many games offer walking, riding horses, flying on dragons, spaceships, speed bikes, and wheeled vehicles. These are all ways to vary the speed and ease of navigating through the environments. Vehicles can allow the player to supersede natural impediments to movements and are sometimes used as a dependency to allowing the player to access parts of the game that they would be otherwise unable to navigate.

CHAPTER 17

Stories and Games

WHY DO GAMES NEED stories? *Do* games need stories? The game *Centipede*, published in the early 1980s by Namco, was a game without an actual story. It was fabulously successful. But games, as they progressed, seemed to quickly become infused with story as a matter of course, and soon after, the slew of first generation of arcade games having an immersive and somewhat designed story in a game was a must-have. But what does a story *do* for a game? How does it enhance gameplay? How does it interact with gameplay? What relationship does the player have with the game?

Stories in games, as stories in a narrative format, have the role of communicating emotional and relational information. The human mind, as we have seen, is not really a fact-memorization machine, as a computer might be considered. The human mind is an association-making entity that creates connections between one thing and another, and the glue that reinforces these associations is the emotions connected to the events. We tend to strengthen those associations if we can relate to that information through our own emotional memory, or if we can vicariously place ourselves in the positions of others for emotions we would like to feel. A story creates a framework inside of which the players' objectives are given meaning and significance from a human perspective.

In an article by Naomi Alderman, a modern author and game designer, she asserts that the game has become a significant and modern narrative device, akin to that of serious literary acknowledgement. The first great works of digital literature are already being written. While *Grand Theft Auto V* might not necessarily be *War and Peace*, Alderman's point that literature and games have slowly been moving toward the point of convergence is not a fallacy. Indeed, game stories are beginning to be considered a vital component of the gameplay.

But what function does the story ultimately serve? Imagine a game in which you are a generic humanoid, given the objective to get from one end of a level to another without getting killed by other generic humanoids firing guns at you. Certainly you might engage in the activity, and participate in the game, but on the other hand, if you are given a character named *Master Chief*, a Spartan supersoldier engineered by earth in a cosmic battle against the Covenant, an intergalactic congress of multiple alien species intent on wiping out humanity, and the only way to stop them is to carry vital intelligence information to the drop ship before they can stop you, the game suddenly comes to life! This uses two important concepts that apply to interactive gaming: immersion and embodiment.

Immersion is the mental state of perceiving yourself to be an active part of the story in progress, and not just a passive or nonessential observer. A game that allows the player to interact with elements of narrative and perspective will have a much higher level of immersion present with both gameplay and story. Immersion enhances gameplay by stimulating all the senses in a similar manner to the real experience, which might not even be technically or physically possible. This is why games often use fantasy, science fiction, or other devices to remove the player from a boring, mundane world and immerse them in a positive departure from reality.

Embodiment is a similar concept, but in the sense of character and the player's relationship to that character. If we look again at the Voodoo Principle, you will see that it functions here once again as a portal for the metaphysical spiritual presence of the player and the character that they're controlling. Embodiment is an artifact of role-playing games especially when the player feels a deep connection to their personal character since they not only designed it in a character creator, but have also invested a significant amount of time mechanically and emotionally into the development of it. It becomes an extension of their ego, and hence, when they play the game, they are much more immersed in the experience. In this way, they get to control the narrative and direction of their personal character, within the rules and confines of the game experience.

In a study published in 2009 in *CyberPsychology & Behavior,* three researchers conducted an electric skin-based reading test on children with games that had a varying level of control over the avatar (or main character) of the game. The skin conductance levels were taken during gameplay in order to measure the arousal level, which would provide some objective understanding (along with questionnaires of participants) of how engaged in the game the children felt while playing. The games had three levels of avatar control; in the first, they were given an existing avatar to play; in the second, they were given a choice of several preexisting avatars; and in the third, they were given full control with a character creator to make their own. The results consistently illustrated that there was a positive correlation between the levels of engagement felt during gameplay with the level of control over the avatar. This is some level of data-based evidence that the concept of embodiment is important on mental *and* chemical levels to the player.

Of course, giving complete character choice to every player in every game would be ridiculous, and some game-based stories are much better when the characters are predefined! But the evidence that elements of a game such as the influence on the character and the player engagement *with* that story is significant. It clearly shows that immersion is a measurable aspect of gameplay, and that game design choices can have a significant effect on that immersion.

17.1 DESIGNING STORIES FOR GAMES

So now that we understand *why* we need or at least desire a story inside of a game and *how* it can affect the player while engaged, we should look at *what* kind of content and framework would be best for game stories. There are many different needs of the gamestory that are quite separate from what we might think of as a classic story format, such as a book, video, film, or broadcast, the main difference being the need for a framework inside of which those story elements can exist as independent objects with which the player can then interact.

Stories for interactive content are quite different from stories for passive consumption. They can't be seen as a single contiguous line that begins at episode 1 and ends at episode 100. This is due to the fact that the player has some level control over the navigation of the story and the elements of characters, perspective, narrative, sequence, and setting. The author of the story has control over these elements as individual pieces (or objects), but not the flow of the elements and how the player interacts with them. Building the framework of the story within which the game will occur takes a special kind of storyteller, one who can fragment the elements into primary components and lay them out in a logical method that works with the method of gameplay.

The very first decision a storyteller designing for a game must make is exactly *how* they want the player to interact with the story. In order to do this, there must be some compromise with the structure of the game and the genre of gameplay. Some games are built to work in certain ways, and that will greatly influence the manner in which the storyteller will build their story elements. Indeed, the same story elements can be used in more than one type of gameplay, and this is why we try to design with the story as a hierarchical list of elements. Before we can even begin to define the nature of game/story interaction, we must first define the genre of gameplay and separate it into certain categories.

17.2 GENRES OF GAMEPLAY

These are simply models of interaction that take into account game mechanics, player input, player objective, and player perspective from a formalized standpoint using successful game franchises and recognized existing frameworks. This may not cover *every* game in existence, but it covers a good amount of current top-selling titles and notable successes.

17.2.1 First-Person Shooters

One of the most popular gameplay genres by far, first-person shooters (FPSs) take up a large percentage of the market share. FPS games are clearly defined by the perspective of the camera, which is positioned at the head of the player, creating the immersive illusion that the player is looking out of the eyes of the character they are controlling. The camera being positioned this way is intended to make the player feel more immersed in the action of the game by generating that illusion that they *are* the character, and not just controlling the character. If you recall in Section II, when discussing the composition of the still image, the camera is equivalent to the viewer's perception of their own eyes, so when the camera in a game uses this technique in a literal sense, it can greatly enhance the sensation of embodiment and immersive sensation!

The *shooter* term comes from the fact that these games are almost universally characterized by having projectile combat weapons, and indeed, the perspective lends itself well to this kind of gameplay. Hand-to-hand and melee-style weapons such as swords, maces, and clubs are usually much better utilized in a different, third-person style of camera perspective due to their close-quarter nature (Figure 17.1).

FIGURE 17.1 A typical, first-person type of perspective in use. The player sees the hands and weapon only from the characters eye perspective.

Despite having a very set type of interaction with the game, FPS games have a very flexible model for game/story interaction, and there is no real set way of delivering story content in them.

17.2.2 Third-Person Action

Third-person action can be almost identical to FPS games in many regards, with the exception of the camera position, which is generally over the shoulder and semi-adaptive. A semi-adaptive camera is a smart camera in the sense that it adjusts with the movement of the character through the environment. The third-person perspective is important because it removes the player from the immersive level of interaction and makes them aware that they are controlling a character, instead of embodying themselves into that character. This removes the level of immersion in some sense and allows the game to take on less-than-real proportions and mechanics of physics or appearances. It also seems to lend itself to much more close-quarter actions such as hand-to-hand combat and navigation through environments with a higher level of interactivity.

Environment interaction is greatly enhanced by this perspective style, based on the greater ability of seeing the environment from a bigger camera angle, and often, the environment will play a much bigger part in this type of gameplay, allowing the storyteller to use it in more creative ways to deliver content (Figure 17.2).

FIGURE 17.2 *Mission Nutrition*, a third-person action game by the author. The player can interact with the environment in more creative ways than a first-person shooter game due to the wider camera angle.

17.2.3 Head-to-Head Fighting

The head-to-head fighting game is a genre that has a very rigid format. Two combatants enter the ring; one combatant leaves victorious (and many times, the other is temporarily killed in some ghastly violently satisfying manner). *Soul Caliber* by Namco and *Mortal Kombat* are two great examples of this classic arcade-derived format that has stood the test of time and still manage to make popular releases. The format is very rigid, which makes a very limited format for a story to occur, and the format is generally very formalized. The fighting games use a simple story mode, where each character is given their own personal motivation, backstory, and Zoroastrian-style of affiliation corresponding to good or evil. The players have converged on the tournament or elimination style of play, where each individual step into the ring and keeps playing until they have been defeated by another entity. The individual story of each character is usually used to tweak or tailor certain combats or possibly training elements to create a cohesive narrative in story mode; by using other certain characters or trials, a coherent story can be pieced together from the disparate elements available (Figure 17.3).

17.2.4 Sports/Racing

Racing sports are another game genre that has a distinct style and format, differing from all others. The wiggle room for creative storytelling is limited, in the sense that these games all focus on the excitement of

FIGURE 17.3 The original *Street Fighter* arcade game, an enduring franchise for Capcom, has been a hallmark of head-to-head fighting games since its introduction.

the real-time racing alone and leave the rest as an afterthought. It is not impossible, however, to construct story elements for these games by using an object-oriented construction. The racers, such as the combatants in the fighting games, can have personalities, backstories, and challenges that pertain to their own personal perspective and narrative, and the progression of the game can move in certain directions based on those stories. Winning the race, or race performance, can have an implication upon the narrative progression by changing the competitors, cutscenes, racetrack settings, or other creative ways to weave a story into an existing format.

Your typical sports game simulations, such as the all-pervasive and monopolistic *Madden NFL* by Electronic Arts, are not something you'd think of as possessing or even desiring to have any type of story elements. But efforts in recent years to offer sports fans some type of story mode have not gone untouched; many sports games now are beginning to develop and offer concepts such as rookie mode and manager modes, where the player can use certain narrative elements in order to construct their own stories inside of the gameplay. These modes have a certain level of interactivity with various characters and personal choices which propel the career of a fledgling professional sports player forward as they aspire to be a top-level player in whatever sport the game is based on. Training camps and player trades from team to team can generate the objectives and create a level of randomness and depth that can captivate some level of game immersion and repeat single-player gameplay. The heart and soul of team-based sports games, however, still tend to be person-to-person competitive play, however, and the majority of effort is still placed into these areas in terms of development.

17.2.5 Platformer

The platformer derives its titles from the oldest of arcade titles by Nintendo, such as *Donkey Kong*, where characters are made to jump from platform to platform, usually suspended in midair or interspersed by empty air. The platformer can be a 2D flat-screen perspective (such as *Super Mario Brothers*; see Figure 17.4) or a fully rendered 3D environment with a third-person camera view, such as *Ratchet and Clank* by Sony. In either case, the platformer game is characterized by a somewhat cartoonish style of movement and graphics (although this need not be the case) and heavy interaction with the environments. There can be a very wide range of story-based elements in the platform style of game, usually in the form of player collections, miniature objectives, and level progression based on puzzle solving and boss fights. The platformer leaves many levels of interaction for the story elements open, giving the storyteller a very flexible structure within which to craft a compelling narrative.

FIGURE 17.4 *Super Mario Brothers* by Nintendo, illustrating classic platformer mechanics with the main character navigating the environment by jumping.

17.2.6 Sandbox

The sandbox genre of gameplay is characterized primarily by its level of openness. The player is placed within an environment with certain rules and parameters, then let go to basically do as they please inside that environment. Objectives are sparse, and options are high, which allows the player to create their own personal story any way they want.

Placed inside that open world, however, are multiple mini-stories, complete with narratives, characters, sequences, and settings. The player then gets to choose which of these they want to pursue, at their own pace. Like threads, these separate stories and interplay between story objects can be designed any way the storyteller wants, giving them the freedom to construct these elements and place them inside the open world.

Grand Theft Auto is a great example and enduring franchise of the sandbox genre. The player is given an environment in which they can do as they please, especially commit violent crimes at will whenever they want with whomever they want. There are multiple missions and stories inside of the game with levels of complexity, but these are not compulsory and can be chosen at will by the player.

The Sims is another sandbox-style game, where building and controlling your own world are the primary components of the game, and indeed there is some discussion over whether this simulation-style of game is actually a game or not, seeing as it does not have a definitive player objective. But it deserves mention here because although the point of the game type is for the player to have total control, there is often story content inside of these games that the player can choose to engage in or shapes the game in some way. External events such as politics or weather can be written in as narrative devices in order to shake things up a little bit and add some chaos or scripted challenges and obstacles for the player.

17.2.7 MMORPG

Massive multiplayer online role-playing games (or MMORPGs for short) are an interesting case for the development of stories, because they offer the potential for huge amounts of content but limited control over the *delivery* of that content. The storyteller, when approaching this type of game, must think in terms of themes, settings, and big-picture mechanics along with smaller, threaded concepts that branch off to the side of the main world.

Since the players have so much control over the game in the sense that they can build their own characters, involve themselves in their own groups, and communicate and decide their own course, the story mechanics of the game have to be created as a setting that the players can choose to enter into and leave at will. So the player characters and their attributes are often entirely out of the storyteller's hands; they must compensate by putting more effort into the setting and NPCs (such as the dungeon-dwelling denizens of a particular module).

17.3 GAMESTORY INTERACTION MODES

Now that the various genres of gameplay have been identified and categorized, it's time to look at the different models of gameplay–story interaction. Since there is no formal theory or cohesive philosophy in terms of using a story inside of a game, there has been a massive amount of experimentation occurring over 20 years of progressive game development. The good thing about this massive amount of organic growth and experimentation is that the successful models have become more and more common, while the unsuccessful models have become less and less common. It mirrors the concepts of evolution, in which less successful species eventually die out and are replaced by the mutations or branches that were able to out-survive their competitors.

The story for the game, which, for convenience, from now on, we will use the term *gamestory*, requires a certain level of unique and balanced design, which work together to create the total experience. Sometimes a story is superimposed on top of an existing game design, which was far more common in the early days of game development. Sometimes a game is superimposed on top of a story, which is the most common device when dealing with things such as movie-based games or comic book hero games, which have varying levels of success in the final product.

The most important thing to take away from this is the *design* factor. You have to design the interplay between the game and the story as well as the player's role in that interplay. You can't just slap them together and hope it will all work out. At the end of this section, there are a few exercises in which you will carefully lay out the design of story and game in order to create the best playable experience. In that exercise, you will start developing the skills to clearly and definitively organize these things into a cohesive design. It will force you to answer questions about the gamestory that you may not have considered when coming up with the original concept.

The successful and identified common models of gamestory interaction are listed in the following sections, along with diagrams and descriptions.

17.3.1 Parallel

Parallel is the most common and probably oldest form of gamestory in existence. *Parallel* is the term I use to describe this form of player/story interaction because the story is told in chunks, which are linear and parallel to the levels and progression of the game. This is what we know as the *cutscene*, or cinematic chunk of story that is shown to the viewer, usually in a passive sense, in order to make the story progress along with the game. The player is generally given an objective to get to the end of that level or game segment, at which point they will be shown the next chapter or episode in the story that progresses. This follows a simple flow and allows a story to be told before and after each segment of gameplay which, hopefully, adds emotional and human context to the purpose of that particular level and its significance to the previous and following clips. It was present in the earliest arcade games of the 1980s, evidenced by such classics as *Donkey Kong* and *Ms. Pacman.*

In parallel gamestories, the player has no real input into the story or narrative other than being able to see it by accessing the cutscene. They simply move from point to point in the game and receive the cutscenes as they go. Although this may seem to be the simplest and most primitive of models, it's actually a really good format for the storyteller to craft their story because they retain control of the sequence and flow of the story (Figure 17.5).

17.3.2 Branching

In the early 1980s, a series of books known as *Choose Your Own Adventure* became wildly popular for children. The premise of this book line was that you could make a choice at the end of each segment and, based upon that choice, flip to various other pages, where your choice would then guide the next segment and, of course, the choices at the end of those segments.

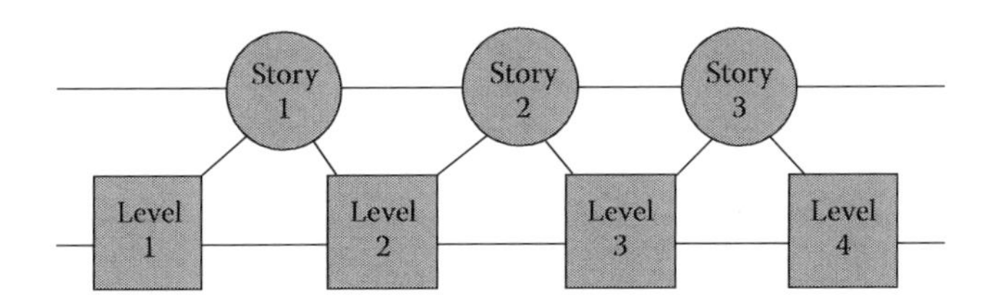

FIGURE 17.5 Diagram for parallel mode of gamestory. You can see a parallel linear progression of both the game and the story as the player progresses through each at the same speed.

This was the first modern interactive entertainment idea, which would later be expanded upon using computers by the exploration of hypertext in the 1987 Apple Computers Hypercard program and others, which would use links from one page of text and images to another. This, of course, along with various parallel developments, would eventually lead to the World Wide Web as we know it today and the formalization of HTML code and browser-based navigation.

The idea of branching storylines is not a new one—but it's an emerging one in the advent of gaming and storytelling. Gamestories with a branching architecture allow the player to choose certain actions, which in turn will change certain aspects of the story and further change the options that the player is given. *Mass Effect*, developed by Bioware and first released by Microsoft in 2007, is the primal example of the concept at work, which gives the player (playing character Commander Shepard) choice over the narrative of the game and events held therein based upon his decisions during gameplay. The game narrative decisions are persistent data that change even circumstances in the sequels that follow, most notably having certain characters be dead or otherwise unavailable based upon the events of the preceding chapter.

Branching storylines are not only of great interest to game developers, but also of great difficulty to the storytellers. Creating the architecture of a branching storyline requires that each branch contain the decisions of previous branches and offer new decisions based upon that branch. The logical analysis and layout of such a system requires either that there be very few branches or that branches generally rep-converge with the main narrative at certain points. Unfortunately the amount of work needed to go into a sincerely deeply branching storyline with thousands of possible outcomes is not very cost effective if done manually, and a good AI-driven procedural storytelling computer has not quite been created that could make it believable just yet! Interestingly enough, the mathematics behind such a thing would be derived from fractal mathematics, which is devoted to calculating a branching algorithmic equation to infinite levels of detail. Such a feat is technically possible and may even be closer than we think. Many open-world space-based games are using such procedural generators to create planets and environments that are infinite in variability and variety. Basing our concepts off of those types of systems, we can easily see how it could be transposed to narrative instead of just setting.

Giving the player choice over the narrative presents an interesting form of gamestory immersion. The choices become a part of the narrative that the player controls; therefore, the story begins to conform to their individual style of play or decision-making. It allows the flexibility of the storyteller to present a choice/consequence model, which can then be used to enhance narrative elements and themes such as morality or cause/effect. It's also interesting to note that the events still move in a linear path—the player choices move the narrative forward, but just in a different branch. Overall, there will always be a guiding hand behind the choice of narrative result which will provide structure, especially if the storyteller wants to limit the choices of the player to what seems morally appropriate for the character they control. For instance, you wouldn't give them the option to kill the entire crew of their ship for no reason just for fun, but you *would* make that an option if it would somehow lead to self-preservation or for their benefit in some manner. Conversely, in an open-architecture sandbox game (see Figures 17.6 and 17.7), you might give them all the options possible and let them choose whatever they want.

In Figures 17.6 and 17.7, you can see some very basic diagrams of how the branching architecture unfolds into the results or varying choices the player encounters. The difference between these two diagrams is that in Figure 17.6, the branches continue to branch (in this case, each decision

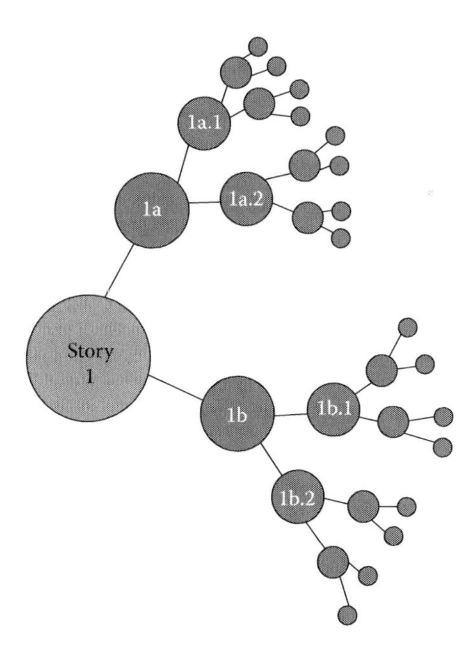

FIGURE 17.6 A nonmerging branching diagram. You can see how the iterations quickly become too dense to create enough viable outcomes for a story to be created.

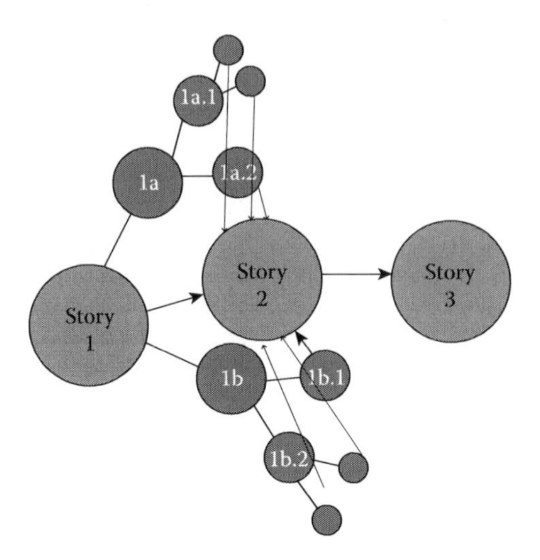

FIGURE 17.7 A merging branching architecture. In this model, you can merge the narrative and elements back into the main story with subtle changes that the player makes as the choices effect circumstances. This provides limiters on how far you go with the choices, and always moves the options back into the main storyline.

is branched into two more decisions, which quickly grows exponentially) ostensibly into infinity, and you can see the rapidity with which the organization structure would become overwhelmed with complexity. In Figure 17.7, you can see how the branches of choice merge back into the main story, which allows persisted data to change certain parts of the main story line without having to lead into completely new branches. This, coincidentally, is how distributed source version control with software development happens using programs such as Git, which is also a branching/merging architecture for changes to data.

17.3.3 Open

Open is the narrative equivalent of a sandbox game, in which the player has a set of circumstances, rules, and various nonplayer or other human player entities that populate the world in which the game takes place. From that point on, the player has an infinite amount of choices within those confines that would lead to more options, much like Figure 17.7, but without any form of central control! This means that the choices that the player makes lead to other varying choices, but these occur entirely within the procedural system of the game and not from any prewritten narrative content. This removes the gamestory entirely in some instances, relegating it to a simple environment, or setting, and some hierarchical rules and game AI, which while interesting for some amount of time can quickly become tedious and repetitive. Early versions of *Grand Theft Auto* games suffered from this repetitive action, which led to a restructuring or adding of preconceived story narrative in the form of threads and side stories the player can participate in. It will quickly become clear from open gamestory architecture that without some sort of cohesive story elements that have been preconceived by a writer, the game seems to become repetitive and boring.

MMORPGs often have this open architecture as a matter of course, with varying levels of input from a storyteller to add the narrative element. MMORPGs can get away with less predefined content, however, because they have a massive amount of human element creating variety instead of the game AI engine or physics and rules. Other human beings provide the much needed unpredictability and social interaction that can substitute for a preconceived and cohesive story.

17.3.4 Scattered

Scattering the story throughout the game is a way to plant elements of narrative, perspective, and character throughout the setting and allow the player to discover it as they navigate through the gameplay. The storyteller loses some control over the sequencing of these elements, but it can greatly enhance the sensation of immersion into the world, since these pieces are found or accessed within the normal course of play.

Bioshock, originally released in 2007 by 2K Games, is a great example of the use of scattered story elements inside of an environment. The player discovers the story they are participating in by opening and finding recordings of what happened to the ruined underwater city of Rapture and its inhabitants. Like many discovery based games, the player begins the journey knowing almost nothing about the story, but slowly picks up on the pieces as they discover artifacts, recordings, journal entries, and newsreels that put it together.

The nice thing about this architecture is the fact that the player is able to choose in most cases whether to pursue the narrative or leave it alone; the option to simply play the game is there (for repeat play or people who are less concerned with gamestory and more concerned with gameplay). For people who want to completely immerse themselves into the story, they can scrounge the environment for every single scrap of it.

This form of storytelling, coincidentally, is nothing new by any means. In fact, it was the narrative device from the original novel by Bram Stoker,

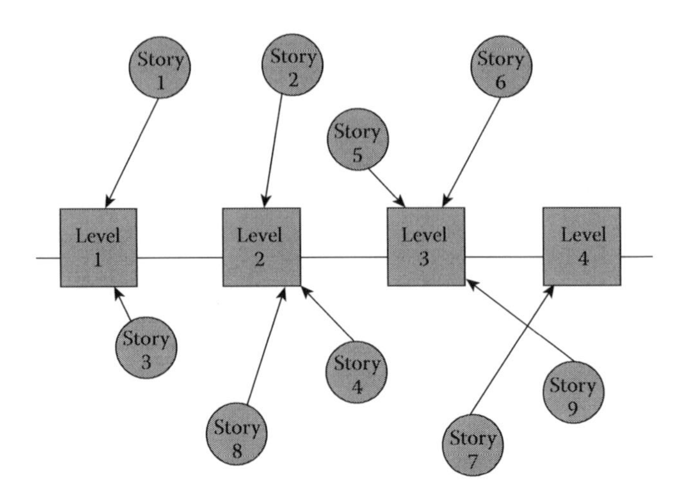

FIGURE 17.8 A diagram depicting the scattered model of gamestory. You can see that the sequence can be in any order the character finds the elements or can be manipulated in a certain order of preference by the storyteller.

Dracula. In this novel, the story is told through various newspaper clippings, journal entries, letters, and other removed third-party perspectives. There is no one central storyteller that recounts the tale. In the case of the gamestory, it lends itself well to the planting of story elements among the levels of gameplay for the player to discover. Figure 17.8 illustrates a diagram of the scattered architecture and how the story can be told out of sequence by multiple parties and perspectives.

17.3.5 Threaded

Threaded stories are offshoots of a primary central storyline. Threads could be considered missions, quests, jobs, or rescues. They generally operate as the varying options that a player can take inside the larger context of the gamestory. They can be either entirely optional, such as the threads inside of *Grand Theft Auto*, or entirely necessary for some forward movement of the larger story, such as a vital mission in a military campaign in *Modern Warfare*.

Threads provide several opportunities for crafting the story inside of a game. They allow the storyteller to generate a tremendous amount of variety in what would be an otherwise repetitive or boring game, they allow the storyteller to continue to craft content even after the game is released (such as adding mission packs or quests in *Warcraft*), and they generate an expansive feel to the total game environment. Threads are commonly used

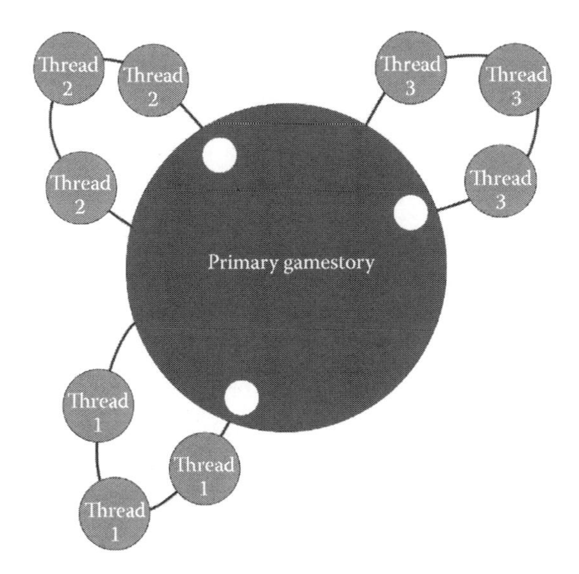

FIGURE 17.9 A diagram of a threaded gamestory architecture.

in big-picture narratives (see Figure 17.9) and can even act as supplemental story content or sequels/offshoots from the main narrative.

Threaded, unlike branching architecture, does not allow the player choices in the threads, only a linear gamestory that flows out of and back into the primary storyline. For this reason, they are far easier to craft for the storyteller, because they can be written as mini-episodes, with independent objectives, goals, rewards, and narratives that are contained within the larger system, but not necessarily creating any dependency upon it. In Figure 17.9, you can see a diagram of the threaded architecture, which has offshoots of threaded content (such as missions or quests) emerging from the primary gamestory, which remains set. The players can then choose to complete the missions or quests for various purposes while the storytellers and game designers can continuously implement new ones to enhance content variability.

17.3.6 Converging

Convergence in terms of gamestory is very similar to converging multiple perspectives, as discussed in Section I. Convergence is a very limited gamestory architecture and is usually used strictly in combat, tournament, and competitive fighting games. The concept is fairly simple: each individual participant/racer/combatant has a unique and compelling backstory which explains why they are at the tournament and what they hope to accomplish at that tournament. They often have a nemesis, opposite, or opposing team that they hope to defeat or destroy by moving through the ranks of the combat tournament or racing circuit. Each individual's story converges upon the current tournament, and if the story mode is turned on, the combatants they will face will be chosen based upon the narrative element. The convergence on the tournament and the selection of opponents are often the full extent of the story in terms of narrative. In some cases, certain upgrades, weapons, or power-ups are available only to characters on a certain team or on an individual basis which increases the variety of outcomes and gameplay as the character works to earn those achievements.

17.4 STORY MODES FOR GAMES

17.4.1 Big Story/Little Story

In Figure 17.9, you can see how the threaded architecture allows smaller stories to occur inside of bigger narrative themes. The side quests, missions, and jobs all have a common element with the larger narrative or context, but only focus on a small part of it. In this way, episodic material can be constructed in a very similar manner to a podcast or a television series. There is an overarching narrative device that smaller stories can be constructed from. These hierarchical story constructs are perfect for games and gamestories because they allow the storyteller to devise chapters, threads, layers, and levels into a much more massive narrative and leave plenty of room for growth! There are a few versions of this construct.

17.4.2 The War Narrative

Earth against the Covenant. Earth vs the martians. Allies against axis. Jedi against Sith. We've seen it a thousand times, in a thousand games, the context of a global, galactic, or universal scale, the bad people and the good people, or just varying factions duke it out for total control over the others. This Zoroastrian concept is as old as storytelling itself and has its roots in the primordial legends of early civilizations such as the Mesopotamians, Syrians, and Babylonians.

The great thing about this construction of narrative device is that it can span hundreds of worlds, planets, and thousands of years, which gives the storyteller plenty of leeway to craft smaller individual tales and narratives. *Halo*, *Star Wars*, *Lord of the Rings*, and *Harry Potter* are just some examples of this bigger universe war-based narrative where there is an eternal struggle between two factions or forces that seems to last forever (or at least span several generations).

17.4.3 The Quest Narrative

A quest, or a specific objective goal, can be useful as a device in both the big picture narrative and the little picture narrative. If we look at Tolkien's classic *Lord of the Rings* trilogy and companion book *The Hobbit*, we can see that a defining quest objective is outlined at the beginning of the book. In *Lord of the Rings*, it is to take the one ring to Mordor and throw it into the fire from which it was once forged. But Tolkien didn't take 20 years to write three dense copy books about a straight trek to Mount Doom so Frodo could chuck the ring in there and go home. Every step of the journey from one place to another became about the more pressing quest at hand. Getting through Moria, combating the army of Saruman with the kingdom of Rohan, defeating the army of Sauron at Gondor, and of course the long, slow trek of Frodo, Sam, and Gollum through each trial and tribulation of their journey, finally culminating in the destruction of the ring, which was the whole point in the beginning of the book.

A quest can have epic proportion, and inside of that single quest, the storyteller can break the story into miniature quests, just as a military campaign is broken into smaller missions for use inside a threaded type of gamestory architecture. Using a global quest can encapsulate the smaller quests, which form a part of the greater whole.

17.4.4 Survival Narrative

Where would we be without the notion of apocalypse? The notion that at some point, everything and everyone would undergo a catastrophic transformation from order to chaos. This movement from order to chaos, and the underlying fear that everything that is now safe, secure, and predictable can go horribly wrong at any moment, pervades our fears and collective consciousness. The idea is not without precedent. Over the course of human history, many civilizations have been destroyed overnight by invasions, earthquakes, meteor impacts, or tidal waves.

From *Ragnarok* to *World War 3* to the *Zombie Epidemic*, the concept of the end times or the cataclysmic destruction of everything previously known is a deep-seated belief in the culture of many religions and the human psyche.

The use of this postapocalyptic world as a literary device in gaming is evidenced by multitudes of popular titles, such as *Fallout*, *Bioshock*, and the ever-present *Resident Evil*; the concept of survival in a world with multiple dangers and limited resources has been a key theme to interactive gamestory content. The narrative device has a very easy way to create multiple offshoots and variations, with the principle theme being to simply survive or reach some place of reprieve from the zombies or radioactive mutations or escape. Survival narratives demand that resources be sparse, limited, and ingenious in their use on the part of the player.

17.4.5 Mystery Narrative

Myst, one of the first incredibly successful horror/mystery games (and mentioned here several times), is a class mystery style of game. *Dead Space* is a similar style of narrative device, albeit set in space. *Portal* is another similar narrative device. The idea is that you have no backstory, you have no recollection of events leading to where you are, you have no idea where you are, and you don't have any idea what your objective *is* even as a player.

The key to this style of narrative device is to lead the player from the dark to the light, by using gamestory setups such as a scattered architecture to slowly inform them of where they are, why they are there, and what they're supposed to be doing. This type of innovative exploration on the player's part can greatly enhance the reward of discovery as the story unfolds before them. The idea behind this style of narrative device is to let that story reveal itself at the proper pace, keeping the player involved just enough to really want to find out more.

17.4.6 Cop/Criminal Narrative

Crime, as a central narrative device, is a great way to construct a large framework inside of which smaller factions, rivalries, missions, and heists can be created as smaller, bite-sized narratives and plot devices. Such a criminal underworld plays the primary role in classics such as *Grand Theft Auto* and *Saints Row*, which emphasize the criminal element as the primary umbrella underneath which the narrative of the game takes place.

Creating the characters, individual stories, and interactions between them is easy to do with the primary objective of two things: money and power. Using these as the motivating tools to build a narrative-driven world is the objective of the storyteller, using the strife between rival factions and criminal enterprises to devise the individual stories.

Reversing this effect is the cop narrative, which will place the player in the shoes of a police officer or other representative of public safety in charge of stopping the crime and preventing the criminals from acting out their crime spree of profiting from theft and illegal sale of narcotics, firearms, etc. The reverse crime narrative is a nice way to balance the tables of this narrative device. So far, it is debatable whether this narrative has actually been attempted in a sandbox style of architecture such as *Grand*

Theft Auto, but it has been successfully employed in other genres of gameplay such as *L.A. Noire* and *SWAT*. *L.A. Noire* is more of a mystery-based narrative device, however, and *SWAT* is certainly based on the concept of the war narrative in that it has a very urban military feel to it.

17.4.7 The Hunting Narrative

The idea of *the hunt* is as old as humanity. Tracking and killing wild animals is such a deeply ingrained element to the nature and, by extension, *definition* of our species. Of course, most people in our first-world economy don't often experience the thrilling and natural sensation of pursuing something for the intent of killing and (and perhaps eating it). But the sensation of hunting can be incredibly primal and cathartic if developed correctly as a gamestory narrative.

Hunting wild game, either real or fantastic, is only part of the options available in the hunting narrative. The thing that you are hunting can be humanoid, or even an actual person, in which case the stakes and the risks increase exponentially. There aren't many games to reference for this narrative device, since most hunting games focus on either big-game simulations or dinosaurs and leave out the tracking aspect altogether. *Manhunt*, released in 2002 by RockStar Games, was a stealth-based game which undertook some of these elements (along with the survival narrative) to an extreme, allowing players to sneak up and strangle other humans in a twisted setting that focused on tactics, hiding, and weapons such as plastic bags. The reception was good in terms of creativity, but many people found the game disturbing to play, due to its graphic nature and the lack of dehumanization of the victims as zombies, aliens, Nazis, or other nonhuman entities (see the Voodoo Principle in Section I for discussion on why this is the case).

But a hunting narrative, with an intelligent creature, can be a compelling element to a game based on the same action. The *Predator* film series, along with the *Alien* franchise, often focus on hunting as a prime element of suspense and narrative device. In many of the films, and some of the derivative games, the player is the one being hunted, and not vice versa. The hunt is a great place for fight/flight reactions, adrenaline-based reward systems, and a good amount of dynamic tension between the roles of the hunter and the hunted, which the storyteller often reverses at some point in the story.

Bounty hunter games are great ways to use this device and have a human element as the hunted individual. The game *Star Wars: Bounty Hunter*, released in 2002 by LucasArts, was a film tie-in using the character of

Jango Fett as a bounty hunter, with the larger context of seeking Dark Jedi Komari Vosa. Throughout the game, there are threaded missions to find and capture various intergalactic criminals for money, along with a primary narrative that continues in a linear format. By using this type of narrative structure, it's very easy to see how a storyteller could create compelling stories for gameplay.

17.5 WRITING THE GAMESTORY

Designing a story for a game requires that we see things not as a whole but as a summation and interplay of various pieces, which the storyteller can create as separate entities that the player will then interact with in a predetermined manner. This requires us to see the world of storytelling a little differently from a novelist or screenwriter. Since the art of writing compelling content for interactive entertainment is in its infancy, there's really no structured body of evidence to say that one way will be more successful or popular than another in terms of *taste*, but there are some objective elements we can begin with in order to better structure our story for the purpose it is intended.

Seeing things as a computer programmer sees things is a good place to start. What does *object-oriented* mean, after all? Without getting too technical about compute programming, *object-oriented* in the sense of a story means that you have a hierarchical system of elements (objects) that have specific attributes and that those attributes are either unique to the object or inherited from other objects. What this does for the programmer is allow them to create these objects at will and change or perform actions based on those created objects. So instead of working things in a linear fashion, like say writing in a new character with a plot line at a certain point in the story, the storyteller can set up a character (object) which the player can interact with at any point in the game and receive the same information or possibly unlock new information carried by the character's attributes.

17.5.1 Character Cards

I like the approach of having cards for each character, like baseball cards, with the pictures and statistics of each player written on the card. Each character has those stats, which, in this case, would be attributes, dependencies, independent narratives, motivations, and relationship to the player character. In this way, you can begin to construct a meaningful story that allows you to design the narrative experience as well as allow the

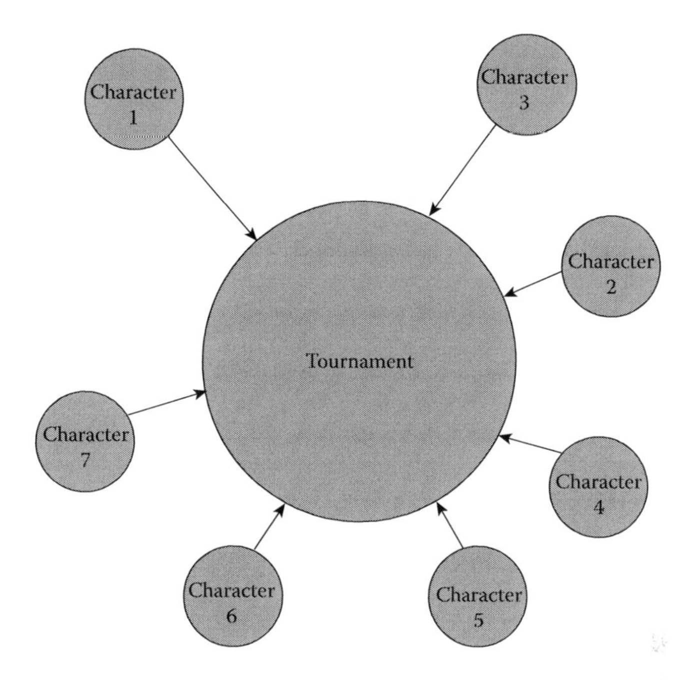

FIGURE 17.10 Converging gamestory.

player to interact with story elements at their own discretion and at their own pace. Figure 17.10 shows a baseball card layout, based on collectible memorabilia from baseball players which were used to list out the individual history, statistics, etc., of each player on a team. Using this format and layout, we can create unique cards for every character in our story, listing out their important elements, attributes, narrative devices, objects and weapons, characteristics, and dependencies from which the narrative content might come from. Figure 17.11 illustrates this concept in an object format, which you can use as a mental or graphical model when laying out the pieces of your gamestory.

17.5.2 Narrative Cards

Continuing our flowchart model for object-oriented gamestory design, we now need to manage the narrative by breaking it up into chunks. Chunking data is a well-known tactic for the organization of information into more easily manageable pieces of information that can be used as design elements. Narrative chunks are small pieces of your overall narrative, which can be then placed inside your game environments or attached to characters who will be providing this information. By stringing them together,

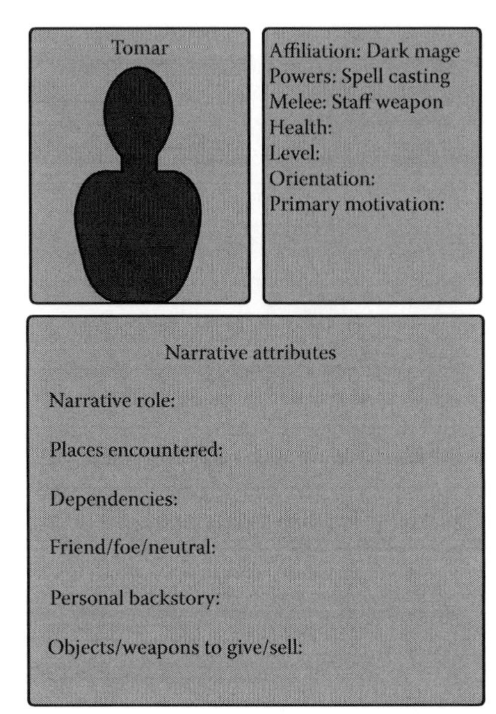

FIGURE 17.11 A character card with important attributes and elements based upon the story character.

you will ultimately be able to construct the entirety of the gamestory narrative, but you want to be able to imagine them as individual pieces of data (once again, like objects) which the player can discover or will be handed at some point. Cutscenes or parallel gamestories are especially easy to use to create individual, unique chunks for building.

When writing the narrative for these chunk card bits, it's a good practice to write out the sequence of events as they happen in order (you can always tell the story *out* of order later if you so desire) and lay them out in order of occurrence, separated like paragraphs or complete actions. When you write these out, you can dispense with the descriptive language and use a factual listing of events. Of course, we will add the descriptive language and storyteller elements later, along with the actual scripts!

17.5.3 Objective Cards

Like narrative cards, objective cards should contain the specific objective of the main gamestory or thread, along with specific dependencies. Dependencies are things that must be achieved or acquired or circumstances

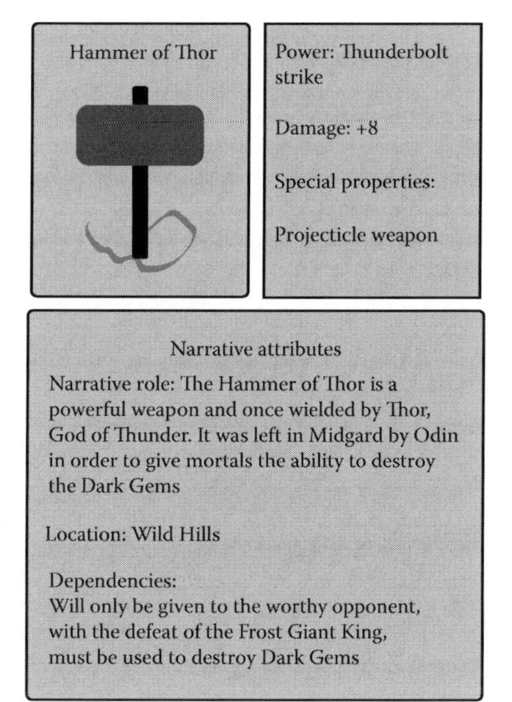

FIGURE 17.12 Objective card with information about a specific goal, along with dependencies and obstacles.

that must changed before an objective can be met. Each objective should have a list of dependencies and obstacles that will prevent the player from reaching the objective (Figure 17.12).

17.5.4 Obstacles Cards

There might be specific obstacles to each individual objective, such as a boss to defeat or some treacherous environment to overcome before reaching or achieving the objective. An obstacle differs from a dependency in that it is something to overcome, and not something that must be acquired.

Objects, weapons, and vehicles (which include horses, camels, pterodactyls, and other animal-enhanced locomotion) are all objects that alter the circumstances in some way of the player moving through the environments and gamestory. In this regard, it is important to list any special items, weapons, or vehicles that will be featured in the gameplay and are essential for the gamestory narrative. Figure 17.13 shows an object card layout, much like the character card layout. This weapon is necessary to

Objective: Locate and obtain Hammer of Thor

Narrative role: The Queen has tasked Tomar with the destruction of Dark Gems, which can only be accomplished if he obtains the Hammer of Thor.

Location: Wild Hills

Obstacle: Must defeat the Frost Giant King in order to be worthy of the Hammer.

FIGURE 17.13 Objects that are essential to the gamestory narrative should have cards built for them.

the gamestory, and so it gets its own individual description and placement in the narrative.

17.5.5 Environment Cards

The environment is the setting of your gamestory, and as such, it must have as much attention to detail of description as possible. Writing down and noting the various environments in your game will help you organize the objects and events that have connections to that particular place and time.

17.6 DESIGNING THE PLAYER EXPERIENCE

Now that everything in your gamestory has been chunked, documented, and converted into objects, you can begin building the gamestory schematic! It's not that hard to do, actually, it just requires you to think more like a person listing a bunch of data than actually writing a story. Don't worry; you can get incredibly creative with your story in a multitude of ways, but in order to break this story into intelligible parts that can then be used as part of an interactive gameplay experience, you must think in lists and links, which in many ways is similar to the original idea of hypertext, which as previously discussed is the interactive formatting of the World Wide Web.

Start by listing out the key events in your narrative, in the order that they happened. Be very careful to note where, when, who, and what as much as you can! This is your opportunity to create links and make chunks of data out of all the important items in your gamestory. Every time you mention an environment, note it with parentheses as such. Do the same with characters, narrative, objects, objectives, dependencies, and anything else you wish to add.

1. Tomar enters the castle (*environment*). He is not sure what he will find. He has been told he must visit the Queen (*character*) in order to find out what his next quest (*objective*) must be.
2. Tomar is shown into the Queen's Throne Room (*environment*) by her ushers. She is waiting for him.
3. The Queen tells Tomar of the Dark Gems (*objects*) (*narrative*) and how, in order to save the kingdom from utter destruction, he must find them and destroy them all (*objective*) by smashing them with the Hammer of Thor (*object/weapon*) (*dependency*), which he can find somewhere in the hills east of the Wild Lands (*area/environment*).
4. The Queen gives Tomar weapons, food, potions (*objects*) and sends him on his way.

Now that we have the basic narrative elements, dependencies, and objective goals, we can start setting up the important elements of the story as pieces on a table, with attributes as part of their descriptions.

Narratives: These are narrative elements, as told by either a narrator or a character.

- Queen's Tale—Tale of power, history, and Dark Gems, narrated by the Queen: *insert detailed script here.*
- Tomar's Story—Personal backstory and motivations; ostensibly, this could be broken down into multiple elements and revealed to the player as they navigate the gamestor, or told all at once up front; narrated by a narrator or Tomar himself.

Environments: Places that the player has visited or even just heard about.

- Castle Entrance—Large, plush, with draped tapestries and winding staircases
- Queen's Throne Room—Majestic and royal; occupied by the Queen
- East of Wild Lands—Nebulous and unknown territory

Characters: Any human, human-like being, or anthropomorphized object

- Tomar—Loyal subject; willing adventurer
- Queen—Wisdom and power, etc.
- Ushers—Nondescript; basic NPC

Global objectives: List large objectives here, but not smaller ones

- Find and destroy Dark Gems

Dependencies: What must be done in order to fulfill the global objective?

- Find Hammer of Thor
- Obtain Hammer of Thor
- Find Dark Gems
- Destroy Dark Gems

Objects: Any object pertinent to the narrative of the gamestory should be listed here, along with its relationship to the story. But leave out little things not pertinent to the story such as food, water, and weapons.

- Hammer of Thor—A legendary weapon of great power, once wielded by the thunder god Thor himself; it is located somewhere east of Wild Lands.
- Dark Gems—Items of great evil power; they have been used to build an army of undead to destroy the Kingdom.

As we can see from the breakdown, it's very easy to turn a few pages of what would be a simple narrative script or chapter into an extremely comprehensive gamestory design document. This is what is known as building the *player experience.* A lot of work and labor go into developing user interface and user experience for software, mobile apps, and websites, but with the advent of entertainment-based games, we also have to think in terms of the player experience or what we want the player to see, hear, and interact with from the very beginning of the game to the very end.

The player experience begins the moment the game is started and ends only when the player ceases to play the game *forever.* The player experience does not necessarily end when they turn the game off! This is because of the extrinsic reward systems and the Voodoo Principle we have created with our design. The game should persist in the player's head in some form or fashion until they are completely done playing the game forever. Different game types will have different levels of persistence, of course, and we have discussed how embodiment and the creation of a custom character will persist with a much higher level of awareness, but a great gamestory, such as a great book or television series, should persist enough to inspire the player to return to the game as frequently as they can.

17.7 ESSENTIAL GAMESTORY PLAYER EXPERIENCE ELEMENTS

17.7.1 Entry

Entering the game is the moment the game begins to engage the player's attention. It's very important that the audiovisual experience immediately locks them into the setting and tone of the gamestory. If our game, let's call it *Tomar's Quest* from now on, starts out with the sounds of laser blasts, spaceships, and explosions, we probably aren't going to be getting in the mood for the medieval fantasy style of gamestory that we have written! Obviously, we want the experience to immediately ground them into the world that they are entering, assisting in our goal of total immersion in the experience. So what kind of audio should we hear? Probably monks chanting, swords clanging, and maybe some fire-breathing dragon sounds for good measure. We want to make sure that we are grounding the player into the setting and preparing them for bloody, medieval barbaric combat.

17.7.2 Objectives

As discussed, the objectives, both small and large, are what will drive your player through your gamestory, so they must be well designed and form an integral part of your design. The important thing here is to give them significant *meaning* to the player's character and the setting you have created. Making the objectives appropriate to your narrative device and your setting will further immerse the player into the experience.

17.7.3 Dependencies

The dependencies, such as the rules of the game, create structure for the player to progress through the levels and missions. They must make a framework that challenges the player to be creative, think actively, and engage the gamestory elements in pursuit of their objectives. Writing dependencies that make sense for a gamestory is important when creating the immersive narrative experience. Once again, the logic and meaning of dependencies is important to weave into the narrative for your gamestory. Is there a reason that Thor's Hammer was hidden away and kept a secret? Why doesn't Thor need it anymore? Or is he just lending it to you for a while until you're done with it? These might be silly questions to ask yourself while writing the elements of the gamestory, but without reasonable answers to reasonable questions, the immersion will start to fall apart if the player begins asking them himself. Of course, it's important not to go into overdetail mode. Just have these dependencies make some kind of natural sense, and don't throw random ones in there for the sake of variety. They should all connect to your narrative in some meaningful way.

17.7.4 Narrative Interaction

Good interaction design is important when you are building a narrative player experience. How is your narrative going to come to the player? In the case of Tomar's Quest for the Hammer of Thor, he gets the initial story of the Dark Gems from the Queen. She is the source of the narrative. You can see that I have built that element into the game, categorized it, and codified it so that I know that part of the narrative comes from a human being, who narrates the story in her own voice. What other devices can we use to deliver narrative other than directly from a character? Drawing from the *Bioshock* example, we could use newsreels, journal entries, radio broadcasts, and memoir recordings to present pieces of our story to the player. There are plenty of ways to get our narrative nuggets into the perspective of the player! We want to make sure that they are congruent with the setting (as such, I would not use newsreels in a fantasy setting, but I *would* perhaps use a magic crystal with a recording instead) and level of technology.

17.7.5 Non-Player Characters

NPCs are vital parts of the narrative, as they represent both character and perspective as they relate to the gamestory. The NPC can be a vessel through which the story is told to the player. Keep in mind that perspective is somewhat locked inside of gameplay; it's almost always through the eyes of the player character. For this reason, NPCs are important methods of delivery for parts of the story that the player is not aware of or needs to discover at certain points during the game.

The NPC can deliver that content to the player as they interact with them, providing the external perspective needed in the game (if so desired). The NPC often supplies the player character with vital information about elements, tactics, enemy movements, dependencies, and plot points that they would not uncover without help. When designing your gamestory, make sure that your character cards for your NPC have very specific lists of narrative elements they are going to deliver, along with the scripts for speeches and the number of vital interactions with the player character. For instance, the Queen in Tomar's Quest will have a specific role, and that role is to provide the player with an objective goal, accompanied by narrative elements that are attached to those objectives. When designing her character, you should list out all possible interactions with Tomar, along with the goals she will give him, the rewards/bonuses she can offer, and the story elements that will go along with each one of those goals or rewards.

17.7.6 Maps

Environments and settings are important to design with a level of congruency and description. The environments should be broken up into smaller areas, which have their own characteristics, inherent obstacles, and even maps if necessary. Maps are a good way to lay out the characteristics of a certain area form a bird's eye view, allowing the game designers to visualize the layout of the background from a topographical standpoint. Tolkien was famous for drawing up semitopographical maps with landscape features such as mountains and forests. These served to enhance the level of immersion in the fictional world of Middle Earth because it allowed the reader to construct a 3D visual model in their head. In the same way, you can build simple maps that can help the game developers and designers visualize the world your gamestory is set in (Figure 17.14).

17.7.7 Objects/Weapons/Vehicles

The objects, weapons, and transport items of your world should be congruent with the level of technology and your setting. For instance, in the film *Avatar*, it was a jungle-like otherworldly landscape, but the world was being invaded by a technologically advanced civilization. So you had a combination of primitive weapons such as spears and bows and flying dinosaur/dragons alongside spaceships and technology elements from science fiction. If you are relegating your gamestory to one level of technology

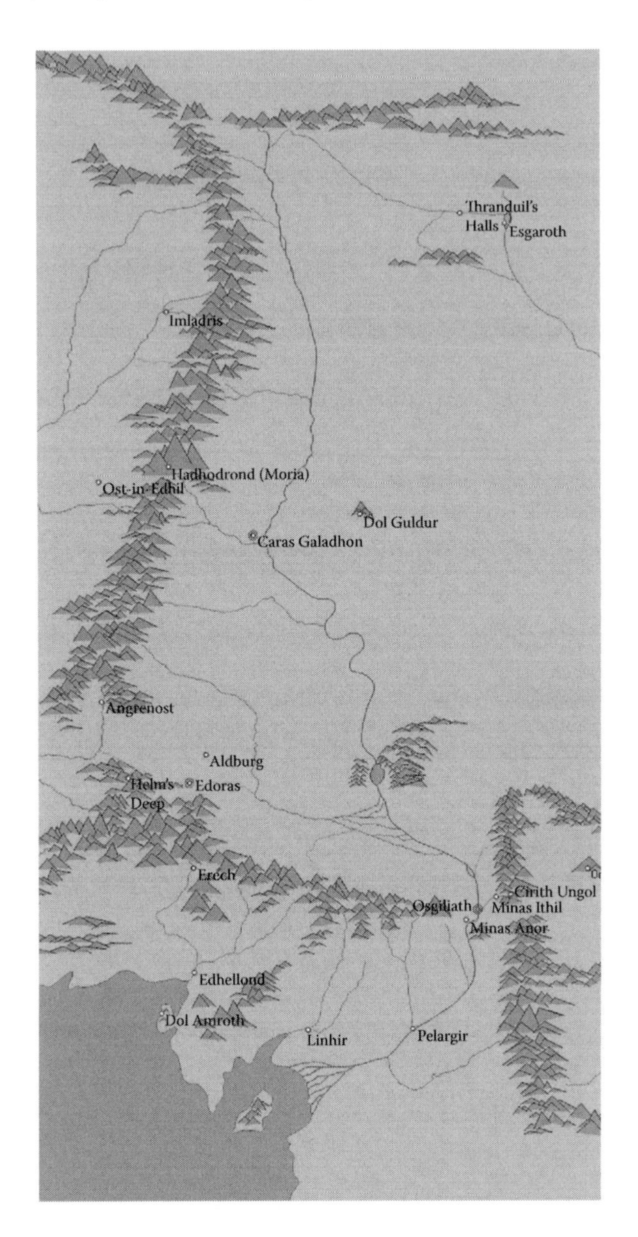

FIGURE 17.14 A Tolkien-like map, with mountain ranges and body of water. Simple maps like this can enhance your environment design greatly.

and time/space, then you should make sure that the weapons and forms of travel reflect that.

Any world you are creating needs to have a well-planned variety in means of transportation. If you plan to have more than just movement on foot, then you should definitely design your vehicles to go with the terrain and level of technology present in your world. Your options for designing vehicles are transportation through certain means, which are usually based on some kind of physical environment. Your physics-based world has several options:

- Ground—The usual way! Options will always be held up by rivers, mountains, and seas.
  - Foot
  - Horse/quadruped
  - Quad-powered wheeled vehicle
  - Motorized wheeled vehicles
  - Hover vehicles
- Air—Anything that flies through the air. Usually, this will get the person where they are going to fastest, and he or she will be able to cross all terrain, including water.
  - Dragon/bird/flying animal
  - Balloon/dirigible/air ship
  - Manual power of flight
  - Propeller airplane
  - Jet-propelled airplane
  - Spaceship/fighter ship
- On water—If you have bodies of water, you need a way to cross them!
  - Swimming
  - Man-powered ship (oars)
  - Wind-powered ship (sails)

    - Motor-powered ship (engine)
    - Magic/other-powered ship (create something cool here)
- Underwater—Some submerged cities in your design? How do you expect those characters to get there?
    - Submerged swimming (Aquaman, Sub-Mariner)
    - Submarine
- Space—What would a science fiction gamestory be without some space travel? Spaceships of all sizes and types exist in this genre.
    - Spaceship
    - Living space creature
- Portals/teleportation—Getting from one part of the world to another without taking forever to get there is an important design feature to stave off boredom if you have really big worlds and to offer some way to travel instantly from one area to the other.
    - Wormholes
    - Magic gates

17.7.8 Time Flow

I'm personally a huge fan of astrophysics and quantum physics, so I have always been fascinated with time and space and the flow of both as they pertain to our understanding of them. But even if you're not a huge nerd such as myself, you're still going to have to start thinking of time and space in terms of relativity as it pertains to your gamestory world.

You don't have to be Einsten, but you *do* have to plan out the time factor in relative terms. If you're going to track time somehow during your game, you're going to have to figure out some relative relationship between our real-world time and the game time. Game time can be a one-to-one ratio, which would mean of course that the sun rising and setting and the hours counted mirror our own. But the problem with game time is that it sometimes pauses, because the player isn't playing the game all the time.

So the first thing you have to figure out, if you need to track time in some manner, is whether or not the time *persists* if the player leaves the game, or if it pauses as well. If it is persistent time, then you can match it to real time with some kind of ratio, let's say 2:1, which would mean that for every one day passing in our real-world time, two days pass in game time. Generally, although not always, game time is sped up relative to real-world time, because the time spent playing the game is usually a small portion of your day (let's hope you're not playing Tomar's Quest 18 hours a day). Now this is important because the passing of time can be relative to perception! If you are doing something really boring, such as waiting for your college lecture class on political economics to end, time will appear to slow down. If you're doing something really fun, such as hanging out with your friends, that same amount of time will seem to go by very fast. The effect goes both ways. Having game time be the same as real-world time can cause the game to seem slow and boring, and speeding up the game time relative to real-world time can make the game seem more active and interesting! So you want to work out how the game time works relative to real-world time and come up with a ratio that makes the game seem to move forward with action, but not so fast that the player gets frustrated.

Nonpersistent time models require another level of consideration. If the game time pauses when the player quits the game, you'll have to figure out where to restart the time when the player begins to play again, which could be at any time of day or night relative to the real-world time, which has not paused of course. If it is nighttime when you start playing the game again, but the game was paused during the daylight, you have a conflict between real-world time and game time. So how do you handle this? You have a few different options.

- Separate game time—Game time is entirely separate from real-world time and counts up from the moment the game begins. Pausing the game pauses game time. Restarting the game restarts game time.
- Jump game time—Game time jumps to the current time and then begins occurring at the ration you previously set. This is great for real-world game time clocks because it will always be the same time in the game as it is in the real world.
- New day game time—Every time the player pauses the game, the character goes to sleep, and every time they restart the game, the player wakes up to a new dawn, and the game time starts ticking from that new dawn moment.

17.7.9 AI

AI stands for artificial intelligence, and you'd better have some in your gamestory design. Although it seems like something the programmer would be taking care of, that's just the code itself to get the game to function properly. What you want to do as the gamestory designer is put in a list of hierarchical motivations and objectives for any and all NPC elements of your game. AI isn't just computer code; it's a list of things that the NPCs are supposed to do, often with some basic logic and prioritization.

A great example here is Isaac Asimov and his iconic three laws of robotics. In many of his science fiction books, Asimov envisioned a world in which robots would be common and proliferate themselves all throughout the human world. The robots' positronic brains, however, were created from a template that would absolutely not function without obeying three primary laws. This safeguard was intended to put humans at ease and protect them from machines that might otherwise harm us since they would have no emotions or natural moral compass. The three laws were as follows:

1. A robot may not injure a human being or, through inaction, allow a human being to come to harm.
2. A robot must obey the orders given to it by human beings except where such orders would conflict with the first law.
3. A robot must protect its own existence as long as such protection does not conflict with the first and second laws.

Notice that there is a hierarchical structure to these laws; the second is only if the first is not violated, and the third can only be obeyed if the first and second laws are not conflicting. So a human can't order a robot to kill another human (incidentally, the *definition* of human was never taken into consideration, a point which Asimov takes into account in later works). The second law would be in conflict with the first law. A robot *can* be ordered to kill another robot, however. And that victim robot would be able to defend itself unless it was ordered by another human not to. There are all kinds of holes in these basic hierarchies, which Asimov then exposes and explored in his novel *I, Robot*.

The point of all this robot stuff is that your NPCs must have some form of logic and motivation, even if it's only a single driving motivational objective. For instance, if you are working on a zombie survival game and you need to develop the AI of the zombies, what would be the primary motivator? I'd say that images in which "eat nonzombies" would be absolutely the first priority! But they could have other priorities as well. So the three laws of zombies that you could develop for your game might be as follows:

1. Eat (nonzombie) humans when (nonzombie) humans are detected.
2. When no (nonzombie) humans are detected, walk forward at slow, limply pace.
3. *If* no (nonzombie) humans are detected *and* energy is critically low, eat zombie humans.

I'm sure you can work out the various details of how this might play out. A zombie with critically low energy might start eating another zombie, who was aimlessly walking forward into a wall, but if the player walks by, they will both quit what they are doing and immediately pursue them!

The most important thing to reiterate is that you should have a plan for your AI. Don't just leave stuff for other people to set up. Your AI will be the intelligent force of your game that works in opposition to or *with* the player character, and so, it is absolutely vital that you create some sort of realistic tendencies in the NPCs.

One of my favorite example games for AI is the all-time classic *Pac-Man*. In the game *Pac-Man*, you are a little yellow ball running through a maze eating pellets, being pursued by four ghosts: Inky, Blinky, Pinky, and Clyde. At first glance, the ghosts would *seem* to have a particularly identical and simple AI. They follow Pac-Man when they can see him, and when the power pellet is eaten, they turn blue and rapidly run away until they are eaten or they return to their normal state. But if you play the game long enough, the ghosts will split apart and begin acting somewhat differently. You will see over time that each ghost has an independently tweaked AI, with nuances causing differences in their behavior. Some of the ghosts, especially the red one named *Blinky*, are faster to target and attack Pac-Man. Other ghosts seem to have slightly different personalities and attack methodologies, with the orange one Clyde seemingly the slowest to adjust and target Pac-Man. The point of this is that the original creator of *Pac-Man*, Toru Iwatani, has previously stated that he made minor tweaks in each ghost's AI pattern in order to generate some level of tension and dynamic behavior differences, and it definitely worked (as a guy who played this game until his hands cramped can attest)!

17.7.10 Persistence

Persistence, as previously described, is the concept that the game goes with the player, even when he or she isn't actually playing the game. How can you, as a gamestory designer, create a sense of persistence? The important thing to remember here is that persistence can be based on several factors, not all of which are under your control. Persistence can be based on the embodiment of a person, in which they have a personal emotional connection to a game character (or characters), or it can be a *narrative* persistence, in which they feel an emotional connection to one or more of the events or situations in the narrative.

In the case of character persistence, there is usually a character creator and developer which is independent of your creation (such as *Warcraft* or other MMORPGs). But character persistence can also occur when the player feels a strong affinity for the characters in the story, NPC, or player character, and want to engage in that immersion as that character hero (or *against* the villain) again. If they are thinking of your characters when they *aren't* playing the game, you can say that you have been successful in your design of persistence. Character persistence also occurs at a global level, when the love for that character and fandom reach the point where they are bigger than the game (such as Master Chief or Solid Snake) and rise above the franchise as an iconic entity unto themselves.

Narrative persistence generally comes from wanting to know what happens next, as in a game that reveals the story in bits and pieces or allows the player to discover them on their own. Discovery is a really important component to generating narrative persistence because it leaves the player hanging, wanting to know more. Proper construction of *when* to tell the player something and *where* in the game to tell them is how you can generate narrative suspense that will last until the next chapter is unveiled.

CHAPTER 18

Activities

Now that you have all the tools necessary to design a great narrative content for interactive games and media, let's get down to it! We need to think about developing all of the ins and outs of a proper gamestory. In order to get you started, we can work on continuing the Tomar's Quest concept discussed in this section. What I want you to do is to fully develop the game design, from beginning to end, using all your interactive narrative powers to do so. Starting out with a preexisting game (OK, a quarter of a preexisting game, quickly jotted down) is a little easier than coming up with a creative idea on your own, but if you want to superimpose the structure of this assignment on something you've been working on in your head or otherwise, feel free.

The important thing is that you take the following structure and use it to design the structure of your gamestory. But I really want you to design the structure with detail, taking the time to fill out every element of gamestory as I present it in the following. Then I want you to take all of those elements and build a gamestory deisgn document, which will also contain a flowchart for the player experience, from the point that they switch on the game until the point that the game ends! The rule of thumb I generally follow is that you can never have *too* much detail. You can always remove elements or fluff later, but it's much harder to insert information into a completed design than it is to remove it.

18.1 WRITING THE SYNOPSIS

Like an executive summary of a business plan, the synopsis of your story will tell the entire thing in a few pages, as if it were a linear short story. In this way, you create a basic narrative map that can be reviewed at any time and elements pulled off of it that need to go into the final game design. I have provided a sample synopsis of Tomar's Quest as follows. It's only a part of an entire game synopsis, which, of course, would take several pages to write, but you can derive the template of how to write one from the text as it is laid out. A complete synopsis will finish with the completion of the game.

18.1.1 Synopsis: Tomar's Quest

Tomar is a warrior of the Bodega clan, who resides in central Molonia under the rule of the wise and just Queen Molon. He has pledged his sword and his service to the Queen as her personal champion, and for this, he has been rewarded justly. He is called to the Queen's palace, one last time, in order to preserve his legacy and receive the most important task of all. While in the audience of the Queen, he is told the tale of the Dark Gem and how the forces of Nibloth the Wicked have recovered them from an ancient site where they had lain protected by the Guardian for eons. Nibloth and his wicked horde have absconded with the powerful gems and are building an army of undead to destroy Molonia and take power over the realm. The Queen tasks Tomar with the destruction of the gems, which can only be done through the power of the Hammer of Thor, which resides in a mysterious temple somewhere west of the Wild Lands Hills.

Armed with only an ancient map of the temple and the Wild Lands, Tomar must journey into the unknown to find the Hammer of Thor and then enter the Bad Lands on his way to the Dark Tower, where Nibloth and his undead army are building the forces of darkness in order to enslave the entire world.

Insert the rest of the story here.

18.2 BUILDING THE ELEMENTS

Here is where we create our objects for the layout and fragmentation of our synopsis. Who are the characters? What are the rules? What is the objective? What are our environments? All these things must be laid out as independent pieces, as covered in this section.

- Global setting
    - Time period
    - Technology level

- Interaction mode
  - Gamestory control (parallel, threaded, scattered, etc.)
  - Level of interaction with narrative (if present)
- NPCs
  - Name
  - Story
  - Attributes
  - AI rules; motivations
  - Dependencies
  - Obstacles
  - Rewards
- Nonplayer, nonpresent, narrative characters (characters mentioned but not actually in game)
  - Name
  - Personal story
  - Relation to story
- Weapons
  - Type
  - Range
  - Powers
- Vehicles
  - Element of travel (air, water, earth)
  - Speed level
  - Obstacles (can't fly over mountains, can't walk over water)
- Physics (this seems silly, but if you are writing for a sci-fi game, it's important to know the levels of gravity, etc.)
  - Gravity
  - Friction

- Global objective
  - Dependencies
- Local objectives
  - Objective 1
    - Dependency
    - Involved characters
  - Objective 2
    - Dependency
    - Involved characters
- Local setting
  - Environments
    - Characteristics
    - Natural obstacles/barriers
    - Narrative significance
- Rules
  - Movement constraints
  - Item dependencies
- Objects/items
  - Purpose
  - Categories
  - Purchasing
  - Currency type
- Narrative elements
  - Narrative 1
    - Objectives
    - Rewards
    - Dependencies

    - Narrative 2
        - Objectives
        - Rewards
        - Dependencies
- Global narrative (the story underneath which this story/quest/mission is taking place)
    - Context of current narrative to global narrative
    - Temporal placement

18.3 GAMESTORY DESIGN FLOWCHART

Create a visual design flowchart, using a graphic program such as Adobe Illustrator or a nonlinear presentation application such as Prezi, and make a comprehensive flowchart that shows the progression of the player experience as they move through the entire game, segment by segment. Create the connections between these elements as arrows with descriptors in as much detail as possible. Use the baseball card concept, as previously mentioned, in order to lay out all the individual pieces as they fit together to form the complete whole.

CHAPTER 19

Conclusion

IN THIS SECTION, WE have learned all about what constitutes *interactivity* and how to design narrative story content for it. The art of writing a story for interactive content is dependent on seeing it not as a single, continuous, linear story, but as a series of objects, pieces, and modules that we can interact with on multiple levels.

The object of this book has been to guide aspiring interactive storytellers through the fragmentation of the theoretical construction of what we understand and define as a *story*. In doing so, we had to break apart the story into fundamental components that can be designed, edited, and manipulated by the storyteller. The first thing we did, in Section I, was start to look at these components from the perspective of the story creator, and not the story viewer. By the end of Section I, you should have been able to deconstruct any story, no matter how big or small, into its separate pieces and look at them under a microscope.

Section I was all about understanding a story as part of language, constructed of not only words but also ideas, thoughts, and structures that create emotional associations in the audience, whether for cathartic entertainment purposes or deliberate, targeted purposes. We learned what the story is, who is telling the story (and who is *listening*), what kind of stories there are to tell, and why we tell those stories. The exercises in Section I were targeted toward becoming an effective storyteller when given a concept, a task, and a deliberate purpose.

In Section II, we learned about media and the use of that media in creating stories. Art, images, drawings, sculpture, Instagram selfies, radio, sound effects, and music were all explored as extensions of our senses of hearing and eyesight. The lessons learned in this section were all about the use of audio/visual information to tell and enhance a story that was written in words.

We can tell a story with only our words, as in a novel, but to think that those words aren't conjuring visual elements in a person's head in lieu of pictures and sounds would be foolish. We learned that our memory and imagination are powerfully media based, with sights, sounds, and otherwise being heavily associated with descriptions in terms of words. So it should be no surprise that adding images and sound to stories and narrative content can lock down a person's imagination and replace their mental images with specific ones, which are now common to everyone watching the story or listening to it. So in essence, the adding of media to a story will remove the imaginative individual versions of it and create a unified version of that story, both in words and audio/visual memory. We can then share our commonality as social creatures by having had the same story-based experience.

In this section, we learned all about interactivity and storytelling. First, we broke down the concepts of *interactivity* and understood just what kinds of input and output we have available as creative storytellers and how those levels of control and synchronicity of input are related. All the levels of input that a user or player have at their disposal are able to be tailored and manipulated to work with our story.

We also learned in this section all the varying formats of interactive media, past, present, and future. In order to generate an interactive experience, there must be some vessel or format through which it can be presented, and the varying formats were explored with their attributes. Choosing some media format will greatly structure and limit the forms of interactivity you can present the audience, which allows for tighter control over the design of that interaction.

Finally, we delved into the most prolific and common form of interactive entertainment, games, and how our desire to craft a story can be intertwined with gameplay and gameplay mechanics. Games were explored in terms of stories and storytelling interaction, which we termed *gamestory*, and all aspects of both gameplay genres and narrative devices were also explored. The design and construction of the player experience was described, and the individual elements as objects with various inputs and outputs was presented to make you understand how to better construct your gamestory to work *with* the gameplay and to allow the game to work with your story.

As I conclude this book, it should have enough content in it to get anyone started in the field of creative storytelling for interactive content. The skills and knowledge presented here are incomplete, as is any technology-based information, but comprehensive in the sense that if you adhere to strong design principles and allow yourself the freedom to see the world of creative narrative in terms of a storyteller, and no longer the audience, you should possess the tools to break down and reconstruct any form of digital interactive story that you so desire. Good luck; now go get creative and design some content!

Index

Page numbers followed by f indicate figures.

D

E

F

J

K

L

M